Code and the City

Software has become essential to the functioning of cities. It is deeply embedded into the systems and infrastructure of the built environment and is entrenched in the management and governance of urban societies. Software-enabled technologies and services enhance the ways in which we understand and plan cities. They have a profound effect on how we manage urban services and utilities.

Code and the City explores the extent and depth of the ways in which software mediates how people work, consume, communicate, travel and play. The reach of these systems is set to become even more pervasive through efforts to create smart cities: cities that employ ICT to underpin and drive their economy and governance. Yet, despite the roll-out of software-enabled systems across all aspects of city life, the relationship between code and the city has barely been explored from a critical social science perspective. This collection of essays seeks to fill that gap, and offers an interdisciplinary examination of the relationship between software and contemporary urbanism.

This book will be of interest to those researching or studying smart cities and urban infrastructure.

Rob Kitchin is Professor and ERC Advanced Investigator in the National Institute for Regional and Spatial Analysis at the National University of Ireland, Maynooth.

Sung-Yueh Perng is a postdoctoral researcher on the *Programmable City* project at the National University of Ireland, Maynooth.

Regions and Cities
Series Editor in Chief:
Susan M. Christopherson, *Cornell University, USA*

Editors
Maryann Feldman, *University of Georgia, USA*
Gernot Grabher, *HafenCity University Hamburg, Germany*
Ron Martin, *University of Cambridge, UK*
Martin Perry, *Massey University, New Zealand*
Kieran P. Donaghy, *Cornell University, USA*

In today's globalised, knowledge-driven and networked world, regions and cities have assumed heightened significance as the interconnected nodes of economic, social and cultural production, and as sites of new modes of economic and territorial governance and policy experimentation. This book series brings together incisive and critically engaged international and interdisciplinary research on this resurgence of regions and cities, and should be of interest to geographers, economists, sociologists, political scientists and cultural scholars, as well as to policy-makers involved in regional and urban development.

For more information on the Regional Studies Association visit www.regionalstudies.org.

There is a **30% discount** available to RSA members on books in the *Regions and Cities* series, and other subject related Taylor and Francis books and e-books including Routledge titles. To order just e-mail alex.robinson@tandf.co.uk, or phone on +44 (0) 20 7017 6924 and declare your RSA membership. You can also visit www.routledge.com and use the discount code: **RSA0901**

97 **Code and the City**
    *Edited by Rob Kitchin and
    Sung-Yueh Perng*

96 **The UK Regional (and National) Economic Problem**
    Philip McCann

95 **Skills and Cities**
Edited by Sako Musterd, Marco Bontje and Jan Rouwendal

94 **Higher Education and the Creative Economy**
Beyond the campus
Edited by Roberta Comunian and Abigail Gilmore

93 **Making Cultural Cities in Asia**
Mobility, assemblage, and the politics of aspirational urbanism
Edited by Jun Wang, Tim Oakes and Yang Yang

92 **Leadership and the City**
Power, strategy and networks in the making of knowledge cities
Markku Sotarauta

91 **Evolutionary Economic Geography**
Theoretical and empirical progress
Edited by Dieter Kogler

90 **Cities in Crisis**
Socio-spatial impacts of the economic crisis in Southern European cities
Edited by Jörg Knieling and Frank Othengrafen

89 **Socio-Economic Segregation in European Capital Cities**
East meets West
Edited by Tiit Tammaru, Szymon Marcińczak, Maarten van Ham and Sako Musterd

88 **People, Places and Policy**
Knowing contemporary Wales through new localities
Edited by Martin Jones, Scott Orford and Victoria Macfarlane

87 **The London Olympics and Urban Development**
The mega-event city
Edited by Gavin Poynter, Valerie Viehoff and Yang Li

86 **Making 21st Century Knowledge Complexes**
Technopoles of the world revisited
Edited by Julie Tian Miao, Paul Benneworth and Nicholas A. Phelps

85 **Soft Spaces in Europe**
Re-negotiating governance, boundaries and borders
Edited by Philip Allmendinger, Graham Haughton, Jörg Knieling and Frank Othengrafen

84 **Regional Worlds: Advancing the Geography of Regions**
Edited by Martin Jones and Anssi Paasi

83 **Place-making and Urban Development**
New challenges for contemporary planning and design
Pier Carlo Palermo and Davide Ponzini

82 **Knowledge, Networks and Policy**
Regional studies in postwar Britain and beyond
James Hopkins

81 **Dynamics of Economic Spaces in the Global Knowledge-based Economy**
Theory and East Asian cases
Sam Ock Park

80 **Urban Competitiveness**
Theory and practice
Peter Karl Kresl and Daniele Letri

79 **Smart Specialisation**
Opportunities and challenges for regional innovation policy
Dominique Foray

78 **The Age of Intelligent Cities**
Smart environments and innovation-for-all strategies
Nicos Komninos

77 **Space and Place in Central and Eastern Europe**
Historical trends and perspectives
Gyula Horváth

76 **Territorial Cohesion in Rural Europe**
The relational turn in rural development
Edited by Andrew K. Copus and Philomena de Lima

75 **The Global Competitiveness of Regions**
Robert Huggins, Hiro Izushi, Daniel Prokop and Piers Thompson

74 **The Social Dynamics of Innovation Networks**
Edited by Roel Rutten, Paul Benneworth, Dessy Irawati and Frans Boekema

73 **The European Territory**
From historical roots to global challenges
Jacques Robert

72 **Urban Innovation Systems**
What makes them tick?
Willem van Winden, Erik Braun, Alexander Otgaar and Jan-Jelle Witte

71 **Shrinking Cities**
A global perspective
Edited by Harry W. Richardson and Chang Woon Nam

70 **Cities, State and Globalization**
City-regional governance in Europe and North America
Tassilo Herrschel

69 **The Creative Class Goes Global**
Edited by Charlotta Mellander, Richard Florida, Bjørn T. Asheim and Meric Gertler

68 **Entrepreneurial Knowledge, Technology and the Transformation of Regions**
Edited by Charlie Karlsson, Börje Johansson and Roger Stough

67 **The Economic Geography of the IT Industry in the Asia Pacific Region**
Edited by Philip Cooke, Glen Searle and Kevin O'Connor

66 **Working Regions**
Reconnecting innovation and production in the knowledge economy
Jennifer Clark

65 **Europe's Changing Geography**
The impact of inter-regional networks
Edited by Nicola Bellini and Ulrich Hilpert

64 **The Value of Arts and Culture for Regional Development**
A Scandinavian perspective
Edited by Lisbeth Lindeborg and Lars Lindkvist

63 **The University and the City**
John Goddard and Paul Vallance

62 **Re-framing Regional Development**
Evolution, innovation and transition
Edited by Philip Cooke

61 **Networking Regionalised Innovative Labour Markets**
Edited by Ulrich Hilpert and Helen Lawton Smith

60 **Leadership and Change in Sustainable Regional Development**
Edited by Markku Sotarauta, Lummina Horlings and Joyce Liddle

59 Regional Development Agencies: The Next Generation?
Networking, knowledge and regional policies
Edited by Nicola Bellini, Mike Danson and Henrik Halkier

58 Community-based Entrepreneurship and Rural Development
Creating favourable conditions for small businesses in Central Europe
Matthias Fink, Stephan Loidl and Richard Lang

57 Creative Industries and Innovation in Europe
Concepts, measures and comparative case studies
Edited by Luciana Lazzeretti

56 Innovation Governance in an Open Economy
Shaping regional nodes in a globalized world
Edited by Annika Rickne, Staffan Laestadius and Henry Etzkowitz

55 Complex Adaptive Innovation Systems
Relatedness and transversality in the evolving region
Philip Cooke

54 Creating Knowledge Locations in Cities
Innovation and integration challenges
Willem van Winden, Luis de Carvalho, Erwin van Tujil, Jeroen van Haaren and Leo van den Berg

53 Regional Development in Northern Europe
Peripherality, marginality and border issues
Edited by Mike Danson and Peter De Souza

52 Promoting Silicon Valleys in Latin America
Luciano Ciravegna

51 Industrial Policy Beyond the Crisis
Regional, national and international perspectives
Edited by David Bailey, Helena Lenihan and Josep-Maria Arauzo-Carod

50 Just Growth
Inclusion and prosperity in America's metropolitan regions
Chris Benner and Manuel Pastor

49 Cultural Political Economy of Small Cities
Edited by Anne Lorentzen and Bas van Heur

48 The Recession and Beyond
Local and regional responses to the downturn
Edited by David Bailey and Caroline Chapain

47 Beyond Territory
Dynamic geographies of knowledge creation, diffusion and innovation
Edited by Harald Bathelt, Maryann Feldman and Dieter F. Kogler

46 Leadership and Place
Edited by Chris Collinge, John Gibney and Chris Mabey

45 Migration in the 21st Century
Rights, outcomes, and policy
Edited by Thomas N. Maloney and Kim Korinek

44 The Futures of the City Region
Edited by Michael Neuman and Angela Hull

43 The Impacts of Automotive Plant Closure
A tale of two cities
Edited by Andrew Beer and Holli Evans

42 Manufacturing in the New Urban Economy
Willem van Winden, Leo van den Berg, Luis Carvalho and Erwin van Tuijl

41 Globalizing Regional Development in East Asia
Production networks, clusters, and entrepreneurship
Edited by Henry Wai-chung Yeung

40 China and Europe
The implications of the rise of China for European space
Edited by Klaus R. Kunzmann, Willy A Schmid and Martina Koll-Schretzenmayr

39 Business Networks in Clusters and Industrial Districts
The governance of the global value chain
Edited by Fiorenza Belussi and Alessia Sammarra

38 Whither Regional Studies?
Edited by Andy Pike

37 Intelligent Cities and Globalisation of Innovation Networks
Nicos Komninos

36 Devolution, Regionalism and Regional Development
The UK experience
Edited by Jonathan Bradbury

35 Creative Regions
Technology, culture and knowledge entrepreneurship
Edited by Philip Cooke and Dafna Schwartz

34 European Cohesion Policy
Willem Molle

33 Geographies of the New Economy
Critical reflections
Edited by Peter W. Daniels, Andrew Leyshon, Michael J. Bradshaw and Jonathan Beaverstock

32 The Rise of the English Regions?
Edited by Irene Hardill, Paul Benneworth, Mark Baker and Leslie Budd

31 Regional Development in the Knowledge Economy
Edited by Philip Cooke and Andrea Piccaluga

30 Regional Competitiveness
Edited by Ron Martin, Michael Kitson and Peter Tyler

29 Clusters and Regional Development
Critical reflections and explorations
Edited by Bjørn Asheim, Philip Cooke and Ron Martin

28 Regions, Spatial Strategies and Sustainable Development
Graham Haughton and David Counsell

27 Sustainable Cities
Graham Haughton and Colin Hunter

26 Geographies of Labour Market Inequality
Edited by Ron Martin and Philip S. Morrison

25 Regional Innovation Strategies
The challenge for less-favoured regions
Edited by Kevin Morgan and Claire Nauwelaers

24 Out of the Ashes?
The social impact of industrial
contraction and regeneration
on Britain's mining communities
David Waddington, Chas Critcher,
Bella Dicks and David Parry

23 Restructuring Industry and Territory
The experience of Europe's regions
Edited by Anna Giunta, Arnoud
Lagendijk and Andy Pike

22 Foreign Direct Investment and the
Global Economy
Corporate and institutional
dynamics of global-localisation
Edited by Nicholas F. Phelps and
Jeremy Alden

21 Community Economic Development
Edited by Graham Haughton

20 Regional Development Agencies
in Europe
Edited by Henrik Halkier, Mike
Danson and Charlotte Damborg

19 Social Exclusion in European Cities
Processes, experiences and responses
Edited by Ali Madanipour, Goran
Cars and Judith Allen

18 Metropolitan Planning in Britain
A comparative study
Edited by Peter Roberts, Kevin
Thomas and Gwyndaf Williams

17 Unemployment and Social Exclusion
Landscapes of labour inequality
Edited by Paul Lawless, Ron Martin
and Sally Hardy

16 Multinationals and European
Integration
Trade, investment and regional
development
Nicholas A. Phelps

15 The Coherence of EU Regional Policy
Contrasting perspectives on
the structural funds
Edited by John Bachtler and Ivan
Turok

14 New Institutional Spaces
TECs and the remaking of economic
governance
Martin Jones, Foreword by Jamie
Peck

13 Regional Policy in Europe
S. S. Artobolevskiy

12 Innovation, Networks and Learning
Regions?
Edited by James Simmie

11 British Regionalism and Devolution
The challenges of state reform and
European integration
Edited by Jonathan Bradbury and
John Mawson

10 Regional Development Strategies
A European perspective
Edited by Jeremy Alden and Philip
Boland

9 Union Retreat and the Regions
The shrinking landscape of
organised labour
Ron Martin, Peter Sunley and Jane
Wills

8 The Regional Dimension of
Transformation in Central
Europe
Grzegorz Gorzelak

7 The Determinants of Small Firm
Growth
An inter-regional study in the United
Kingdom 1986–90
Richard Barkham, Graham Gudgin,
Mark Hart and Eric Hanvey

6 **The Regional Imperative**
Regional planning and governance
in Britain, Europe and the United
States
Urlan A. Wannop

5 **An Enlarged Europe**
Regions in competition?
*Edited by Sally Hardy, Mark Hart,
Louis Albrechts and Anastasios Katos*

4 **Spatial Policy in a Divided Nation**
*Edited by Richard T. Harrison and
Mark Hart*

3 **Regional Development in the 1990s**
The British Isles in transition
*Edited by Peter Townroe and Ron
Martin*

2 **Retreat from the Regions**
Corporate change and the closure of
factories
Stephen Fothergill and Nigel Guy

1 **Beyond Green Belts**
Managing urban growth in the 21st
century
Edited by John Herington

Code and the City

**Edited by Rob Kitchin
and Sung-Yueh Perng**

LONDON AND NEW YORK

First published 2016
by Routledge
2 Park Square, Milton Park, Abingdon, Oxon OX14 4RN

and by Routledge
711 Third Avenue, New York, NY 10017

Routledge is an imprint of the Taylor & Francis Group, an informa business

© 2016 selection and editorial matter, Rob Kitchin and Sung-Yueh Perng; individual chapters, the contributors

The right of the editors to be identified as the author of the editorial material, and of the authors for their individual chapters, has been asserted in accordance with sections 77 and 78 of the Copyright, Designs and Patents Act 1988.

All rights reserved. No part of this book may be reprinted or reproduced or utilised in any form or by any electronic, mechanical or other means, now known or hereafter invented, including photocopying and recording, or in any information storage or retrieval system, without permission in writing from the publishers.

Trademark notice: Product or corporate names may be trademarks or registered trademarks, and are used only for identification and explanation without intent to infringe.

British Library Cataloguing in Publication Data
A catalogue record for this book is available from the British Library

Library of Congress Cataloging in Publication Data
Names: Kitchin, Rob, editor. | Perng, Sung-Yueh.
Title: Code and the city / edited by Rob Kitchin and Sung-Yueh Perng.
Description: New York : Routledge, 2016.
Identifiers: LCCN 2015041564 | ISBN 9781138922105 (hardback) |
    ISBN 9781138922112 (pbk.) | ISBN 9781315685991 (ebook)
Subjects: LCSH: Municipal services–Technological innovations. | Cities and
    towns–Growth. | Management information systems.
Classification: LCC HD4431 .C543 2016 | DDC 363.60285–dc23
LC record available at http://lccn.loc.gov/2015041564

ISBN: 978-1-138-92210-5 (hbk)
ISBN: 978-1-138-92211-2 (pbk)
ISBN: 978-1-315-68599-1 (ebk)

Typeset in Times New Roman
by Servis Filmsetting Ltd, Stockport, Cheshire

Contents

List of figures	xiii
List of tables	xv
List of contributors	xvi

1	Code and the city: introduction	1
	ROB KITCHIN AND SUNG-YUEH PERNG	

PART I
Code, coding, infrastructure and cities   **13**

2	From a single line of code to an entire city: reframing the conceptual terrain of code/space	15
	ROB KITCHIN	
3	The Internet of Urban Things	27
	PAUL DOURISH	
4	Interfacing urban intelligence	49
	SHANNON MATTERN	
5	Abstract urbanism	61
	MATTHEW FULLER AND GRAHAM HARWOOD	
6	Code traffic: code repositories, crowds and urban life	72
	ADRIAN MACKENZIE	

PART II
Locative social media and mobile computing   **89**

7	Digital social interactions in the city: reflecting on location-based social networks	91
	LUIGINA CIOLFI AND GABRIELA AVRAM	

xii *Contents*

8 Feeling place in the city: strange ontologies and
location-based social media 105
LEIGHTON EVANS

9 Curating the city: urban interfaces and locative media as
experimental platforms for cultural data 116
NANNA VERHOEFF AND CLANCY WILMOTT

10 Moving applications: a multilayered approach to mobile
computing 130
JAMES MERRICKS WHITE

11 Exploring urban social media: *Selfiecity* and *On Broadway* 146
LEV MANOVICH

PART III
Governance, politics and knowledge **161**

12 Digital urbanism in crises 163
MONIKA BÜSCHER, XAROULA KERASIDOU, MICHAEL
LIEGL AND KATRINA PETERSEN

13 Coding alternative modes of governance: learning from
experimental 'peer-to-peer cities' 178
ALISON POWELL

14 Encountering the city at hacking events 190
SOPHIA MAALSEN AND SUNG-YUEH PERNG

15 Semantic cities: coded geopolitics and the rise of the
Semantic Web 200
HEATHER FORD AND MARK GRAHAM

16 Cities and context: the codification of small areas
through geodemographic classification 215
ALEX SINGLETON

Index 236

Figures

2.1	Digital technology stacks	20
2.2	Conceptualising the constitution of a digital socio-technical system	21
2.3	Conceptual framework for programmable urbanism	23
3.1	USB ports incorporated into a US power socket	31
3.2	The 2004 map of the National Lambda Rail optical fibre network displays a remarkable similarity to a map of the ARPANet in 1974	39
6.1	Event counts for the GitHub team	78
6.2	Repositories worked on by the GitHub team	79
6.3	`Bootstrap` repositories with more than 100 forks since 2012	85
7.1	Tips for Sheffield train station	98
7.2	Tips for the Crucible Theatre, Sheffield	98
7.3	Tips used as private banter at a Limerick pub	99
7.4	User photographs of Limerick's Milk Market	101
9.1	*Saving Face* installation	117
10.1	From left to right: Benkler's model, Zittrain's model and the proposed model	133
10.2	From left to right: Hailo tour feature (location refinement), taxis near Muckross Parade, tracking the driver in real time and automatic card payment	135
10.3	Clockwise from top left: Moves interface mode (temporal representation), two views of Moves interface mode (spatial representation) and third-party services built using the Moves API	138
10.4	Left: MMapper Processing sketch. Right: Move-O-Scope Web application	140
11.1	50,000 Instagram photos shared in Tokyo in 2012	147
11.2	50,000 Instagram photos shared in Bangkok in 2012	147
11.3	Imageplot showing distribution of selfie photos in five cities according to sex and degree of smile	150
11.4	Screenshot from *Selfiexploratory* application	152

xiv *Figures*

11.5	Data and image layers used to create the interface for navigating a city street in *On Broadway* project	153
11.6	Screenshot from *On Broadway* application, showing a zoomed-in view centred on Time Square	154
11.7	Interaction with *On Broadway* installation at New York Public Library	155
12.1	A displaced Haitian fixes mobile phones in a tent city near Port au Prince, Haiti (24 January 2010)	164
12.2	Ushahidi Haiti Project situation room in Boston	169
15.1	Results of a search for 'Paris' on Google (4 December 2014)	202
15.2	Section of the Jerusalem infobox on English Wikipedia as at 13 July 2014	205
15.3	Screenshot of Google results after clicking on the population figure for Jerusalem (19 January 2015)	208
15.4	Screenshots after clicking on 'feedback' and the 'Wrong?' hyperlink above the Jerusalem headline on google.com	209
15.5	Screenshot of Google Public Data Explorer Forum as at 21 December 2014	210
16.1	Supergroup level Output Area Classification – UK	224
16.2	Supergroup level Output Area Classification – Liverpool	225
16.3	An 'elbow criterion' plot used to consider an appropriate number of supergroup clusters in a Liverpool Output Area Classification	226
16.4	Supergroup level Liverpool Output Area Classification	227
16.5	Liverpool Output Area Classification supergroups	229

Tables

2.1	Apparatus and elements of a data assemblage	19
6.1	20 early and recent repositories on Github.com	83
6.2	Most-forked repositories on GitHub in January 2013	84
6.3	Most-forked `bootstrap`-related repositories during January 2013	85
12.1	Example of messages sent by Haitians	167
12.2	Crowdsourcing funding for Haiti 'first responders'	169
12.3	Excerpt from a chat running alongside the Mission 4636 effort	170
16.1	2011 Output Area Classification input variables	221
16.2	2011 Output Area Classification hierarchy	222
16.3	Liverpool Output Area Classification labels and brief descriptions	228
16.4	Percentage of output areas assigned to Output Area Classification supergroups (rows) and Liverpool Output Area Classification supergroups (columns)	230

Contributors

Gabriela Avram is Lecturer in Digital Media and Interaction Design, and Senior Researcher at the Interaction Design Centre, University of Limerick, Ireland. Building on a background in computer-supported cooperative work and knowledge management, her research currently focuses on practices in cultural heritage organisations and urban communities, and on facilitating technology adoption. Her previous work includes studying distributed work practices in software development and the uses of social media for work purposes.

Monika Büscher is Professor of Sociology at the Centre for Mobilities Research at Lancaster University. She researches the digital dimensions of contemporary 'mobile lives', with a focus on ethics and crises. In 2011, she was awarded an honorary doctorate by Roskilde University, Denmark. She edits the book series *Changing Mobilities* with Peter Adey.

Luigina Ciolfi is Reader in Communication at Sheffield Hallam University, UK. She holds a Laurea (University of Siena) and a PhD (University of Limerick) in Human–Computer Interaction. She studies socio-technical systems in settings such as heritage sites, public spaces and professional organisations, as well as practices in the design of interactive systems.

Paul Dourish is Professor of Informatics in the Donald Bren School of Information and Computer Sciences at University of California, Irvine with courtesy appointments in Computer Science and Anthropology. His research focuses on information technology as a site of social and cultural production, combining topics in human–computer interaction, ubiquitous computing and science and technology studies. His most recent book (with Genevieve Bell) is *Divining a Digital Future: Mess and Mythology in Ubiquitous Computing* (MIT Press, 2011).

Leighton Evans received a PhD in the Philosophy of Technology and Digital Media from Swansea University in 2013. He is a lecturer in digital media cultures at the University of Brighton, and was formerly a postdoctoral researcher on the *Programmable City* project at Maynooth University, funded by the European Research Council. Leighton is the author of *Locative Social Media: Place in the Digital Age* (Palgrave, 2015).

Heather Ford is University Fellow in Digital Research Methods at the University of Leeds School of Media and Communication. With a background in Internet rights activism, working with several organisations, including Creative Commons, Privacy International, the Association for Progressive Communications and Ushahidi, her research interests include issues around the governance of digital platforms, media power in networked information environments, and the design and politics of software platforms.

Matthew Fuller is Professor of Cultural Studies and Director of the Centre for Cultural Studies, Goldsmiths, University of London. His books include (with Andrew Goffey) *Evil Media* (MIT, 2012) and he is a co-editor of *Computational Culture, a Journal of Software Studies.*

Mark Graham is Associate Professor and Senior Research Fellow at the Oxford Internet Institute. His research focuses on Internet and information geographies, and the overlaps between ICTs and economic development. His recent books include *Society and the Internet* (OUP, 2014, edited with William H. Dutton) and *Research and Fieldwork in Development* (Routledge, 2014, with Daniel Hammett and Chasca Twyman).

Graham Harwood is part of the celebrated artists' group YoHa, where he works with his partner Matusko Yokokoji. He also teaches at the Centre for Cultural Studies, Goldsmiths, University of London.

Xaroula Kerasidou is a research associate at the Centre for Mobilities Research, Lancaster University. Her research interests lie within the field of feminist science and technology studies, where she focuses on the material and semiotic practices of technoscience. Currently, she works on the EU FP7 funded project *SecInCoRe* (www.secincore.eu).

Rob Kitchin is a professor and ERC Advanced Investigator at the National University of Ireland, Maynooth. He is currently a principal investigator for the Programmable City project, Digital Repository of Ireland, All-Island Research Observatory and the Dublin Dashboard. He was the 2013 recipient of the Royal Irish Academy's Gold Medal for the Social Sciences.

Michael Liegl is postdoctoral researcher and coordinator of the graduate program *Loose Connections: Collectivity in Urban and Digital Spaces* at the University of Hamburg. Central to his research are socio-technical assemblages formed by the hybridization of online and offline practices. His research focuses on digitally mediated collaboration in disaster management and digital art, creative work, mobility patterns and collectivisation in digital mobile dating practices.

xviii *Contributors*

Sophia Maalsen is a postdoctoral research fellow at Macquarie University, working on the ARC-funded grant, *Governing Urban Energy Transitions: Reconfiguring Spaces, Sites, Subjects*, with Professor Robyn Dowling and Professor Pauline McGuirk. Sophia is an urban and cultural geographer, and also writes on feminist and music geographies.

Adrian Mackenzie is Professor in Technological Cultures, Department of Sociology, Lancaster University and has published work on technology: *Transductions: Bodies and Machines at Speed*, (2002/6); *Cutting Code: Software and Sociality* (2006), and *Wirelessness: Radical Empiricism in Network Cultures* (2010). He is currently working on an archaeology of machine learning and its associated transformations. He codirects the Centre for Science Studies, Lancaster University, UK.

Lev Manovich is the author of seven books including *Software Takes Command* (Bloomsbury Academic, 2013) and *The Language of New Media* (MIT Press, 2001). He is Director of the Software Studies Initiative, which works on the analysis and visualisation of big visual cultural data. He appeared on the *List of 25 People Shaping the Future of Design* (2013) and a list of 50 'most interesting people building the future' (The Verge, 2014).

Shannon Mattern is Associate Professor of Media Studies at The New School. She writes about media infrastructures, libraries, archives and other media spaces. She is the author of *The New Downtown Library* (Minnesota, 2007), *Deep Mapping the Media City* (Minnesota, 2015) and writes regularly for *Places*, a landscape and urbanism journal.

Sung-Yueh Perng is a postdoctoral researcher on the ERC funded Programmable City project at Maynooth University. He received a PhD in Sociology from Lancaster University; his current research focuses on distributed, collaborative and embodied practices in civic hacking and the incorporation of personal analytics into urban lives.

Katrina Petersen is Research Associate at Lancaster University working on the *SecInCoRe* project focusing on the design of a culturally and ethically conscious disaster information sharing system for the EU. Her main research is on visualising risk, disaster maps and how to communicate between diverse groups.

Alison Powell is Assistant Professor at the London School of Economics and Programme Director of the MSc course in Media and Communication (Data and Society). Her research examines how people's values influence the way technology is built, and how discourses, practices and governance structures are produced in relation to new technological systems. She is especially interested in open source cultures.

Contributors xix

Alex Singleton is Professor of Geographic Information Science at the University of Liverpool. His research concerns the development of an empirically informed critique of the ways in which geodemographic methods can be refined for effective yet ethical use in public resource allocation applications.

Nanna Verhoeff is Associate Professor at the Department of Media and Culture Studies at Utrecht University. She publishes on emerging and changing media cultures of early cinema, mobile and location-based arts and media, and urban screens and interfaces. Her books include *The West in Early Cinema* (Amsterdam UP, 2006) and *Mobile Screens* (Amsterdam UP, 2012).

James Merricks White is studying for a PhD with the *Programmable City* project at Maynooth University. He is researching the role played by standards and processes of standardisation in the development of digital technologies in the city.

Clancy Wilmott is a PhD student at the University of Manchester. Her research focuses on the impact of digital mobile mapping practices on place-making, wayfinding and the spatial imagination in three post-colonial cities: Hong Kong, Sydney and Los Angeles. She is also affiliated to the *Charting the Digital* research project led by Sybille Lammes, which is funded by the European Research Council.

1 Code and the city

Introduction

Rob Kitchin and Sung-Yueh Perng

> The modern city exists as a haze of software instructions. Nearly every urban practice is becoming mediated by code.
>
> (Amin and Thrift 2002: 125)

Over the past few decades, software has become essential to the functioning of cities. Urban systems and the physical and social infrastructure of the city are increasingly composed of and mediated by software-enabled technologies, and the management and governance of society framed by and undertaken through interconnecting socio-technical systems. A diverse range of public and private organisations now deploy digital technologies to monitor, regulate and control their infrastructure and the delivery of services using coded assemblages of hardware (such as chips, boards, sensors, actuators, transponders, meters, wires, batteries, screens, etc., combined into digital devices), software (e.g., firmware, middleware, operating systems, programs, apps), flows of data and interfaces, which are networked together (via various forms of Internet connections: e.g., wired, wireless, radio, satellite) (Kitchin and Dodge 2011).

Such coded assemblages now exist with respect to urban government (e.g., city services, public administration), utilities (e.g., energy, water, lighting), transportation (both car-based and public transit), public and private surveillance and security, emergency response, communications (e.g., mobile phone networks, the Internet), financial institutions and retail chains, environmental monitoring (of pollution, environmental risk, weather), and other services. All kinds of websites and apps exist – including information and data portals, crowdsourced maps and encyclopaedias, and reviews of shops, accommodation, etc. – that provide insights about urban environments, resources, services and pressing issues, as well as providing a means to source further data. A large percentage of people now traverse their cities carrying a relatively powerful computer in the form of a smartphone that hosts locative social media platforms, such as Twitter, Foursquare and Tinder, enabling and facilitating new forms of social interaction and socio-spatial behaviour, and location-based services providing spatially contextual information and recommendations.

2 *Rob Kitchin and Sung-Yueh Perng*

Indeed, interacting with software has become an everyday occurrence for people, to the extent that it is mostly treated as routine and habit, operating as a 'technological unconscious' that is only noticed when it performs incorrectly or fails (Thrift 2004; Kitchin and Dodge 2011). Moreover, such is the pervasiveness of digital technologies and networks, it is impossible now to live outside their orbit, even if one possesses no digital devices and resides within an analogue home, as all key infrastructures are coded and national governments deploy digital systems in managing their affairs. Whether one is relaxing at home, travelling across a city, engaging in work, undertaking consumption, or communicating with friends and family, these are now activities that are mediated by code.

Digital technologies and services, then, are increasingly important to how we understand and plan cities, how we manage urban services and utilities, and how we live urban lives, helping to produce what have been termed 'smart cities': densely instrumented urban systems that can be monitored, managed and regulated in real time (see Townsend 2013; Kitchin 2014), whose data can be used to better depict, model and predict urban processes and simulate future urban development (Batty *et al.*, 2012), and whose deployment facilitates new forms of digital subjectivity, citizenship, participation and political action (Isin and Ruppert 2015).

And yet, despite the rapid development and deployment of digital technologies for augmenting and facilitating city management and urban life, and the creation and roll-out of new forms of networked urbanism, it is fair to say that, in contrast with the thousands of academic studies and the experimentation of companies seeking to develop, test and implement new technological products, *critical analyses* of the relationship between code and cities are small in number, underdeveloped conceptually and lacking detailed empirical case materials. The speed of technological innovation and material deployment, and the power of the discursive regimes driving their adoption, is outpacing and outflanking critical reflection and intervention. Moreover, critical social scientists and humanities scholars are still struggling to get to grips conceptually with a series of interrelated phenomena – code, ubiquitous computing, big data, locative social media, mobile computing, networked urbanism and smart cities – at the same time as trying to map out and dissect their consequences and implications.

The book

Code and the City is designed to add to and extend the theoretical and empirical work conducted to date, providing both new conceptual thinking and illustrative examples of the relationship between software and the urban. It is not focused specifically on the notion and creation of smart cities, but rather on the technologies, networks and relationships that enable their production. As such, the book is interested in charting and understanding the recursive relationship between code and the city: how the city is translated into code,

Code and the city: introduction 3

and how code reshapes the city. To do this, the book brings together an interdisciplinary group of authors (from geography, sociology, media studies, cultural studies, communications, informatics and computer science), as critically examining this recursive relationship requires a variety of expertise and knowledge and for these to be brought into dialogue. As well as a range of disciplinary and theoretical perspectives, to illustrate the diversity of different coded assemblages and the coded production of space, the chapters also detail a number of empirical examples, including the Internet of Things, community wireless, locative social media and other apps, urban art installations, code libraries, search engines, geodemographics, city interfaces, hackathons and crowdsourced emergency response.

The chapters were initially prepared for a workshop at the National University of Ireland, Maynooth, in September 2014, which was funded by the European Research Council through an Advanced Investigator Award to Rob Kitchin for *The Programmable City* (project ERC-2012-AdG-323636-SOFTCITY). The workshop met the travel costs of a carefully selected group of researchers, enabling them to attend. Each paper was drafted and submitted in advance of the meeting, extensively discussed at the workshop and subsequently revised for publication in this volume. A second volume based on a similar workshop held in September 2015, *Data and the City*, will hopefully form a companion book. To provide a structure, we have divided the book into three sections, each with five papers.

Code, coding, infrastructure and cities

The first section considers the relationship between code and the city in a broad sense, focusing on code, its production, and how it is being embedded into cities and used to reshape city life.

In Chapter 2, Rob Kitchin argues that, to date, the literature focusing on the relationship between code and the city has a number of shortcomings. He posits that studies that concentrate on code are often narrow in remit, fading out the city, and tend to fetishise and potentially decontextualise code at the expense of the wider socio-technical assemblage within which it is embedded. Studies that focus on the city tend to examine the effects of code, but rarely unpack the constitution and mechanics of the code producing those effects. To try and provide a more holistic account of the relationship between code and the city, he forwards two interlinked conceptual frameworks. The first places code within a wider socio-technical assemblage. The second conceives the city as being composed of millions of such assemblages. The latter, Kitchin contends, aims to provide a means of productively building a conceptual and empirical understanding of code and the city that scales from individual lines of code to the complexity of an entire urban system.

Much of the rhetoric and creation of smart city technologies revolves around the production of an Internet of Urban Things and urban computing – networked devices, sensors and actuators embedded into the fabric of buildings and the infrastructure of cities. Paul Dourish critically examines, as two parallel discourses, the Internet of Things and smart cities, in order to identify points of connection and to read the pragmatics and politics of deployment of each through the other. In the first part of his essay, Dourish traces the development of the Internet of Things and provides a set of observations concerning its networked nature, its temporality, its scaling, its operation and relations to people. In the second part, he turns his attention to smart cities, applying the same framework of observation. Dourish notes that both the Internet of Things and smart cities are plagued by tensions between holistic design and piecemeal accumulation, temporalities of development, and disparities in control and management. The consequence he contends is that, in contrast to the marketing hype, smart cities evolve in a piecemeal, gradual, disparate manner, under the control of different groups, shaped by politics, and consists of a hodge-podge of technologies using varying standards and protocols, and builds on an array of existing technology and infrastructure. There is no master plan, but rather lots of patching, hacking, jury-rigging and settling. In so much as smart cities exist, they are 'accidental smart cities'. Dourish argues that an understanding of the Internet of Urban Things necessitates examining their socio-technical assemblage, with serious attention paid to the 'technical stack', their temporalities, their politics and the participation they engender.

Much information about cities is presently accessed through screen interfaces, which present particular urban visions. Shannon Mattern critiques the 'widgetisation' of urban resources through such coded media and provides a rubric for thinking about the kinds and sources of data that underpin these systems, the design and implementation of such systems, and the people for whom such systems are created and deployed. How these coded urban dashboard and city operating systems are being deployed to produce smart cities, Mattern argues, reflects a certain kind of instrumental rationality that serves particular corporate and government interests and shifts urban vision and interaction from collective endeavour to personal consumption and convenience: translating urban sociality and spatiality 'from *our* messy city into *my* efficient city'. Mattern contends that much more consideration needs to be paid, on the one hand, to unpacking how urban interfaces are framed, designed and work, and, on the other, on how to design interfaces for urban citizens that are open, transparent, creative and imaginative and open up possibilities rather than limiting conduct and facilitating command and control. Such an approach would facilitate thinking about the relationship between technology, people and cities; what kind of cities we want and what kind of citizens we want to be in the era of smart cities.

For Matthew Fuller and Graham Harwood, the increasing use of computation to manage and control cities necessitates the production of a certain kind of abstract urbanism. Abstract in the sense that the logics of computation are underpinned by processes of abstraction, reduction and empiricism that inherently frame social and spatial processes with respect to defined

Code and the city: introduction 5

rule sets. They trace the rationale and logic of computational models of urban processes, especially simulations, back to game theory, developed in the 1940s and racial segregation modelling, from the 1960s, through to agent-based models designed to simulate how individuals of differing characteristics behave in the city under different conditions. For Fuller and Harwood, computers are abstract machines that may make claims to objectivity but are in fact thoroughly political through the choices made with regards to mathematical structures underpinning the models and encoded in software. As such, while social simulations express forms of emergence, they do so within a field of defined constraints. And yet, despite their limitations, models and modelisations are being ever-more integrated into the design and operation of city spaces and services, and urban issues are becoming computational problems. Fuller and Harwood thus argue that, as computation is increasingly embedded into urban life, and software becomes a city-making force, it is crucial that its processes of abstraction and reduction, and the consequences thereof, are exposed and examined.

In Chapter 6, Adrian Mackenzie asks and answers two key questions. In what frame and at what levels of abstraction does the density and plurality of code in the city become legible or even enumerable? What has happened to the cycling through and rewriting of code over the last 15 years? Drawing on Thrift and French (2002), he discusses three geographies of trafficking code through cities: a geography of writing code (where code writing takes place), a geography of power and control (how code defines and enacts rule of urban conduct and interlinks systems) and a geography of indeterminancy (how code produces emergent spaces). Mackenzie argues that, over the past 15 years, a reordering of code traffic has occurred, with the clustered production of code being decentred through a much more networked flow of code. He illustrates his argument through an examination of GitHub, an enormous code repository initially centred in San Francisco, but now with branches and users distributed globally. Code, he details, travels between different bits of software and GitHub acts as both a platform for social coding and a terminus for code traffic that rechannels and reshapes the code that passes through it. Mackenzie concludes that the production of code is less like a machine, a system or an assemblage but more like a crowd, and that, given the mergers, coalescences, branching and replication of bodies of code within code repositories, there is no single operational level at which code governs cities. As such, code needs to be viewed as a mixing process that reconfigures the infrastructure, logistics and circulation of individuals in cities; to make sense of such code means examining the traffic in code – how it moves and takes shape – rather than isolated pieces of software, systems or applications.

Locative social media and mobile computing

The second section considers the relationship between code, locative social media and mobile computing, focusing on how smartphones in particular and

6   *Rob Kitchin and Sung-Yueh Perng*

the locative social media apps they enable are mediating how people interact with the city and each other, and how the large quantities of data generated from such apps can be used to explore and analyse these relationships.

With the rise of smartphones, location-based social media has become an increasingly popular means of documenting and mediating interactions with city spaces and places. Drawing on initial studies of Foursquare – an app that links and shares location, activity, tips and photos – and their own research of Foursquare use in Limerick, Ireland, and Sheffield, UK, Luigina Ciolfi and Gabriela Avram examine the technological support of human activities and the relationship between code, digital agency and the physical world. In particular, they explore: how location-based social networks (LBSNs) are used by individuals, and how they influence socio-spatial behaviour and frame place perception, as well as being used strategically with respect to self-presentation; and how LBSN interactions are rematerialised in the physical world and also feed back into how the software works. Their findings highlight how digital social interactions are increasingly interwoven with urban spaces and places, producing new kinds of code-mediated socio-spatial behaviours and practices.

Similarly, Leighton Evans, also focusing his analysis on Foursquare, argues that the use of location-based social media can result in deep and novel understandings of locations. He contends that the crowdsourced contributions of other users and the information pushed by the app help individuals to rapidly attune themselves to places. Drawing on Heidegger's phenomenology and Sloterdijk's theory of spheres, he explores how the moment that place is appreciated as *place* (that is, as a meaningful existential locale) can be reconciled with the delegation of the epistemologies of placehood to a computational device and location-based social media application. Drawing on data from an ethnographic study of Foursquare users, code and computational devices are contextualised as a constant foregrounding presence in the city. The engagement of the user, device, code and data in understanding place is a moment of phenomenological revelation that is co-constituent of all these elements, wherein code is the membrane that allows information to flow and influence, and yet is withdrawn and opaque to users. As such, the computationally mediated spatial behaviours of LBSNs, and thus the relationship between code and the city, operates largely beyond the circumspection of their users. Consequently, Evans argues, it is important to theorise and empirically examine the phenomenological unfolding of urban computational praxes in order to appreciate their diverse affects and effects.

Screen interfaces to interactively access, explore and engage with information are becoming an increasingly common feature of many urban spaces. In some cases, these screen interfaces are art works that layer together spaces, software, databases and interactive touchscreen technology and are designed as thinking machines to prompt critical reflection on such urban technology and the datafication and codification of urban culture. In Chapter 9, Nanna Verhoeff and Clancy Wilmott examine in detail one such art installation,

Code and the city: introduction 7

Saving Face, created by artists Karen Lancel and Herman Maat, which links a large, public urban screen with a smaller screen housed in a kiosk, wherein participants are invited to add their face to a database, with a composite image of all participants being projected on the large screen. Verhoeff and Wilmott contend that *Saving Face*, and other similar works, enable consideration of: the specificities of the use of mobile, interactive and networked media; the performativity and embodiment of engaging with such media; and how the city is reflected back into media artworks. They contend that such artworks can be understood as curatorial laboratories for embodied criticality. Moreover, as theoretical objects, they suggest that such projects allow us to investigate layering and location design principles for urban interfaces. Through their analysis, Verhoeff and Wilmott consider the dispositif of urban interfaces, the participatory agency of the individual in the act of interfacing, the installation as a public event, and the curation of cultural data and spaces. In so doing, they start to develop heuristic tools for the critical evaluation of urban interfaces or as interfaces of cultural curation.

Through an analysis of the taxi service application, Hailo, and the personal life-logging application, Moves, James Merricks White argues that it is not enough to examine the relationship between code and the city in order to understand the work and effects of these apps. Rather, he contends, they rely on a vast network of interlocking technologies with a complex spatial topology. White forwards a multilayered model, what he calls a 'socio-technical stack', consisting of four interlocking and hierarchically organised components – hardware, code, data(base) and media interfaces – designed to provide a heuristic for the critical examination of mobile applications that does not fetishise any particular layer, such as code, at the expense of others. His examination of Hailo demonstrates how the reconfiguration of hardware and telecommunications infrastructure is crucial in disrupting traditional radio-based taxi businesses and raises a number of legal and regulatory issues. Moves, in contrast, is an example of how app-generated data can exceed the software configurations in which it is represented, and provide a platform for other apps. Placing software in its wider technical stack, and framing that stack within its wider socio-technical assemblage, White contends, enables the political and economic entanglements of these apps and the mutual constitution of computation and the city to be deciphered.

Lev Manovich has been at the forefront of developing new cultural analytics – the analysis of massive digital, cultural datasets, especially those generated via social media, such as Instagram, Twitter and Foursquare, using computational and visualisation techniques. Through a series of related projects, Manovich has compared the characteristics and content of social media for different cities and how best to extract and communicate meaningful information from the millions of photos and other data generated by people within cities daily. In Chapter 11, Manovich details the process of constructing new cultural analytics for two projects. *Selfiecity* is a dataset of selfie photos shared via Instagram in five cities. To determine whether these photos

8   Rob Kitchin and Sung-Yueh Perng

differ in style and content between cities, Manovich and his team created a number of different types of visualisations, including blend video montages, imageplots and *Selfiexploratory*, an interactive website. *On Broadway* is a multimodal, interactive data visualisation for a single street that blends together data harvested from Instagram, Twitter, Foursquare, Google Street View, taxi pick-ups and drop-offs, and economic indicators from the US Census Bureau, and plotted into 100-metre wide rectangles positioned every 30 metres along 13.5 miles of Broadway, New York. The idea is to enable citizens to explore the rich, cultural 'big data' relating to a place they either visit or live. Together, the two projects reveal the extent to which new locative social media are generating vast troves of cultural data about cities and their inhabitants. Manovich argues that while such datasets open up the possibility of new forms of surveillance, they also create new opportunities for computational cultural analytics to inform and delight citizens.

Governance, politics and knowledge

The third section examines the urban politics of code; how it is deployed to manage cities in times of crisis, how alternative coded assemblages can be produced by communities through civic hacking, and the politics of how code is used to make sense of and produce knowledge about cities.

In times of crisis, such as an earthquake, the digitally networked infrastructure can be severely disrupted, but it can also provide a means to quickly and effectively connect and organise emergency responses both locally and globally. Monika Büscher and her colleagues discuss the latter in Chapter 12, examining digital urbanism under conditions of crisis. Drawing on the examples of the earthquakes in Haiti (2010) and Japan (2011), they detail how the use of mobile phones, cloud computing, locative social media, distributed mapping and networked logistics were used to locate survivors and coordinate relief efforts, and enabled people located at a distance to contribute productively to localised trauma through language translation, topping up phone payments, mapping work and documenting damage. The use of new ICT technologies, and how they could rescale and reterritorialise emergency responses, has proven to be a disruptive innovation, changing established practices and taken-for-granted social and organisational conventions, economic and political models, and notions of humanity and justice. However, while these technologies have undoubted benefits, Büscher and colleagues detail that they facilitate surveillance, qualculation and automation. Moreover, they use their case studies to consider wider philosophical questions concerning the relationship between people and technology, the ethics of care, and how to design better IT for crisis response.

The majority of smart city initiatives that deploy coded infrastructure are owned and managed by companies and states and are deployed through top-down governance via systems of centralised control. Alison Powell, in contrast, considers alternative, bottom-up, participatory visions of the

Code and the city: introduction 9

relationship between code and the city and what they might mean for the governance of urban space. She does so through an examination of peer-to-peer urbanism, as produced through the discourse, practices and architectures of community wireless networks, which are owned and run by local communities. Such peer-to-peer networks, Powell contends, enact a 'politics of the minor' – localised political interventions that disrupt the dominant order – and create new forms of technological citizenship. They therefore illustrate the possibilities of alternative ways of producing coded cities that have different organisational practices, modes of architecture, political sensibilities and spatial formations. However, they are also vulnerable to erasure or absorption by the dominant order, as has happened with many community wireless networks. Nonetheless, they highlight that there is no teleological inevitability to how smart cities will unfold.

Hackathons and civic hacking have become popular events in which individuals collaborate to produce technological solutions to urban problems. Sophia Maalsen and Sung-Yueh Perng examine how hackathons take place, how the coding produced within them seeks to address urban problems, and the implications and challenges that emerge in that process, by drawing on their ethnographic participant observation of Code for Ireland events in Dublin, Ireland. In particular, Maalsen and Perng focus on the placing of hackathons, examining the role of the venue, its spatial arrangements and the fluidity and messiness of the hackathon process, the relationship between individuals and the collective hack, and the productive tension between what the participants want to do and what the government or companies running the hackathon desire. In the process, Maalsen and Perng reflect on how hackathons seek to translate the problems of the city into apps that seek to provide answers and, in turn, transform ways of living. They conclude, however, that the events are often more effective in facilitating networking and providing a social experience than producing apps that effect change.

Heather Ford and Mark Graham examine how places are codified in data and data structures, and linked and represented through the Semantic Web, to produce digital representations that augment knowledge about cities. In particular, they focus on Google's Knowledge Graph, which links, structures and shares data from Wikipedia, UNdata and other sites, to provide snapshot information about places in relation to searches without the need to visit other sites. In combination, Google and Wikipedia's algorithms and databanks determine how a city is presented. This is far from a neutral process, however, with a locale's political context often embedded into its digital layers. Ford and Graham illustrate this by examining how different language versions of Wikipedia, as well as Wikidata, Freebase and Google, present information about Jerusalem, a highly contested city. Their analysis highlights how the intersections of people, practices, tools, laws, and geopolitics produce different, contested codified versions of Jerusalem, depending on language version (English vs Hebrew vs Arabic), but that nuances, provenance, agency of

10 *Rob Kitchin and Sung-Yueh Perng*

editors and transparency in politics are often obscured. Ford and Graham conclude that the messy political informational layers of cities are presently becoming more accessible to machines and more opaque to humans; structured to enable an automatic production of geographical knowledge, but one that obscures heterogeneity and presents a narrowly framed view of cities.

Alex Singleton's chapter provides a detailed illustration of the abstract urbanism identified by Fuller and Harwood, presenting the codification of geodemographic classifications, their history and their use. Geodemographic models group areas into categories based on shared population and built-environment characteristics, using practices of abstraction, reduction and representation. These models are then used for a variety of purposes, including area-based social policy formulation and targeted marketing, having diverse effects on city life. Singleton details how constructing these models is both a science and an art, involving the use of statistics and computation, but also builder judgement and experience to create classifications that seemingly best represent the characteristics of a place. He also details how the models can be influenced by scaling, zones, input variables, measurement, weights, transformations and clustering methods. Singleton illustrates the effect of the geographical extent of the classification boundaries on the geodemographics produced by comparing the same method applied to the UK and Liverpool. He argues that such urban codification has great utility, but also that the methods deployed to create them need to be open in nature so that the process of abstract urbanism is transparent and open to scrutiny and challenge.

Code and the city

Taken together, the chapters highlight the diverse ways in which the city and code are being co-produced and how this, in turn, is reshaping urban infrastructures, management, knowledge and living. Several themes that cut across the chapters advance the debate as to how best to make sense of the relationship between code and the city. We highlight three that we think demand particular attention.

First, what is at stake is the transformation of urban infrastructures, knowledge and everyday practices through their enduring and emergent associations with code. There is a pressing need, then, to understand the nature and work of code in the city. At the same time, we need to be mindful of fetishising code at the expense of the full socio-technical assemblage that constitutes digital technologies and their enactment. Software-enabled technologies consist of amalgams of infrastructure, hardware, operating systems, software and data that are bolted together and work in conjunction to perform their work. How the city is rendered as models and captured in code as algorithms is a crucial element in the reterritorialisation of the city through a computational or mathematical logic (see Chapter 5). This abstract urbanism is, however, enacted through coded assemblages that work in contingent and contextual ways, dependent upon a range of social, cultural, political, legal and economic forces that shape how they are constructed and operate (see Chapters 2 to 4 and 10). These coded assemblages have varying temporalities and scalings (see Chapter 4); there is a geography and sociology to the process through which they are created (see Chapters 6, 13, 14 and 16); and they work not in isolation but in relation to other coded assemblages to create a dense network of coexisting, collaborating and competing infrastructures and systems.

Second, these assemblages are not flat ontologies, composed of horizontal, equally weighted networks of association. Nor are they neutral, objective, non-ideological in their conception and functioning. Rather, they are full of politics and power, and asymmetrical, hierarchical and contested relations (see Chapters 4 and 12 to 15). Digital technologies operate within, recast and reproduce political economies: they form the apparatus of the state, the engines of capital accumulation for business, and can be deployed and recast in acts of resistance and transgression by citizens. They are created to enact the desires of their producers and deployers and are expressions of power that work to (re)produce particular socio-spatial configurations, at the same time as they are challenged and subverted (see Chapters 13 and 15).

Third, there is performativity to the creation and enactment of coded assemblages, with them unfolding in contingent, relational, contextual and embodied ways (see Chapters 6 to 9). There is no teleological inevitability or set path dependency to how digital technologies transduce and reterritorialise cities; how they are created, deployed and used; how they produce and communicate geographical knowledge; and how they enable new forms of spatial behaviour and place making (see Chapters 7 and 8). Rather, they emerge and evolve through diverse practices, often in piecemeal, distributed, embodied and disparate ways (see Chapters 3, 12 and 13), but also through more carefully delineated but nonetheless emergent processes (see Chapters 6, 11, 15 and 16).

Taken together, these three observations point to the need for critical scholarship that can encapsulate two outcomes that are often difficult to achieve simultaneously. On the one hand, there is a need for more holistic accounts that seek to place the relationship between code and the city in a wider context. On the other, there is a need for detailed, nuanced, empirically rich accounts that tease apart complex, contingent, relational processes and unpack how coded assemblages are formulated, produced and work. Moreover, much more normative and ethical thinking needs to take place with respect to what kinds of coded cities we wish to build and inhabit. Collectively, we believe the chapters in *Code and the City* produce such breadth and depth and begin to map routes for thinking creatively about future socio-spatial relations, providing useful insights into how digital technologies are enabling new forms of programmable urbanism. We hope that you similarly find the book a stimulating, informative and constructive read.

12 *Rob Kitchin and Sung-Yueh Perng*

Acknowledgements

The research for this work was funded by a European Research Council Advanced Investigator Award to Rob Kitchin, entitled *The Programmable City* (ERC-2012-AdG-323636-SOFTCITY).

References

Amin, A. and Thrift, N. (2002) *Cities: Reimagining the Urban*, London: Polity.

Batty, M., Axhausen, K.W., Giannotti, F., Pozdnoukhov, A., Bazzani, A., Wachowicz, M., Ouzounis, G. and Portugali, Y. (2012) 'Smart cities of the future', *European Physical Journal Special Topics*, 214: 481–518.

Isin, E. and Ruppert, E. (2015) *Being Digital Citizens*, New York: Rowan and Littlefield.

Kitchin, R. (2014) 'The real-time city? Big data and smart urbanism', *GeoJournal* 79(1): 1–14.

Kitchin, R. and Dodge, M. (2011) *Code/Space: Software and Everyday Life*, Cambridge, MA: MIT Press.

Thrift, N. (2004) 'Remembering the technological unconscious by foregrounding knowledges of position', *Environment and Planning D: Society and Space*, 22(1): 175–90.

Thrift, N. and French, S. (2002) 'The automatic production of space', *Transactions of the Institute of British Geographers*, 27(3): 309–35.

Townsend, A. (2013) *Smart Cities: Big Data, Civic Hackers, and the Quest for a New Utopia*. New York: W.W. Norton and Co.

Part I

Code, coding, infrastructure and cities

2 From a single line of code to an entire city

Reframing the conceptual terrain of code/space

Rob Kitchin

Introduction

Thousands of papers and reports document the development of new digital technologies and their potential impact on cities and citizens, or have examined the role software plays in managing urban infrastructures and practices. The vast majority of these studies, however, focus on the technical development of new innovations and the production, deployment and effects of software from a non-critical, technological, engineering and governance perspective. A relatively small proportion take a more critical perspective, detailing how certain digital technologies produce new socio-spatial practices and effects (such as spatial sorting, algorithmic regulation, anticipatory governance and control creep) and forms of networked urbanism and their wider social, political and economic consequences to urban life (e.g., Mitchell 1995; Graham and Marvin 2001; Graham 2005; Foth 2008; Shepard 2011). Only in a handful of cases, however, has critical and conceptual attention been focused on the nature of software itself, its underlying code, and its relationship to urban management, governance and everyday practices from a more social, cultural and political perspective (e.g., Thrift and French 2002; Mackenzie 2006; Kitchin and Dodge 2011; Kelley 2014).

Drawing inspiration from software studies – a new field that takes software, and its production and deployment, as its object of critical analysis (see Fuller 2008; Berry 2011; Manovich 2013) – these critical interventions consider the ways in which cities and citizens are translated into code and how this code is then used to reshape cities and mediate the lives of their inhabitants. The principal argument forwarded is that:

- Code is an actant that possesses 'secondary agency' (Mackenzie 2006), that is, it is ceded the power to process data and to make automated, automatic and autonomous decisions and actions, thus making aspects of the city sentient (Dodge and Kitchin 2007; Shepard 2011).
- Code transduces space, that is, it alters the unfolding production of space through its deployment (Dodge and Kitchin 2005).

16   *Rob Kitchin*

- The city becomes programmable, that is, open to recoding and remediation, but also to being buggy and hackable (Kitchin 2011; Townsend 2013).

Code, it is thus argued, through its work as an actant, produces forms of coded space, wherein code augments or mediates the production of space but is not essential to its production, and code/space, wherein code is essential to a space being produced as intended (Kitchin and Dodge 2011). Much of the city is now produced as code/space, wherein if the code fails, the space is not transduced as desired (e.g., if checkout software in a supermarket crashes then a space is transduced as a warehouse instead of a supermarket, or if check-in software in an airport fails then the space is transduced as a large waiting room – in both cases there is no longer any manual way to process transactions; code and space are mutually constituted). Moreover, code and forms of automated management (a mode of algorithmic governance produced by software wherein technologies are enabled to make automated, automatic and autonomous decisions about how to process information and act without human oversight) are actively and extensively employed in the management and governance of urban systems, especially with respect to critical infrastructure and utilities (e.g., transport, energy, water) and policing, security and surveillance.

My book with Martin Dodge, *Code/Space: Software and Everyday Life* (2011), was an attempt to provide an overarching, holistic conceptual framework for thinking about code and the city and to make sense of the changes that digital technologies were making to the urban condition. The book sought to take ideas and observations from urban studies and software studies and work them through each other, both as a way to better understand the nature of software, and its role in everyday life, and the changing form and function of city infrastructure and urban life. We illustrated our arguments by documenting how software was reshaping travel, home and work. As with all such texts, it was provisional – a staging post rather than definitive guide – and it very much fetishised software as a key medium and operator in shaping the urban condition.

In this chapter, I want to revisit some of the conceptual ideas that Martin Dodge and I developed and to rework and extend them, focusing particularly on deepening and widening our conceptualisation of code and software, to frame them within the wider socio-technical assemblage in which they are developed and work, and to consider how these socio-technical assemblages coalesce and interact to produce the city. The rest of the chapter is divided into two sections. The first focuses on code itself and the importance of delving into the nuts and bolts and mechanics of its constitution and operation, while at the same time not overly fetishising code at the expense of the wider socio-technical assemblage within which it is embedded. The second focuses on how these socio-technical assemblages are framed within the wider discursive and material technological terrain and urban landscape, and interact and scale to produce densely instrumented cities consisting of millions of coded objects and systems, all in dynamic flux. In this sense, the two sections are trying to find a way of dealing with the issue of productively building a conceptual understanding that scales from individual lines of code to the complexity of an entire urban system; of building a conceptual edifice that moves beyond marrying software studies to urban studies. This is no easy challenge, and I would see the arguments I make as another provisional step that others will hopefully help develop and make more robust.

Thinking about code and the city

In *Code/Space*, Martin Dodge and I argued that software needed to be understood as being both a product of the world and a producer of the world. Code – the lines of declarations, procedures, commands and algorithms, expressed in different languages (assembly, scripting, procedural, etc.) – that, when compiled, create software are not simply the result of a neutral, technical exercise. Rather, coding needs to be understood as a complex and contingent process, shaped by the abilities and worldviews of programmers and engineers, working in companies or on their own time, situated in social, political and economic contexts (Rosenburg 2007). Software development occurs in a collaborative framework, with individuals performing as part of a team or re-appropriating code from libraries or ideas from websites, books and magazines. Often, several teams will work on different aspects of the same program, which are then stitched together. Teams can have different visions about what they are trying to achieve, and have different skill levels to tackle the job at hand. Software, then, is not an immaterial, stable, value-free product; it is a complex, multifaceted, mutable set of relations created through diverse sets of discursive, economic and material practices rooted in particular locales. Moreover, this software does not simply represent the world, but actively participates in it, transducing space, reshaping work, transforming practices, and so on (Dourish 2001).

We argued for a need to, on the one hand, delve further into the nature of code itself, and in particular to start to unpick how coding is actively practised and code created in context, and, on the other, to examine the work that code does in the world. Here, I want to focus on the former. In trying to make sense of code and coding with respect to urban systems, we advocated: (1) a focus on the code itself, deconstructing the lines of code and examining the ways in which elements of the world, and ways to think about and process them, are captured and formalised in sets of interlinked algorithms, and excavating how the code and algorithms evolve through revisions and editions, as they incorporate new ideas, ambitions, policy and law; (2) ethnographies of coders and coding projects, including their wider social, political and economic framing. In other words, we posited a very software studies approach to making sense of code and cities.

18   *Rob Kitchin*

I am still of the view that an in-depth focus on code and coding would be an enormously profitable endeavour. Given the huge growth in forms of algorithmic governance – everything from recommendation systems, to automated forms of surveillance, to profiling and sorting – it is becoming increasingly important to understand the aetiology of code (how algorithms are constructed and operate), how they are utilised, and to tease apart their inherent politics (see Gillespie 2014; Kitchin 2014b). This is evident in two recent, excellent software studies texts: Montfort *et al.*'s (2012) *10 Print*, a detailed analysis of a single, but iconic, line of code; and Manovich's (2013) *Software Takes Command*, in which he provides an in-depth genealogy of the 'softwarisation' of cultural media – art, photos, film, television, music – that has taken place since the 1970s. That said, I have a major concern with this approach in and of itself: it adopts an analytical lens that over-fetishises and potentially decontextualises code at the expense of its wider assemblage of production and use.

Since the publication of *Code/Space*, I have written another monograph – *The Data Revolution* (Kitchin 2014a) – which I loosely think of as the third book in a trilogy of sorts (*Mapping Cyberspace* (Dodge and Kitchin 2001): infrastructure; *Code/Space*: software; *The Data Revolution*: data) and started a large, five-year European Research Council funded project, *The Programmable City*, which involves ten subprojects focused on the intersections of ubiquitous computing, software, big data and the creation of smart cities. Both endeavours have highlighted that the relationship between code and the city is complex and diverse. Code and software are critical to networked urbanism, but so too are data, platforms, hardware, interfaces and users. And none of these can be fully understood without being considered in relation to one another, nor outside of their wider context. This has been brought home to me in two ways, which when combined provide a path forward.

First, in *The Data Revolution*, I developed an argument that to fully comprehend an open data system, or a big data product, or a research data infrastructure, one needs to examine its entire data assemblage (see Table 2.1). The apparatuses and elements detailed in Table 2.1 interact with and shape each other through a contingent and complex web of multifaceted relations. And just as data are a product of the assemblage, the assemblage is structured and managed to produce those data (Ribes and Jackson 2013). Data and their assemblage are thus mutually constituted, bound together in a set of contingent, relational and contextual discursive and material practices and relations. This argument can be equally extended to code or software (indeed, this is an extension of a discussion first expressed in *Code/Space*). For example, an app such as Foursquare or a city geographical information system (GIS) consist of a large amalgam of apparatuses and elements that shape how they are conceived, developed, administered, operated, and interactions with them deployed. A GIS is underpinned by a realist system of thought; it pulls together and combines hundreds of analytical and visualisation algorithms

From a line of code to an entire city   19

Table 2.1 Apparatus and elements of a data assemblage

Apparatus	*Elements*
Systems of thought	Modes of thinking, philosophies, theories, models, ideologies, rationalities, etc.
Forms of knowledge	Research texts, manuals, magazines, websites, experience, word of mouth, chat forums, etc.
Finance	Business models, investment, venture capital, grants, philanthropy, profit, etc.
Political economy	Policy, tax regimes, incentive instruments, public and political opinion, etc.
Governmentalities and legalities	Data standards, file formats, system requirements, protocols, regulations, laws, licensing, intellectual property regimes, ethical considerations, etc.
Materialities and infrastructures	Paper and pen, computers, digital devices, sensors, scanners, databases, networks, servers, buildings, etc.
Practices	Techniques, ways of doing, learnt behaviours, scientific conventions, etc.
Organisations and institutions	Archives, corporations, consultants, manufacturers, retailers, government agencies, universities, conferences, clubs and societies, committees and boards, communities of practice, etc.
Subjectivities and communities	Of data producers, experts, curators, managers, analysts, scientists, politicians, users, citizens, etc.
Places	Laboratories, offices, field sites, data centres, server farms, business parks, etc., and their agglomerations
Marketplace	For data, its derivatives (e.g., text, tables, graphs, maps), analysts, analytic software, interpretations, etc.

Source: Kitchin 2014a: 25

and dozens of datasets and has to be able to handle lots of different data formats, standards and protocols; it has a diverse set of accompanying forms of supporting documentation, in both trade and academic journals; the system and its data are maintained, updated and used by many collaborating stakeholders, through a diverse set of practices, undertaken by many workers, using a range of materials and infrastructures; its operational costs are a source of contention; its use is shaped by legal frameworks and regulations; it is one part of a multibillion-dollar industry and community of practice; and so on. And GISs continue to evolve and mutate as 'new ideas and knowledges emerge, technologies are invented, organisations change, business models are created, the political economy alters, regulations and laws are introduced and repealed, skill sets develop, debates take place, and markets grow or shrink' (Kitchin and Lauriault 2014). They are thus always in a state of becoming. One cannot fully grasp the constitution, operation and work of a GIS by concentrating attention on its code, despite the fact that without code a GIS could not exist. It has to be framed as a socio-technical assemblage.

Second, I have been trying to assemble my thoughts with respect to making conceptual sense of algorithms (Kitchin 2014b) and interfaces (Kitchin et al. 2015), drawing on related, but distinctly labelled literature (e.g., critical code studies, human–computer interaction, new media studies), thus adding to my existing ideas with respect to infrastructure, code and data. This has led to a consideration, drawing on the discussion and conceptual diagrams of Montfort et al. (2012), Bogost and Montfort (n.d.), van Dijck (2013, detailed in Chapter 10) and Chapter 10 (see Figure 2.1), of the make-up of the digital technology stack (the elements that work *together*), underpinning particular digital innovations, products or services that are deployed in cities. In my version of the stack, there are six elements: material platform (infrastructure – hardware), code platform (operating system), data(base), code or algorithms (software), interface, and reception or operation (user or usage). Each layer has effects with regards to the others. For example, the hardware influences the choice of operating system, which shapes the choice of programming environment; the form and extent of the data influence how algorithms are constructed, as do user expectations and patterns of use; the interface is constrained by the hardware and shapes user experience of a technology, and so on (Montfort et al. (2012) provide a nice discussion about how a single line of code and its output is affected by what language it is expressed in, what parameters are selected and what hardware it is run on). Prioritising code, at the expense of the rest of the stack, places a constraint on developing a holistic, socio-technical understanding of how a digital technology is conceived and works in practice (Chapter 10). This holistic approach is also currently limited by each layer in the stack being the focus of a particular field of study – new media studies, human–computer interaction, software studies, critical data studies or platform studies (see Figure 2.1).

Taken together, the notion of a data assemblage and technology stack has led to the creation of an initial wider conceptual framing for *The Programmable City*, a project that intertwines these ideas into an overarching notion of a digital socio-technical assemblage (see Figure 2.2). Within this perspective, code or software is just one element, albeit a critical one, in a much wider assemblage that frames the interrelationship between code and the city. Making sense of a socio-technical assemblage involves drawing

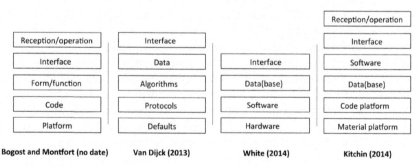

Figure 2.1 Digital technology stacks

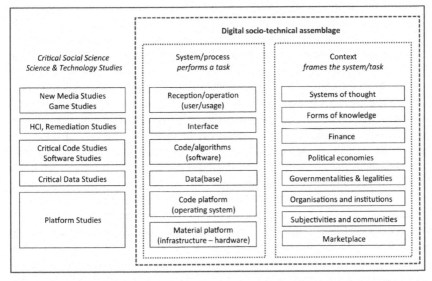

Figure 2.2 Conceptualising the constitution of a digital socio-technical system

on ideas and empirical insights from a range of fields within critical social science and science and technology studies, including new media studies, game studies, human–computer interaction, software studies, critical code studies, critical data studies and platform studies, as well as anthropology, sociology, political science, economics and human geography. Unpacking a digital socio-technical assemblage, then, is no easy task, but is manageable as a large case study, given that it is focused on a single assemblage, such as a program, app or system. The city, however, consists of millions of interconnected socio-technical assemblages, working in concert and contest to transduce the urban condition. A key question then is how to make sense of this dense, interconnected web of assemblages that are constantly working in dynamic flux. It is to this conundrum I now turn.

Thinking about code and the city

The problem with examining individual socio-technical assemblages in detail is that the city largely disappears from view. Certain elements are examined, but in isolation, meaning that a more holistic understanding of how various systems combine and interact to produce the whole is never formulated. Clearly, cities are large, complex, multifaceted, open systems and it is all but impossible to fully comprehend all their interlocking systems. Nevertheless, it is possible to map out the ways in which socio-technical assemblages (mis) align, work together, compete, coalesce to form larger assemblages, and so on. To date, very little detailed empirical research has been conducted on how socio-technical assemblages are framed within the wider discursive and

22   Rob Kitchin

material technological terrain and urban landscape, and how they interact and scale to produce densely instrumented cities. Yet such research would usefully illustrate how networked urbanism is being built and functions in practice.

In contrast, the field of urban studies suffers from the converse problem. Since the early 1990s, as noted in Chapter 1, a fairly substantial literature on the development of networked urbanism and smart cities has emerged. These studies have focused on examining the effects of networked, digital infrastructure on the management and regulation of various urban systems, and urban governance and economy more broadly, providing useful insights into how software-enabled technologies are transforming cities and urban life. However, there is a major omission in such work: it discusses the effects of digital socio-technical assemblages, but rarely unpacks the constitution and mechanics of those assemblages. For example, a paper might discuss anticipatory governance and its effects on civil liberties, or the security vulnerabilities of the Internet of Things and its consequences with respect to privacy, without explicating the specific ways in which systems are configured, code and algorithms work, data are parsed and analysed, users interface, engage, resist, and so on. In part, this is because the socio-technical assemblages are blackboxed; it takes a little more effort to leverage access or to undertake approaches that would shine a light into the box (see Kitchin 2014b), but it is mainly to do with adopting a viewpoint that examines effects rather than causes. In *Code/Space*, Dodge and I illustrated this by comparing approaches that examine the underlying epidemiology of ill-health and the effects of ill-health on the world. Our argument was that while one can gain an understanding of the relationship between health and society by studying how ill-health affects social relations, one can gain deeper insights by also considering the specifics of different diseases, their aetiology, and how these manifest themselves in shaping social relations. Similarly, one could examine how telematic networks shape traffic management without studying how such effects are manifestly the result of how the telematic assemblage is constituted and configured, with rules and procedures formalised within algorithms and code.

It seems to me, therefore, that we have a major disconnect in the literature. Science and technology scholars are focused on the nature of specific elements of socio-technical systems. Urban scholars are focused on the embedding of digital technologies into urban environments and their social, political and economic effects. Occasionally, these perspectives meet, but largely they remain apart. A key question, for me at least, is how to marry them into a conceptual whole, or at least place them in productive tension. The solution seems to be to scale the socio-technical perspective up, and drill the urban studies focus down so that they overlap in view and epistemology.

Figure 2.3 provides an initial attempt at setting out a conceptual framework for what I term 'programmable urbanism' – the instrumented, mutable form of smart cities – that scales between individual socio-technical assemblages and their components to the city and their dense interconnection and embedding

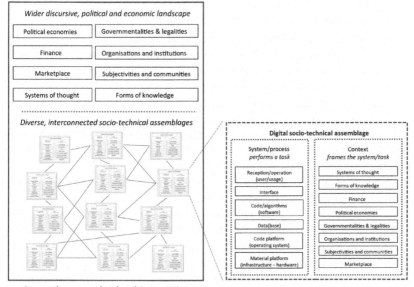

Figure 2.3 Conceptual framework for programmable urbanism

within a wider discursive, political and economic landscape. The framework thus seeks to promote and support research that attempts to simultaneously unpack socio-technical assemblages *and* chart their interconnections and interdependencies, and how they scale to frame and create city life. It thus aims to produce a holistic analysis, examining how programmable urbanism is framed within a wider discursive, political and economic landscape (the rhetoric of smart cities, for example) and how it is built, functions and has effects in practice. The apparatus of 'political economies', 'finance', 'governmentalities and legalities', etc. appear in each socio-technical assemblage, and the wider landscape of smart cities, to denote that there are a multitude of discursive and material elements at play, some supporting individual assemblages and others the broader terrain of city policy, which often align but can also be in conflict. For example, smart city policy within a city might generally support technocratic forms of governance, but preclude some forms owing to legal interventions. Yet there could be an active discursive field supporting the roll-out of precluded socio-technical assemblages.

Enacting this framework through empirical study would be an arduous task for an individual, but it is certainly not beyond the bounds of a research team or network of collaborators. It would also be possible to draw insights by stitching together findings and ideas from across the literature to create a synoptic analysis. It therefore seems plausible that its vision could be realised, enabling us to gain an enhanced understanding of the relationship between code and the city that scales from lines of code to the city in action.

24   *Rob Kitchin*

Conclusion

Cities are rapidly becoming composed of digitally mediated components and infrastructures, their systems augmented and mediated by software, with widespread consequences for how they are managed, governed and experienced. A smart city is not a vision of a future city, as often depicted in the media; it already exists in practice through the millions of interconnected, digital socio-technical assemblages embedded into the fabric of cities that frame how people travel, communicate, manage, play, consume, work, and so on. The challenge for critical scholars is to understand the tightening bonds between code and the city: how such bonds are configured and work in practice, and what they mean for how cities operate and for citizen's lives.

My argument in this chapter is that while there has been much progress in examining programmable urbanism, there is much conceptual and empirical work to be done. To date, the literatures concerning, respectively, code and the city have remained quite divided, and both have shortcomings. On the one hand, studies that focus on code are narrow in remit, fading out the city, and tend to fetishise code at the expense of the wider socio-technical assemblage within which it is embedded. On the other hand, studies that focus on the city tend to examine the effects of code but rarely unpack the constitution and mechanics of the code producing those effects.

My contention is that we need to marry the ideas within these two literatures to provide a more holistic account of the relationship between code and the city. Building on ideas initially developed in *Code/Space* (Kitchin and Dodge 2011), I have forwarded two, interlinked conceptual frameworks. The first places code within a wider socio-technical assemblage. The second conceives the city as being composed of millions of such assemblages. In so doing, the latter seeks to provide a means of productively building a conceptual and empirical understanding of programmable urbanism that scales from individual lines of code to the complexity of an entire urban system. It is certainly not comprehensive in scope or captures the complex processes and interdependencies at play. But it does, I believe, provide an initial scaffold for seeking to scale software studies up towards the city and to drill urban studies down towards code.

Acknowledgements

The research for this work was funded by a European Research Council Advanced Investigator Award to Rob Kitchin, entitled *The Programmable City* (ERC-2012-AdG-323636-SOFTCITY).

References

Berry, D. (2011) *The Philosophy of Software: Code and Mediation in the Digital Age*, Basingstoke: Palgrave Macmillan.

From a line of code to an entire city 25

Bogost, I. and Montfort, N. (n.d.) 'Levels', *Platform Studies*, available from http://platformstudies.com/levels.html [accessed 7 August 2014].

Dodge, M. and Kitchin, R. (2001) *Mapping Cyberspace*, London: Routledge.

Dodge, M. and Kitchin, R. (2005) 'Code and the transduction of space', *Annals of the Association of American Geographers*, 95(1): 162–80.

Dodge, M. and Kitchin, R. (2007) 'The automatic management of drivers and driving spaces', *Geoforum*, 38(2): 264–75.

Dourish, P. (2001) *Where the Action Is*, Cambridge, MA: MIT Press.

Foth, M. (2008) *Handbook of Research on Urban Informatics: The Practice and Promise of the Real-time City*, New York: Information Science Reference.

Fuller, M. (2008) *Software Studies: A Lexicon*. Cambridge, MA: MIT Press.

Gillespie, T. (2014) 'The relevance of algorithms', in T. Gillespie, P.J. Boczkowski and K.A. Foot (eds) *Media Technologies: Essays on Communication, Materiality, and Society*, Cambridge, MA: MIT Press.

Graham, S.D.N. (2005) 'Software-sorted geographies', *Progress in Human Geography*, 29(5): 562–80.

Graham, S. and Marvin, S. (2001) *Splintering Urbanism: Networked Infrastructures, Technological Mobilities and the Urban Condition*, London: Routledge.

Kelley, M.J. (2014) 'The semantic production of space: pervasive computing and the urban landscape', *Environment and Planning A*, 46(4): 837–51.

Kitchin, R. (2011) 'The programmable city', *Environment and Planning B*, 38: 945–51.

Kitchin, R. (2014a) *The Data Revolution: Big Data, Open Data, Data Infrastructures and Their Consequences*, London: Sage.

Kitchin, R. (2014b) 'Thinking critically about algorithms'. Programmable City Working Paper 5, *Social Science Research Network*, available from http://ssrn.com/abstract=2515786 [accessed 16 November 2015].

Kitchin, R. and Dodge, M. (2011) *Code/Space: Software and Everyday Life*, Cambridge, MA: MIT Press.

Kitchin, R. and Lauriault, T. (2014) 'Towards critical data studies: charting and unpacking data assemblages and their work', Programmable City Working Paper 2, *Social Science Research Network*, available from http://ssrn.com/abstract=2474112 [accessed 24 August 2015].

Kitchin, R., Lauriault, T. and McArdle, G. (2015) 'Knowing and governing cities through urban indicators, city benchmarking and real-time dashboards', *Regional Studies, Regional Science*, 2: 1–28.

Mackenzie, A. (2006) *Cutting Code: Software and Sociality*, New York: Peter Lang.

Manovich, L. (2013) *Software Takes Command*, London: Bloomsbury.

Mitchell, W.J. (1995) *City of Bits: Space, Place and the Infobahn*, Cambridge, MA: MIT Press.

Montfort, N., Baudoin, P., Bell, J., Bogost, I., Douglass, J., Marino, M.C., Mateas, M., Reas, C., Sample, M. and Vawter, N. (2012) *10 PRINT CHR$(205.5+RND(1)); :GOTO 10*, Cambridge, MA: MIT Press.

Ribes, D. and Jackson, S.J. (2013) 'Data bite man: the work of sustaining long-term study', in L. Gitelman (ed.) *'Raw Data' is an Oxymoron*, Cambridge, MA: MIT Press.

Rosenberg, S. (2007) *Dreaming in Code: Two Dozen Programmers, Three Years, 4,732 Bugs, and One Quest for Transcendent Software*, New York: Three Rivers Press.

Shepard, M. (2011) *Sentient City: Ubiquitous Computing, Architecture, and the Future of Urban Space*, Cambridge, MA: MIT Press.

Thrift, N. and French, S. (2002) 'The automatic production of space', *Transactions of the Institute of British Geographers*, 27(3): 309–35.

Townsend, A. (2013) *Smart Cities: Big Data, Civic Hackers, and the Quest for a New Utopia*, New York: W.W. Norton and Co.

van Dijck, J. (2013) *The Culture of Connectivity: A Critical History of Social Media*, Oxford: Oxford University Press.

3 The Internet of Urban Things

Paul Dourish

Introduction

The history of computer culture is one of successive waves of colonisation – the colonisation of everyday life by digital systems. Once confined to air-conditioned server rooms in large institutional settings, digital systems have moved to fully colonise the office, and then the home, and then spaces of entertainment. Current developments revolve around two new sites of colonisation. One is the 'smart city' – urban space reconfigured through the widespread deployment of sensing and computational systems, linking everyday space into the 'Cloud' and bringing the technologies of data analytics into the infrastructure of city life. The other goes under the label of the 'Internet of Things' – a drive to incorporate networked computation into the fabric and furniture of daily life, and particularly into 'smart' versions of everyday objects, such as door locks, refrigerators, power switches, lightbulbs, pedometers and thermostats. Sensor-enabled and network-connected, these devices will be able – so the marketing material assures us – to incorporate computational intelligence into all aspects of our engagement with our everyday life, and operate seamlessly together, turning the home into a single computational system rather than a collection of disparate components, appliances and services.

These two developments are linked. Urban computing involves the same sorts of embedded sensor and wireless communication technology that are at the heart of the Internet of Things (IoT) agenda, while the IoT promises to be able to apply the same sorts of statistical machine learning or 'big data' algorithms that are often presented in the context of urban computing. That said, the rhetorical schemes that surround them are quite different. Urban computing tends to be described in terms of urban management, security and resource management, while the IoT arguments are focused primarily on convenience and luxury. Their sites of impact are different too – city managers, service providers and urban planners on the one hand, and consumers and homeowners on the other.[1]

In this article, my goal is to take more seriously the idea that these two constellations of technology and rhetorical practice have important things in

28 *Paul Dourish*

common – both in terms of underlying facilities and in terms of the imaginary futures that they evoke. I want to think about what they might have to say to each other if we approach them as parallel discourses. In particular, I want to try to re-examine some of the rhetorics of code and the city that this volume is broadly examining and see them through the light of the Internet of Things. This involves, in places, taking a more technical reading of the foundations of sensor-based computing, but then following that through to see how the pragmatics and the politics are linked.

The Internet of Things

In the late 1980s, at Xerox's Palo Alto Research Center, Computer Science Laboratory director Mark Weiser initiated a wide-ranging research project into what he dubbed 'ubiquitous computing' (Weiser 1991). 'UbiComp' (as it became known) constituted, in Weiser's words, a third wave of computing. In the first wave, a single mainframe computer had served the needs of hundreds or even thousands of users. In the second wave – the wave of 'personal computing' – the mantra had been 'one person, one computer': the primary site of interaction was a single computer that served the needs of one person (one person at a time, at least). In UbiComp's third wave, Weiser argued, a single person would interact with tens, hundreds or thousands of devices – some large, some small, some visible, some hidden. Rather than being devices that we would need to sit down and use, these devices would surround us – they would be embedded in our everyday environment, incorporated into door knobs, beds, pens and walls, augmenting the capacities of whiteboards, books, picture frames and television sets, and communicating with each other wirelessly to create coherent and collective computational experiences.

UbiComp became a major focus of research attention for the computer science community – one so significant, in fact, that it has been argued that it essentially disappeared as a topic in itself, suffusing itself into every other domain of computer science research (Abowd 2012). At the same time, it also provided a fruitful site for encounters between computer science and social science, turning, as it did, the stuff of everyday life into a site of computational encounter (e.g., Dourish and Bell 2011).

The current marketing label for much of what was once understood as UbiComp is 'the Internet of Things'. This speaks particularly to UbiComp's concern with digital embeddedness – with the idea that everyday objects and devices might now become 'smart' through the incorporation of small, cheap digital processing capabilities, sensors, actuators and wireless communication devices. The rhetoric of the IoT is an attempt to reinvigorate research and development activity around smart devices at a moment when the market might otherwise turn its attention to the migration of technological capacity into the 'Cloud'. If cloud computing is an attempt to consolidate computational capacity in a small number of centralised sites, then the Internet of Things is an attempt to decentralise it once more and distribute it through myriad devices in every home, in every room and at every opportunity. At the same time, of course, it is also a piece of corporate marketing – one that asserts the ongoing relevance of hardware manufacturers and device providers at a time when investment and popular attention had shifted towards the online services provided by Internet start-ups.

If the term 'ubiquitous computing' was one only a nerd could love, then the term 'Internet of Things' is surely one that does the same for marketers. However, if we can put to one side the inherent awkwardness of the term, and the question of why a rebranding was necessary at all, then we might find some utility in thinking it through – its invocation of the Internet, its thing-centredness, the way that problems are formed, the way that data flows are imagined, and so forth. In the next few pages, I will pick up in turn a series of observations sparked by the rhetoric of the Internet of Things that might provide us with some lenses through which we can examine similar questions in the smart city.

The Internet of Things is not the Internet

'Internet of Things' is a marketing term as much as a technical one, and in consequence, strict technical definitions are hard to come by. Nonetheless, despite the fuzziness of the categories, it is reasonable to conclude that, in general, the Internet of Things is *not* the Internet. And the ways in which it is not are instructive.

The key technological achievement of the Internet was the creation of a network protocol infrastructure – a means of transmitting data – that could operate seamlessly over a range of network infrastructures, including wireless, satellite, broadband and point-to-point channels. The TCP/IP protocol 'stack' – most importantly, IP, the internetwork protocol – is the defining feature of the Internet, making it possible to establish connections directly between different hosts on different networks.

While accessibility from the Internet is an important feature for IoT applications – for the purposes, say, of monitoring energy usage from your laptop or controlling lights from your phone – these are in many ways not Internet applications themselves because there is no end-to-end connection between the Internet device and many IoT devices. In other words, IoT devices are not themselves connected to the Internet.

This may seem like a nigglingly small technical point, or even a meaningless detail. What does it matter whether IoT devices are on the Internet or not, if we can control them or monitor them from the Internet? However, this seemingly small point has some important consequences. One is that it means that those properties that we typically ascribe to the Internet – expansibility, openness, interoperability, and so on – may not apply in the case of the IoT. (As I have argued elsewhere, they may apply less in the case of the Internet than we might think, too, but that is a different topic (Dourish 2015a).) If one of the essential features of the Internet is that, because everything

30 *Paul Dourish*

communicates using IP, then everything can communicate with everything else, then that is most certainly not the case with the Internet of Things, in which specialised gateways, controllers, hubs and proxies, introduced by a variety of manufacturers and running a profusion of sometimes-proprietary network protocols, are widespread. New devices do not necessarily interoperate, and their connections – if they can connect at all – must be mediated by other devices that understand how to mediate between them. Arguably, there is no Internet of Things because there are many networks of things – incompatible ones.

The temporal dynamics of things

One of the fundamental ideas that the term 'Internet of Things' seems designed to convey is novelty. Just as 'the Internet' has brought innovation, revolution and disruption to all sorts of services and industries, so the story goes, now it can do the same for 'things'. The label seems to promise that the world of 'things' will now move at the speed of the Internet – at the apparently dizzying pace at which new businesses, new services and new technologies appear online. The term, then, embodies a temporal contradiction right off the bat. The reason that we might want to harness the temporal dynamics of the Internet to the world of otherwise stable and static things is that things do not, themselves, experience the same pace of innovation, revolution and disruption. 'Things' do not seem to be caught up in quite such a breathless hype cycle. 'Things' do not demonstrate the pace of the Internet – that is why we need the Internet of Things, is the claim. How are we to understand the temporal dynamics at work when these are brought together?

We might take a leaf out of Stewart Brand's playbook, in his capacity as someone for whom both the Internet and things have mattered (Brand 1987; 1995; Turner 2006). In *How Buildings Learn*, Brand proposes a model for thinking about the way that buildings change and evolve. What he calls 'shearing layers' (an elaboration of a concept originally coined by architect Frank Duffy) are six elements of a building that coexist – site, structure, skin, services, space and stuff. They are organised according to their rate of change. Stuff – the contents of the building, such as furniture, ornaments, and the objects of everyday life – moves and changes frequently. The space plan – the layout of rooms – changes too, as the house is remodelled, but changes less often than the 'stuff'. The next least frequent sites of change are the services of the building – infrastructures that connect the building to the outside world, such as gas, electricity, water and sewage. The building's 'skin' – its exterior cladding – changes even less frequently, although it might be renewed over many decades. The fundamental structure of the building – its mechanical core, foundations and load-bearing beams – is subject to change only rarely, and changeable but least dynamic of all is the building's site – its location and orientation (most commonly, the site lasts longer than the structure itself).

The Internet of Urban Things

A similar analysis might be usefully directed towards the Internet itself, which comprises many different elements of both physical and digital infrastructure that evolve at different rates. However, a more significant issue here concerns the way that the Internet of Things, as a point of encounter between digital technologies and domestic or urban infrastructure, requires a melding of the temporal dynamics of the two. It is a well-worn idea that technology – particularly software-based technology – changes quickly. There are a lot of mistaken assumptions bound up in that easy claim (there is much that is old in the most modern technology, particularly when we delve into the guts of operating systems and programming languages), but nonetheless we need to pay attention to the different rates of change of different parts of the IoT system.

A simple but telling example is represented by the power socket shown in Figure 3.1. In addition to standard US NEMA 5-15R power sockets, it also provides two USB type-A plugs that can be used to charge devices such as

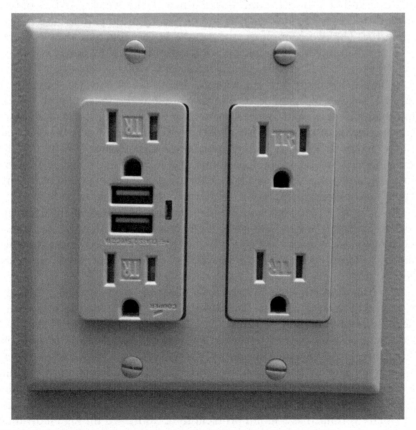

Figure 3.1 USB ports incorporated into a US power socket
Source and copyright: 2014 Killian Murphy, reproduced by permission.

32 *Paul Dourish*

mobile phones. For people who find themselves struggling to find the right adapter at the right time, or are tired of the ever-expanding battery of connectors, cables and adapters that we carry around with us, these can be of considerable value – I have more than once been pleased to find them when staying with a friend or checking into a hotel. But the plug embodies the very different dynamics of analogue and digital infrastructures.

NEMA – the National Electrical Manufacturers' Association – was established in 1926 and the NEMA 5 socket was standardised over 60 years ago, in the early 1950s, becoming widespread in the 1960s. (It is based on an earlier 2-pin standard that is still operative today – including in parts of my own 1930 home.) By contrast, the USB type-A connector was standardised in 1995. Apple was widely ridiculed when, in 1998, it introduced the first personal computer to eschew then-standard PC ports (such as parallel, serial and PS/2 connections) and provide only USB ports for all devices. As it turned out, most other manufacturers quickly followed suit. If Apple's bet on the USB port was in any way prophetic, then we might want to note that Apple recently (early 2015) introduced a new device which provides only a single digital port, the new, smaller and physically incompatible USB type C connector. The two connectors, then, embody very different ideas of infrastructural lifetime. Most people do not want to replace the power outlets in their houses every 17 years. (I clearly have not.)

Arguably, for many IoT applications, the situation is worse. Computers only a few years old may become incompatible with modern, more secure, implementations of Wi-Fi wireless networking. A ten-year-old Web browser is incapable of displaying most modern websites. The objects that become 'smart' in the IoT world are generally those that change slowly, but the embeddedness of IoT technologies implies a form of fixity that is in many ways incompatible with the cycle of software development and deployment. Apple's most recent releases of iOS will run only on phones manufactured in the last couple of years; on Android, the situation is even worse, since Google does not design the handsets itself, with the result that Google has pretty much given up on backward compatibility for Android, and most Android phones will only ever run the version of the operating system that they were shipped with.

It is important to note that Brand's shearing layer analysis, although organised in terms of a simple linearity of change, speaks also for other complexities in the evolution of infrastructure. Writing about the problems and opportunities associated with the use of advanced technology for sustainable energy use, Dillahunt and colleagues (2009; 2010) have emphasised the different degrees of control over building fabric available to different groups, and in particular the challenges that low-income communities may face in implementing technological shifts – a particular problem when environmental sustainability is framed as a moral problem to be addressed through individual acts of consumer choice (DiSalvo *et al.* 2010; Dourish 2010). This issue will be returned to in more detail later.

The IoT's scale problem

The very idea of the 'Internet of Things' is one that responds in some sense to a shift in scale that has taken place over the lifetime of the Internet. Early in its history, the devices that were connected via the Internet (or its predecessor, ARPANet) were large computers – mainframes and minicomputers that generally filled large air-conditioned rooms and required special facilities for their upkeep. Even the first Internet routers – interface message processors – were delivered on trucks and installed via fork-lift. (A common stop on tours of my campus is a nearby engineering building where some discoloured panels five or six stories off the ground show where the first computers were installed via crane when it turned out that they were too large to fit through any door.) The premise of the 'Internet of Things' – that objects as small as switches, valves and button-panels might now be connected to the Internet – reflects the idea that the objects that the Internet connects are now of a quite different order.

Discussions of scale frequently founder on the failure to acknowledge the difference between 'scale' and 'size'. 'Size' encompasses problems of growth, of number, of multiplicity and of limits. 'Scale' focuses on the emergence of different kinds of objects at different classes of size. So, for example, my arm comprises tens of millions of cells; but the emergence of an 'arm' as an object of attention is not merely a question of size. Questions of size and of scale are both relevant here. We will begin with a problem of size, and in particular, the size of the Internet address space.

Perhaps unexpectedly, one technological shift that industry observers have suggested that the IoT may trigger is the switch from the current generation of internet protocols (known as IPv4) to the next generation (known as IPv6). IPv6 is not, at this stage, new; it was standardised in 1998. However, adoption has been slow, at best, since IPv4 is widely deployed and adequate for many purposes. While IPv6 incorporates several technological innovations, the most pressing problem that it resolves is that the IPv4 address space is close to being exhausted; there are almost no new IPv4 network addresses available for new Internet-connected devices. Now, as explored earlier, many IoT devices do not actually use Internet protocols anyway, and those that do make use of partial solutions (like the use of network address translation, a protocol mechanism built into most domestic network gateways) that provide a simple, if clunky, workaround. However, the vision of truly Internet-connected things – many more of them than the traditional computers for which the Internet was designed – would seem to provide further impetus for the adoption of IPv6, which vastly expands the 'address space' (the number of devices that can be individually identified by IP addresses) and so eases the congestion problems that have bedevilled IPv4 over the last several years. Arguably, the widespread switch from IPv4 to IPv6 will be more consequential for other devices – desktop computers, laptops, tablets and mobile phones – than for the unconventional IoT devices, but the IoT might nonetheless provide the trigger for the transition.

34 *Paul Dourish*

The problem of addressing is matched by a related problem, which is that of control. A world of smart devices poses a significant problem for monitoring and management. Arguably, one of the key enabling technologies for the Internet of Things is not an IoT device at all – the smartphone. 'Control from your phone' is perhaps the one common feature of IoT pitches. Arguably, this is an issue not of size but of scale – that is, of the units of control and the organisation of interfaces. How are devices collected together for the purpose of control? How is it that, in the Internet of Things, a new set of considerations – not of network nodes or organisations but of homes, rooms, zones and families – emerge as relevant objects of technical attention? The multiplicity of devices and the difficulties of controlling so many with a single user interface require that new scalar features, such as homes and rooms, emerge as technical objects. This is not simply a matter of network topology – the structure of the way that different networks connect together – but rather of new kinds of ways in which the human logic of physical space must be represented to the computer system in order to make the network of things manageable.

In other words, the embedding of technologies into new sorts of spaces, as implied by the Internet of Things, requires too that those spaces become visible and legible to the structures of control – both social and technical – upon which those technologies are founded. Critically, this reconfiguration of sizes and scales associated with myriad small devices and the smartphone as a universal interface involves one other key element – the 'Cloud'. However, since the role of the Cloud as a mediating entity raises other important issues, it is best to raise it separately as part of an examination of the role of the user in the Internet of Things.

IoT routes around the user

In John Gilmore's well-worn aphorism, the Internet is argued to 'treat censorship as damage and route around it'. The technical logic of the Internet supports many potential paths between a start-point and an end-point, so that data can follow the path of least resistance, 'routing around' congestion or temporary technical problems – or, in Gilmore's metaphor, human intervention. In the Internet of Things, however, it is often the user who is being routed around.

In traditional Internet applications, human users are on one end of a connection, if not both. So, a connection might link a human user to a game server, or a pair of human users via a video connection, or a human user to a website. In the Internet of Things, however, at least one end of the connection is guaranteed to be, well, a thing – and, most probably, what the thing connects to is a server or cloud-based service (to which it reports its status, activity logs or sensor data readings). Devices that form part of the Internet of Things are often particularly inscrutable, offering little more than a glowing or flashing LED as a signal of activity. They communicate not with people, but with other digital infrastructures. One's access to this information

The Internet of Urban Things   35

is, at best, limited and mediated. The 'smart meter' that regulates and measures the electrical service in my house, for example, does not communicate directly to me, but rather to my electricity provider – and even when I buy another IoT device, a gateway that connects to the smart meter, this gateway sends the data to another service, where I can access it only indirectly and in manners determined by the Cloud service provider. In the Internet of Things, users are at best of secondary relevance. Where once we thought simply of people being 'on the Internet', the key move of the Internet of Things is not that it is an Internet of Users that has been extended to incorporate things too, but that it is an Internet of Things first in which users potentially play no part.

Given that the IoT is frequently deployed in settings with a significant personal stake – domestic spaces, personal transportation and health monitoring, for example – this explicit attempt to 'route around' the user raises a number of important considerations. One is the consequence for 'audit' – for determining the validity of information and for monitoring the extent of the data flow.

An example of the importance of data audit: When I moved from the UK to the USA, I requested copies of my medical records so that I could provide details of my medical history to my US physician. Only with extreme reluctance did my British GP practice agree to do this, and the records I received were still, they emphasised, partial (since medical notes were, they argued, the property of the physician and not the patient). When I had the chance to review the records, I discovered that many of them were not mine at all, but actually were records of my father's medical history, from many years before. While the clues were there to be read (most especially notes of patient age at time of treatment), I had never had the opportunity to review or audit them, and so it was over a decade before this ever came to light.

Verifying content, then, is a critical function in any information system, but one that is systematically erased in the architecture of many Internet of Things applications. A related function of audit is that it provides for an assessment of the information that is being transmitted (including content, volume and frequency). One consequence of the opaque nature of communication in the Internet of Things is the nature of the sensor data stream set-up. Is there monitoring in real time? Does the device (e.g., a motion-activated smart light) transmit sensor data (motion data) or process it locally? How detailed are the available sensor data? Where are they being transmitted? Are the data encrypted? When the user is in the loop, these questions are easy to answer. When communication is enabled device-to-device or device-to-Cloud without a user channel, answering them is difficult or impossible.

The final question that is raised here is that of ownership. Who owns the data generated by and transmitted on the Internet of Things? What kinds of contractual and voluntary agreements govern the relationship between devices, users, storage and service providers? How are responsibilities, for stewardship, accuracy and responsiveness for example, distributed between

36　*Paul Dourish*

these? A recent text examines cloud computing from a legal rather than a technical perspective and demonstrates unequivocally that contemporary legal arrangements are inadequate to the challenges thrown up by cloud computing, particularly in the public sector (Millard 2013).

The Cloud plays a critical enabling role in the Internet of Things, partly because of the issues of scale addressed earlier. The very distribution of digital capacity implied by the Internet of Things – the embedding of computational capacities into so many objects and elements – requires a point of integration, a coming together that can integrate information and action, make sense of sensor readings, correlate information streams and produce coherent analyses. This happens, in general, in the Cloud. The Cloud's role is central, then, even as these issues of audit, assessment and ownership are thrown into question. The Internet of Things addresses its user in quite different ways from those we have come to expect.

Smart cities and the Internet of Things

Our motivation for examining the rhetorical and technical strategies behind current interest in the Internet of Things has been as a backdrop for exploring some questions related to digital technology in urban settings. Fundamental IoT technologies are often aspects of an urban computing story – embedded sensors, distributed networking, cloud-based integration and large-scale data analytics all have a part to play in how we imagine the encounter between code and the city. However, I am more interested here in how the relationship between social and technical that we have seen at work in the analysis of the IoT provides a context that can illuminate discussions of urban computing.

First, we need to think a little about code and the city. There are at least two separate stories about the relationship between code and the city that need to be borne in mind.

The first, the conventional narrative, is the somewhat breathless account of a city whose every operational feature, from traffic flow to crime prevention, air quality management and service billing is digitised, integrated and managed in real time through a combination of human action and algorithmic enhancement. In the smart city, flows of people, goods and activities are mirrored by, and often anticipated by, flows of data and algorithmic attention that ensure seamless hand-off between different functional units. As Greenfield (2014) notes, it is a rhetoric that is manifestly impractical and fantastical, but it is significant nonetheless because of its power to animate processes of civic decision making and investment, the relationship that it imagines between public and private interests, the patterns of investment to which it is already giving rise, and the very sense of inevitability that it seeks to promote.

The second is what we might call, to adapt a phrase from Edwards and Grinter (2001), the 'accidentally smart city'. Edwards and Grinter were writing about the way that images of the 'smart home' were deployed in UbiComp

The Internet of Urban Things 37

research. Given the prevalence of arguments about seamlessness and holism at work in those accounts, Edwards and Grinter argued that, to the extent that conventional homes can be thought of as 'smart', they are accidentally smart, rather than smart by design. They are not designed as 'smart' from the outset, nor do they become 'smart' in one sweeping moment. They become smart slowly, over time, without perhaps much design intent. They acquire digital capacities slowly and cumulatively – a network at first, a digital power meter later, an Internet-connected digital video recorder or television further down the line, wireless networks of different sorts, games machines, and so on. These devices enter the home separately, and over time. They are not designed to be 'of a piece'; they may or may not talk to each other, or they may do so with different degrees of success. They are built to different standards (or different variants of the same standard) with varying degrees of compatibility. They occupy different parts of the home, with different degrees of accommodation (devices in my own home are connected sometimes wirelessly and sometimes by wireline where old, thick walls from 1930 prove less compatible with wireless signals than walls of contemporary construction). In the accidentally smart home, there is no unified design perspective; in the accidentally smart home, the struggle to get things to work together is one of continual improvisation and compromise. It is a familiar picture.

Similarly then, the story of the accidentally smart city is not of one in which a single strategy and coherent design approach yields an urban space in which information is woven into the fabric. Instead, the city becomes smart in the same piecemeal, gradual, disparate manner in which the home becomes smart – little by little, one piece at a time, under the control of different groups, without a master plan, and with a lot of patching, hacking, jury-rigging and settling. Unlike the homogenising gaze that James Scott (1998) suggests in *Seeing Like a State*, the characteristic of high modernist states, legal scholar Marianne Valverde (2011) suggests that 'seeing like a city' is fragmented. Cities, she observes, are not managed by formal grids; they do not offer or conform to uniform accounts. Instead, cities are patchworks of overlapping, related but not-quite-consonant regions of regulation and management – tax assessment districts, construction zones, postal routes, school catchment areas, political wards, historical districts, council districts, police precincts and more. Sometimes these line up; sometimes they do not. Sometimes they are defined with respect to infrastructure; sometimes they are defined with respect to historical and social convention. Sometimes they are visible to citizens; sometimes they are purely matters of professional practice.

These are two accounts of the smart city, but we can see significant parallels with the case of the Internet of Things. Holistic design versus piecemeal accumulation, the dynamics of the development of technology and infrastructure, and disparities in control and management are issues that plague both systems. Of course there is more to this than mere analogy; to a large extent, the technical platforms for both urban computing (at least in the first, more triumphal, account) and the Internet of Things are the same – these

38 *Paul Dourish*

are both conjunctions of distributed sensing, large-scale communication and data analytics. They have a good deal in common because they are two versions of the same design imperative.

So, can we use the understanding of the Internet of Things to reopen questions around smart cities? Can we turn in particular to the topics discussed here – protocols, ownership, audit, scale and temporal dynamics – to unpack the relationship between code and the city?

Protocols and their politics

As Bowker and Star (1999) observe in their classic study of infrastructures, new infrastructures are built upon old. They follow paths that are already laid down. In the UK, for example, major roads follow the paths of roads built during the Roman occupation (such as Dere Street, Watling Street and Ermin Street, parts of whose routes are now followed by highways, including the A1, the A2 and the A5). Much the same is true of Internet highways. Networks are built to connect centres of computation; computational facilities are located where the networks are accessible; and over successive generations of technology, the same patterns recur (see Figure 3.2).

These patterns of network evolution produce uneven sites of dense interconnection. For example, about 30 miles north of my house in Long Beach, California, in the southern part of downtown Los Angeles, a 35-storey server farm and Internet packet exchange known as One Wilshire is the most densely networked building in the USA. It is a point where many networks converge – extensions from trans-Pacific cables (Starosielski 2015) and points of presence for major network providers, such as Level 3, Tata Communications, TeliaSonera, AT&T, Verizon and Cogent. Since the Internet is a network of networks, those networks have to meet somewhere, and One Wilshire is a place they meet. So significant is One Wilshire in the fabric of western US Internet connectivity that I have been unable to find a single network path from my home to any network destination that does not go through One Wilshire. This is a matter of concern for multiple reasons, not least in light of Snowden's revelations about National Security Agency surveillance at points of network density (Greenwald 2014).

Ethernet pioneer Bob Metcalfe observed that the value of a network increases exponentially (rather than linearly) with the number of people who are on it. That same observation is also true of network connection points. If I am a network service provider, I need to be connected to other networks; if I am located in One Wilshire, then I am within easy reach of many. Indeed, the very density of network connections within One Wilshire makes it almost impossible for any provider to leave – or for a new entrant to consider locating elsewhere. The new networks go where the old networks already run, because that is where the interconnections are.

As sites like One Wilshire demonstrate, we can read the topology of Internet connectivity on two levels – one of designed structure, and one of emergent

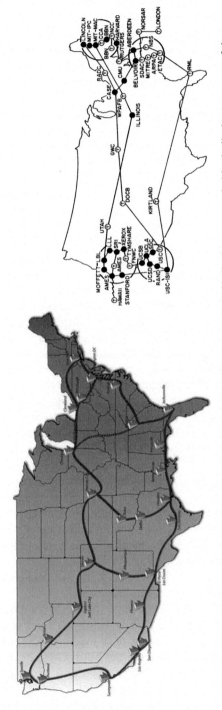

Figure 3.2 The 2004 map of the National Lambda Rail optical fibre network (left) displays a remarkable similarity to a map of the ARPANet in 1974 (right). In many cases, not only are the same cities connected, but often the same sites within those cities – perhaps some of the same buildings?

40 *Paul Dourish*

structure. The designed structure of the Internet – that is, the structure encoded in its fundamental design principles – is entirely open. In contrast with network designs based on fixed structures, such as rings, stars and trees, the design of the Internet allows for *ad-hoc* interconnections between component networks and so for an entirely arbitrary topology (Dourish 2015b). However, in practice, commercial efficiencies have resulted in the emergence of a series of regional networks that provide high-speed interconnections in specific areas, and high-speed long-haul networks that connect regions and countries. Different corporations specialise in the provision of different sorts of network, and so different classes of network – transit carriers, tier 1 providers, and so on – emerge within a hierarchical structure. The emergent structure is necessarily more particular than the designed structure, but, more interestingly, reflecting not just technical but also market arrangements, it is specifically hierarchical and considerably more structured than the designed structure. The 'openness' and 'resilience' that characterise the ways in which we think about the Internet may be features of the Internet as designed but turn out to be less true as properties of the Internet as implemented. More significantly, protocols implemented and incorporated into the Internet Protocol suite after the initial design – protocols designed to solve problems that emerged in the context of an implemented, running network – reinforce and encode aspects of this hierarchical structure (Dourish 2015a; 2015b).

Again, as we saw with the case of the IoT, the specific protocols in question – the technical realities that lie below the banner of 'the Internet' – need to be taken into account when we want to consider the properties of that network, or the kinds of social arrangement that can be enacted through it. Addressing modes, connection architectures and arrangements for naming and routing need to be accounted for, because they are deeply coupled with organisation and institutional arrangements. In the case of the Internet of Things, we noted that the way that the 'Internet' becomes present – or fails to materialise – in the Internet of Things has consequences for the ability of a user to become involved, and in particular can obscure the flows of information within circuits of transmission that essentially route around the user. In the case of urban computing, we might similarly be concerned about the nature of the flows created. While urban computing efforts are touted as ways of promoting democratic or civic engagement, providing smoother access to municipal services or ensuring equality of information and access, we should bear in mind the ways that specific protocol designs often lend themselves to reinforcing rather than reconfiguring traditional inequities.

It is useful in this regard to contrast conventional urban computing efforts with what is sometimes known as 'DIY networking' – efforts essentially to create 'new Internets', ones that often attempt to maintain some of the technical infrastructure of the conventional Internet but reassess its institutional arrangements (e.g., Antoniadis *et al.* 2008; Gaved and Mulholland 2008; Jungnickel 2014; Powell 2011). These 'alternate Internets' are alternate in various ways – in their instantiated structures, in their systems of regulation,

The Internet of Urban Things 41

in their patterns of evolution, and in their suites of applications and uses – although they often rely on the same protocol foundations as the commercial Internet. They demonstrate the different ways that a single protocol framework can be deployed with different politics – and sometimes with the limits upon particular frameworks. The fact that these are often themselves spatially constituted – sometimes urban, sometimes rural, but always situated – is particularly relevant to the discussions that arise throughout this volume, demonstrating an alternative entwining of technological opportunity and regional vision to that manifested by most 'smart city' efforts.

Citizenship

The problems of the presence or absence of the user in the Internet of Things become problems of the presence or absence of the citizen in the smart city. Greenfield (2014) has written perceptively of the role of the citizen in visions of the smart city, with a particular focus on prototypical spaces such as New Songdo City in South Korea. As he has noted, the role of 'citizen' is not a primary one for residents of these spaces; they are workers, consumers, and, perhaps, occupants first, and citizens only secondarily, if at all. The smart city is a centre of entertainment, and provides opportunities for leisure, for travel and for consumption, but it is not designed for political participation, for moral or spiritual development or even for collective association. While places like New Songdo City represent one version of a smart city vision, other encounters between code and the city are those of the 'accidentally smart city' – a newly (and unevenly) informed space with its own history and characteristics. This is the smart city vision espoused by those who see opportunities for more efficient digital management of existing city services and structures. However, although this is a different conception of the smart city, it shares with the first a somewhat marginal role for residents as citizens. Just as the Internet of Things 'routes around' the user by directly connecting objects to commercial entities and only incidentally perhaps to us, so too do smart cities frequently 'route around' their citizens.

Of course, many smart-city projects are constituted precisely in order to promote the connection between citizens and city administrators, and the potential for supporting engagement, activism and community are important aspects of e-government programmes in general (e.g., Homburg 2008), including in urban or municipal contexts. The challenge is to be able to do so in ways that foster participation of diverse groups. Pelle Ehn and colleagues at Malmö University have explored opportunities to address these questions through a range of projects that have adapted techniques developed in the participatory design movement in the context of diverse urban populations, particularly with immigrant and other marginalised communities (Ehn *et al.* 2014). Even when technology can be fruitfully harnessed to capitalise on the energy and interest of citizen groups, disconnects between their interests and those in positions of power and influence remain significant. Light *et al.*

42 *Paul Dourish*

(2009) have documented a project that was, in many ways, remarkably successful in terms of engagement, and yet left participants feeling frustrated that their concerns met with little interest or response from officials. Projects such as those documented by Ehn and Light and their colleagues are just the sort that are regularly held up to exemplify the way that digital technologies provide a new platform for enrolling people in civic participation activities and for harnessing citizen creativity in a reformulated encounter with urban governance. The technological platforms may be new, but they are deployed in the context of age-old problems.

Scale

How do we, as urban residents and citizens, experience the smart city? Digital infrastructures produce new grids and logics through which our relationship with the city is mediated (Dourish and Bell 2011). Users of Global Positioning System (GPS) navigation systems describe the joys of deliberately 'getting lost', knowing that technology can always point their way home, opening up new opportunities for exploring space (Leshed *et al.* 2008); students discuss the ways that their movements around a university campus are shaped by the availability of power outlets to charge digital devices (Barkhuus and Dourish 2004). Perhaps more interesting though is the possibility that technology may remediate our experience not just of spatial structure but of spatial scale.

Several years ago, a group of colleagues and I studied spatial practices amongst paroled sex offenders whose location was being tracked with GPS units bound to their ankles (Troshynski *et al.* 2008; Shklovski *et al.* 2009; Shklovski *et al.* 2015). At the time, this was a pilot program, and our study was piggy-backed on a feasibility evaluation that the state of California was conducting in order to determine whether this sort of monitoring was useful and practical; as it happened, a ballot proposition was passed which introduced mandatory lifetime GPS tracking for sex offenders before the feasibility trial was conducted. We went into the study with an interest in how location-based technologies served as a lens through which urban space was experienced. What did it mean, for instance, to move around the city but maintain a two-thousand-foot exclusion radius from every park, playground, school, library or swimming pool? How does one manage one's movements through space in the face of these conditions, and how does technology reveal the space to you as being organised in such a way as to facilitate legal wayfinding?

The answer, as it turned out, was that it does not. One reason is significant, if prosaic – not only can one not ask Google Maps to plot a route from A to B maintaining those exclusion zones, but many of the participants in the pilot program were also prevented by their parole conditions from using the Internet anyway. However, more significantly, conventional urban spaces are simply so densely dotted with exclusionary hazards that our parolees found that it was simply impractical to move around the city in any conventional

The Internet of Urban Things 43

sense. Their solution was not to figure out which side of the street was further away from hazards that might land them back in jail; their solution instead was to move to places – exurbs, rural towns and unincorporated areas – where such amenities as a library or a public swimming pool, or even a school, were not to be found. In the group meetings that were part of their parole regime, they would exchange information about where such 'safe' places might be found. In other words, the shift that had taken place for them was a shift in scale. The exclusions were framed in terms of feet, but the changes that they experienced were those of miles – not so much a simple displacement (walking along one street rather than another so as to maintain greater distance from a school), but rather a search on a different scale for different places where dangers did not lurk so densely.

In the case of the IoT, we saw that forms of human scale that had previously not been issues of technical concern now became manifest within the interface and interaction, represented digitally. In the case of GPS navigation for the parolees, an inverse pattern emerges, where technologies that putatively represent the city at the scale of streets or metres create an experiential structure that operates at the level of towns or kilometres. In both cases, a complex interplay emerges between the scales of representation and the scales of experience, an interplay that depends significantly on patterns of action rather than simply upon design. Given their grounding within systems of practice that give them meaning, these scales too have their temporal dimensions, as understandings of spatial structure – the social organisation of space (e.g., Kelleher 2003) and the cultural dimensions of movement (e.g., Munn 1996) – themselves evolve over time.

Temporalities

The problems of the encounters between old and new and of the problematic persistence of infrastructure that we saw in the Internet of Things are no less true, and arguably more so, in the case of the smart city. That is, just as we saw how the Internet of Things must operate in a world in which infrastructure has a lifetime longer than we might ever want to imagine, so too, when building the infrastructure of the smart city, what you are building is not the glitteringly new urban infrastructure of blockbuster sci-fi movies; what you are building is the next London Underground, something to be encountered by millions daily as more than faintly Victorian but so deeply embedded in the practice of the city that it can never become anything else. The smart city often involves taking all the problems of the Internet of Things, embedding them in concrete and burying them under city streets that can only ever be dug up again at the cost of a good deal of traffic disturbance and pedestrian grumbling.

However, there is a second and perhaps most significant issue concerning infrastructural persistence in the case of the city, and this leads to the kinds of values associated with age in urban experience. While 'building for the ages'

44 *Paul Dourish*

is rarely a rallying cry for urban designers in the early twenty-first century, 'designed obsolescence' is even less effective, even if it has been the watchword of the computer industry. The smart city, in other words, is a celebration both of the new and the old, of the kinds of permanence that allow us to enjoy the Renaissance splendour of Florence and, at the same time, the pressures that prevent people from using last year's power supply with this year's laptop.

Temporal contradictions of a similar sort came to light in recent work with colleagues studying the Cassini mission to Saturn (Vertesi and Dourish 2011; Mazmanian *et al.* 2014). Cassini is arguably engaged in the most advanced navigation ever of a NASA mission; although probes have gone much farther on ballistic orbits, Cassini is explicitly flown though the Saturn system, and nobody has ever flown a spacecraft so far away in such a complex space for so long. In these terms, it is undoubtedly a cutting-edge project. However, at the same time, it is something of a dinosaur. Designed in the 1980s using technological platforms developed in the 1970s, it was built and launched in the 1990s to arrive at Saturn in 2004, at which point the scientific mission could begin. By definition, then, by the time the science began, the spacecraft was, in design terms, obsolete; the ground systems significantly predate the development of contemporary software platforms (including not only bespoke systems at NASA, but commercial programming languages and operating systems). To work on Cassini, then, is to work in a temporal double bind, operating on the cutting edge and the trailing edge simultaneously.

This temporal double bind underscores the problematic rhetoric of temporality in smart cities and urban computing – one that is not unique to those sites, by any means, but is pervasive in contemporary culture. Useful antidotes to aspects of this rhetoric are to be found in recent examinations of the way in which rhetorics of novelty and the pace of change are used to narrate problems and opportunities in daily life. Edgerton (2011), for example, presents a series of compelling examples that undercut conventional arguments about technological progress by showing how old technologies persist amongst the new despite our blindness to them (e.g., the significant role played by horses for transportation and haulage during World War II); Wajcman (2014) critically examines the idea that digital technology is responsible for a sense of the increasing pace of life in the twenty-first century. Examinations of this sort provide us with a useful conceptual foundation for resisting univocal accounts of novelty in urban computing and looking at the more complicated temporal texture within which these accounts are embedded.

Conclusions

What might we take away from this exploration? The analogy between the technologies and discourses of the Internet of Things and those of urban computing is intriguing, but the analogy itself is not, in the end, a hugely substantive one. What it suggests or reveals is more important than the analogy itself.

The first entailment is the need to be able to approach technological interventions in ways that incorporate the whole technical 'stack', as well as its social and political considerations. Social scientists have long argued for the need to be able to form socio-technical understandings that do not hive off the social and the cultural from the technical, but understand them as being thoroughly entwined and mutually constitutive. However, within those discussions, technology itself is often left largely unexamined. I have argued elsewhere that discussions of the socio-technical implications of 'the Internet' are largely meaningless unless we grapple in detail with what the Internet specifically is, in contradistinction to other possible digital networking configurations (Dourish 2015b). Similarly, any account of the role of Internet technologies in urban computing needs to be able to examine how protocol configurations render 'Internet' arguments – about openness, for instance, or about access, or about adaptability – more or less effective.

A second consideration that we see arise out of the analogy between these two technological regimes is the resituating of power and control in digital environments. Digital environments reconfigure social and technical infrastructures by taking centralised phenomena and distributing them and by relying upon or producing new forms of concentration – of power, of logic, of action, of control and of visibility. The Internet of Things is based on a distribution of computational power but also on a shift in the points of connection – from the home to the Cloud, from the desktop to the mobile.

The third point concerns the way that accounts of old and new technologies lend meaning and justification to different accounts of the incorporation of digital technology into the fabric of daily life. One particularly prevalent account, for instance, holds that technology changes quickly (and inevitably) while human or social responses are sluggish and faltering. One might just as well, of course, note that the source of technological change is itself human and organisational, while conventional technologies embed within them a whole history of archaeological artefacts – today's most fashionable smartphone apps incorporate software architectures from the 1990s, network protocols from the 1980s and operating system kernels from the 1970s. There is more to the temporality of technology than a single dimension.

Fourth, this perspective calls for renewed attention to the questions of participation engendered through technological platforms. While many in the technology design community have argued for the adoption of so-called participatory design techniques as a way to engage people with civic structures through technology, a number of researchers have drawn attention to the problems of marginalisation and selective participation that are often at the heart of these projects (e.g., Ehn *et al.* 2014; McCarthy and Wright 2015). The widely recognised problems of minority participation in science and technology, both in academia and in industry, speak to problems of seeing technological projects as inherently democratic and inclusive. Using information technology as the tool of urban change may shift but not necessarily open up the sites of power and agency.

46 *Paul Dourish*

The encounters between code and the city, then, are telling not because they move us beyond existing questions of urban control, management, representation and participation. They are telling precisely because of the ways in which they continue to make those questions relevant.

Acknowledgements

I am grateful to Adam Greenfield, Kat Jungnickel, Rob Kitchin, Ann Light, Alison Powell, Irina Shklovski and participants in the *Code and the City* workshop at the National University of Ireland and the *Dagstuhl Seminar on DIY Networking* for conversations that inspired aspects of this discussion. Melissa Mazmanian and Phoebe Sengers provided useful and generous comments on an incomplete draft. Colleagues in the Intel Science and Technology Center for Social Computing, especially Ken Anderson, Ian Bogost, Carl DiSalvo and Tom Jenkins, have been of tremendous value in framing thinking about the Internet of Things.

Note

1 I should note that I am focusing my examples here on a domestic account of the Internet of Things, which, while prominent, is not, by any means, the only one. Similar arguments, and indeed the same labels, are applied in such domains as workplace and factory automation, for example, which are similarly seen as major IoT application areas. I draw my examples from the domestic space primarily because it is likely to be more familiar to a majority of readers but the central issues apply more broadly.

References

Abowd, G. (2012) 'What next, UbiComp? Celebrating an intellectual disappearing act', *Proceedings of ACM Conference of Ubiquitous Computing*, 31–40.

Antoniadis, P., Le Grand, B., Satsiou, A., Tassiulas, L., Aguiar, R., Barraca, J.P. and Sargento, S. (2008) 'Community building over neighborhood wireless mesh networks', *IEEE Society and Technology*, 27(1): 48–56.

Barkhuus, L. and Dourish, P. (2004) 'Everyday encounters with ubiquitous computing in a campus environment', *Proceedings of the Sixth International Conference on Ubiquitous Computing UbiComp 2004*, 232–49.

Bowker, G.C. and Star, S.L. (1999) *Sorting Things Out: Classification and Its Consequences*, Cambridge, MA: MIT Press.

Brand, S. (1987) *The Media Lab: Inventing the Future at MIT*, New York: Viking Press.

Brand, S. (1995) *How Buildings Learn: What Happens after They're Built*, New York: Viking Press.

Dillahunt, T., Mankoff, J., Paulos, E. and Fussell, S. (2009) 'It's not all about green: energy use in low-income communities', *Proceedings of the 11th International Conference on Ubiquitous Computing*, 255–64.

Dillahunt, T., Mankoff, J. and Paulos, E. (2010) 'Understanding conflict between

The Internet of Urban Things   47

landlords and tenants: implications for energy sensing and feedback', *Proceedings of the 12th International Conference on Ubiquitous Computing*, 149–58.

DiSalvo, C., Sengers, P. and Brynjarsdóttir, H. (2010) 'Mapping the landscape of sustainable HCI', *Proceedings of ACM Conference on Human Factors in Computing Systems CHI 2010*, 1975–84.

Dourish, P. (2010) 'HCI and environmental sustainability: the politics of design and the design of politics', *Proceedings of ACM Conference on Designing Interactive Systems DIS 2010*, 1–10.

Dourish, P. (2015a) 'Packets, protocols, and proximity: the materialities of Internet routing', in L. Parks and N. Starosielski (eds) *Signal Traffic: Critical Studies of Media Infrastructures*, Champaign, IL: University of Illinois Press.

Dourish, P. (2015b) 'Not the Internet, but this Internet: how othernets illuminate our feudal Internet', *Proceedings of Critical Alternatives (Fifth Decennial Aarhus Conference)*, Aarhus, Denmark, 157–68.

Dourish, P. and Bell, G. (2011) *Divining a Digital Future: Mess and Mythology in Ubiquitous Computing*, Cambridge, MA: MIT Press.

Edgerton, D. (2011) *The Shock of the Old: Technology and Global History since 1900*, Oxford: Oxford University Press.

Edwards, K. and Grinter, R. (2001) 'At home with ubiquitous computing: seven challenges', *Proceedings of International Conference on Ubiquitous Computing UbiComp*, 256–72.

Ehn, P., Nilsson, E. and Topgaard, R. (2014) *Making Futures: Marginal Notes on Innovation, Design, and Democracy*, Cambridge, MA: MIT Press.

Gaved, M. and Mulholland, P. (2008) 'Pioneers, subcultures, and cooperatives: the grassroots augmentation of urban places', in A. Aurigi and F. De Cindio (eds) *Augmented Urban Spaces: Articulating the Physical and Electronic City*, Aldershot: Ashgate.

Greenfield, A. (2014) *The City Is Here For You to Use. Part 1: Against the Smart City*, New York: Do Projects.

Greenwald, G. (2014) *No Place to Hide: Edward Snowden, the NSA, and the US Surveillance State*, New York: Metropolitan Books.

Homburg, V. (2008) *Understanding E-Government: Information Systems in Public Administration*, London: Routledge.

Jungnickel, K. (2014) *DiY WiFi: Re-imagining Connectivity*, Basingstoke: Palgrave Macmillan.

Kelleher, W. (2003) *The Troubles in Ballybogoin: Memory and Identity in Northern Ireland*, Ann Arbor, MI: University of Michigan Press.

Leshed, G., Velden, T., Rieger, O., Kot, B. and Sengers, P. (2008) 'In-car GPS navigation: engagement with and disconnection from the environment', *Proceedings of ACM Conference on Human Factors in Computing Systems, CHI 2008*, 1675–84.

Light, A., Simpson, G., Weaver, L. and Healey, P. (2009) 'Geezers, turbines, fantasy personas: making the everyday into the future', *Proceedings of ACM Conference on Creativity and Cognition CandC'09*, 39–48.

McCarthy, J. and Wright, P. (2015) *Taking [A]part: The Politics and Aesthetics of Participation in Experience-Centered Design*, Cambridge, MA: MIT Press.

Mazmanian, M., Cohn, M. and Dourish, P. (2014) 'Dynamic reconfiguration in planetary exploration: a sociomaterial ethnography', *MIS Quarterly*, 38(3): 831–48.

Millard, C. (ed.) (2013) *Cloud Computing Law*, Oxford, UK: Oxford University Press.

48 *Paul Dourish*

Munn, N. (1996) 'Excluded spaces: the figure in the Australian aboriginal landscape', *Critical Inquiry*, 22(3), 446–65.

Powell, A. (2011) 'Metaphors, models and communicative spaces: designing local wireless infrastructure', *Canadian Journal of Communication*, 36(1): 91–114.

Scott, J. (1998) *Seeing Like a State: How Certain Schemes to Improve the Human Condition Have Failed*, New Haven, CT: Yale University Press.

Shklovski, I., Vertesi, J., Troshynski, E. and Dourish, P. (2009) 'The commodification of location: dynamics of power in location-based systems', *Proceedings of International Conference on Ubiquitous Computing UbiComp 2009*, 11–20.

Shklovski, I., Troshynski, E. and Dourish, P. (2015) 'Mobile technologies and spatiotemporal configurations of institutional practice', *Journal of the Association for Information Science and Technology*, 66(10): 2098–115.

Starosielski, N. (2015) *The Undersea Network*, Durham, NC: Duke University Press.

Troshynski, E., Lee, C. and Dourish, P. (2008) 'Accountabilities of presence: reframing location-based systems', *Proceedings of ACM Conference on Human Factors in Computing Systems CHI 2008*, 487–96.

Turner, F. (2006) *From Counterculture to Cyberculture: Stewart Brand, the Whole Earth Network, and the Rise of Digital Utopianism*, Chicago, IL: University of Chicago Press.

Valverde, M. (2011) 'Seeing like a city: the dialectic of modern and premodern ways of seeing in urban governance', *Law and Society Review*, 45(2): 277–312.

Vertesi, J. and Dourish, P. (2011) 'The value of data: considering the context of production in data economies', *Proceedings of ACM 2011 Conference on Computer-Supported Cooperative Work*, 533–42.

Wajcman, J. (2014) *Pressed for Time: The Acceleration of Life in Digital Capitalism*, Chicago, IL: University of Chicago Press.

Weiser, M. (1991) 'The computer for the 21st century', *Scientific American*, 265: 94–104.

4 Interfacing urban intelligence

Shannon Mattern

Introduction

As more cities become 'smart', we are beginning to see the political and epistemological contradictions of urban 'sentience' writ large in steel and silicon. Underlying all the personalised data streams and purported opportunities for public engagement is still, almost always, a 'black-box' control system. We citizens are empowered to report failed trash pick-ups or rank our favourite hospitals, but *not* entitled to know what happens to our personal data each time we pass through a toll booth. We often have little understanding of how and where the mediation of urban systems takes place within the city itself.

City governments, technology companies and design firms – the entities teaming up to construct these highly networked future-cities – have prototyped various interfaces through which citizens can engage with the smart city. But those prototypes embody institutional values that are not always aligned with the values of citizens who have a 'right to the city' (Lefebvre 1996; 2003). Judging from the promotional materials released by corporate smart city makers, you would think that one of the chief preoccupations of the smart city is reflecting its own data consumption and hyperefficient activity back to itself. At its heart is a 'control centre' lined with screens that serves in part to visualise and celebrate the city's supposedly hyperrational operation. Rio's Ops Centre, designed by IBM, integrates data from 30 city agencies; its layered screens feature transit video feeds, weather information and maps of crime statistics and power failures, as well as other snafus (Singer 2012). The city is thus partitioned into atomised projects, services and flows, each competing for technicians' attention. We see a similar 'widgetisation' in Arup's proposed dashboard for Melbourne staff: *This is Your City in Real Time.*[1]

Governments and their citizens need to think more deeply about these designs. What does it mean to 'modularise' urban services? To offer a map-based snapshot of something as complicated as 'public health'? To permit users to filter data streams of interest? To dedicate prime screen space to 'fast-moving' data while pushing relatively static urban dimensions to the bottom of the screen? What kind of intelligence do these windowed screens manifest?

If the Ops Centre dashboard has received too little critical analysis, the public interface has received almost none at all. Some smart city proposals represent the public interface as a schematic mock-up, with apparently little regard for interaction design. Others proffer a completely blank slate. (Intel renders its Sustainable Connected Cities interfaces as tiny, benevolent explosions).[2] The range of imagined programs and services is shockingly narrow: typically the street interface is little more than a conduit of transit information, commercial locations and reviews, and information about tourist attractions and cultural resources.

Many city governments have developed Web portals to showcase their open data, and they host hackathons and competitions, usually resulting in apps that serve a single function – finding farmers' markets, for instance, or measuring air quality – and rarely survive without sufficient institutional support (Again, the 'widgetisation' of urban resources.) Almost always, they frame their users as *sources* of data, who feed the urban algorithmic machines, and as *consumers* of data, concerned primarily with *their own* efficient navigation and consumption of the city. These interfaces to the smart city suggest that we have traded in our environmental wisdom, political agency and social responsibility for corporately managed situational information, instrumental rationality, and personal consumption and convenience. We seem ready to translate *our* messy city into *my* efficient city.

Assuming that greater populations will find themselves residing in networked, intelligent megalopolises, we need to give more serious consideration to designing urban interfaces for urban *citizens*, who have a right to know what is going on inside those black boxes – a right to engage with the operating system as more than mere reporters-of-potholes-and-power-outages. We need to focus attention on the 'bleed points' between the concrete and digital and social city, those zones where citizens can investigate the entwinement of various infrastructures and publics.[3]

Examining existing and proposed, even speculative, interfaces allows us to ask ourselves what kind of a 'public face' we want to front our cities, and, even more importantly, what kinds of intelligence and agency – technological *and* human – we want our cities to embody. We need to consider how these interfaces structure their inputs and outputs, how they illuminate and obfuscate various dimensions of the city, how they frame interaction, how that interaction both reflects and informs the relationship between citizens and cities and, ultimately, how these interfaces shape people's identities as urban subjects. We will need to challenge the common equation of 'interface' with 'screen', and the implications of reducing urban complexity to a two-dimensional visualisation. Can we – *and I do believe that this must be a collaborative, interdisciplinary enterprise* – envision interfaces that honour the multidimensionality and collectivity of the city, the many kinds of intelligence it encompasses, and the diverse ways in which people can enact their agency as urban subjects?

The urban stack

In his 1997 book *Interface Culture*, Steven Johnson defines the interface as 'software that shapes the interaction between user and computer. The interface serves as a kind of translator, mediating between the two parties, making one sensible to the other' (Johnson 1997: 14).[4] Branden Hookway (2011: 14) agrees that the interface does its work 'as the zone or threshold that must be worked through in order [for the user] to be able to relate to technology'.[5] In that working-through, the interface structures the user's agency and identity and constructs him or her as a 'subject', which is different from a mere 'user', in that the subject's identity shifts in response to contextual variations and is informed by historical, cultural and political forces.

However, the zone between person and machine is only the most visible type of interface. Computer systems are commonly modelled as a 'stack' of protocols of varying degrees of concreteness or abstraction – from the physical Ethernet hardware to the abstract application interface – with interfaces between every layer of this stack (Solomon 2013; Bratton 2016).[6] Alexander Galloway (2012: 54) defines 'interface' broadly as 'a general technique of mediation evident at all levels'. At the *user* level, the technique might be graphical, sonic, motion-tracking, gestural, tangible or embodied, or of another variety (see also Dourish 2001; Homecker and Buur 2006).

Thus, we might think of future city technologies as an 'urban stack'. At the highest level, we find all those zoomable maps and apps that translate urban data into something useful. Today, the most ubiquitous vehicle for this digested and visualised data is the mobile phone.[7] The widespread availability of open data via smartphone apps (and globally via text messaging) has inspired many urban residents to explore 'deeper' down the stack, to understand how local systems work behind the scenes: how their water arrives at their homes, for example, or where their garbage goes when disposed. I have written elsewhere about 'infrastructural tourism' and DIY data-science projects that connect citizens with those often-obfuscated networks (Mattern 2013a; 2013b; Tironi *et al.* 2014).

Yet much of what is 'beneath' or 'behind' the user interface remains inaccessible and unintelligible. Powering these public-facing interfaces are highly sophisticated technical and administrative networks that integrate urban services and infrastructures – water, power, police and fire services, snow removal, etc. – with computer operating systems.[8] Living PlanIT, for instance, 'owns and monetises' the Urban Operating System (UOS™) – with projects in the UK, the Netherlands and Portugal – which 'extracts, aggregates, analyses and manages sensor data' in urban environments, thereby 'harvesting useful intelligence and also enabling management, control and greater efficiency for many city services'.[9] Control and efficiency: these are the values – and the *ends* of intelligence – built into this system. Yet citizens do not come into contact with the operating system; they merely reap its efficient rewards. The obfuscation of the operating system – largely intentional and perhaps even necessary, to the extent that it enables us to focus attention on the data most immediately relevant to our urban experiences – is also risky. We forget just how extensively these layered interfaces structure our communication and sociality, how they delimit our agency, and how they are defining the terrain we are interfacing *with*.

How might we conceive of interfaces that allow us to monitor those aggregators and protocols, and even deeper levels of the urban stack – the code, the hardware, etc. – that undergird integrated (and often proprietary) urban operating systems? Below the human–computer level of the urban stack, we have the wireless networks that transport the data from and to us, and the application programmer interfaces (APIs) that allow various entities to build apps that tap into our cities' open data.[10] Particularly, given the complexity of these networks, and the profound implications their algorithms can have for urban politics and our identities as urban 'subjects', we should have a means of looking inside the box, if not tinkering with the code.

Observers have long sought to wrap their heads around complex urban operations and to picture the totality of the urban domain. The rise of print in the fifteenth century brought new maps, guidebooks and public posters that shaped residents' comprehension of and interaction with their cities (San Juan 2001; Wilson 2005). The explosion of newspapers in the late nineteenth century likewise offered a new means of 'overviewing' the expanding, increasingly diverse, polyglot metropolis. The inventions of panoramic and aerial photography and, eventually, satellite imagery offered ever-more comprehensive, scalable representations of cities – and our places within them (Bruno 2002; Vidler 2011: 317–28; Parks 2012; Haffner 2013; Huhtamo 2013; Kurgan 2013). Today, media facades, public screens, ambient interfaces, responsive architectures and other forms of 'public interactives' are transforming our physical environments into interfaces in their own right. In the Melbourne proposal,[11] Arup envisioned screens embedded in architectural facades, at transit stations, on the sides of trams, and hanging from posts on every block. Even local waterways, the designers suggested, could become 'ambient' conduits for visually (and perhaps sonically and haptically) sharing information about their own workings.

Yet I have to wonder: interfaces to *what*? What is the 'city' they propose to put us in relation *with*, and how deep into the stack does that relation go? In too many cases, the 'city on the screen' is little more than a set of measureable events, trackable movements and rateable services. Could we develop urban interfaces that actually help us wade through, make sense of – and critically engage with – the oceans of data generated by our cities and presented to us in edited form? Could alternative modes of presentation encourage us to think about the biases, affordances and limitations built into our tools and techniques of data representation? Could we 'read' our urban interfaces – our windows into the urban operating system – as a means of assessing the ethos of urban development, ensuring that our cities' operations are upholding an open, democratic ethic?[12]

Interfacing urban intelligence   53

Interface critique

The most prevalent ways of thinking about human–computer interaction are framed by values central to *engineering*. According to media scholar Johanna Drucker (2011: 1), the evaluation of interfaces typically involves 'scenarios that chunk tasks and behaviours into carefully segmented decision trees' and 'endlessly iterative cycles of "task specification" and "deliverables"' (see also Drucker 2013). Such thinking tends to equate the 'human' in human–computer interaction with an efficiency-minded 'user'. This is, of course, how much smart cities discourse frames inhabitants, too – as efficiency-minded, affect-less consumers of urban resources. But if we want our cities to embrace a wider set of experiences and values – serendipity, ambiguity, even productive, 'seamful' inefficiency – and to facilitate more diverse forms of human agency, what should we be looking for in those interfaces between the city and its inhabitants?[13]

I offer a rubric for how we might evaluate our urban interfaces. We should consider:

- The *materiality, scale, location and orientation* of the interface. If it is a screen: where is it sited, how big is it, is it oriented in landscape or portrait or another mode, does it move, what kinds of viewing practices does it promote? If there is audio: where are the speakers, what is their reach, and what kind of listening practices do they foster?
- The *modalities of interaction* with the interface. Do we merely *look at* dynamically presented data? Can we touch the screen and make things happen? Can we speak into the air and expect it to hear us, or do we have to press a button to awaken Siri? Can we gesticulate naturally, or do we have to wear a special glove, or carry a special wand, in order for it to recognise our movements?
- The *basic composition* of elements on the screen – or in the soundtrack or object – and how they work together across time and space.
- How the interface provides a *sense of orientation*. How do we understand where we are within the 'grand scheme' of the interface – how closely we are 'zoomed in' and how much context the interface is providing – or the landscape or timeframe it is representing?
- How the interface *'frames' its content*: how it chunks and segments – via boxes and buttons and borders, both graphic and conceptual – various data streams and activities.
- The *modalities of presentation* – audio, visual, textual, etc. – the interface affords. What visual, verbal, sonic languages does the interface use to frame content into fundamental categories?
- The *data models* that undergird the interface's content and structure our interaction with it: how sliders, dialogue boxes, drop-down menus, and other GUI elements organise content – as a qualitative or quantitative value, as a set of discrete entities or a continuum, as an open field or a set

54 Shannon Mattern

of controlled choices, etc. – and thereby embody an *epistemology and a method of interpretation*.

- The acts of interpretive translation that take place at the *hinges and portals* between layers of interfaces: how we use *allegories or metaphors* – the desktop, the file folder or even our mental image of the city-as-network – to 'translate', imperfectly, between different layers of the stack.

- *To whom the interface speaks, whom it excludes, and how*. Who are the intended and actual audiences? How does the underlying database categorise user types and shape how we understand our social roles and expected behaviour? This issue is of particular concern, given the striking lack of racial, gender and socio-economic diversity in much discourse and development of 'smart cities'.

- *What kinds of information or experience are simply not representable* through a graphic or gestural user interface, on a zoomable map, via data visualisation or sonification? While some content or levels of the protocol stack may be intentionally hidden – for the sake of 'public' security, for instance, or to protect Cisco's and IBM's intellectual property – Galloway (2012: 91) argues that some things are unrepresentable, in large part because we have yet to create 'adequate visualisations' of our network culture and control society. Yet we should also consider the possibility that some aspects of our cities are not, and will never be, machine-readable (Greenfield 2012).[14] Affect, for example. Or beauty. In our interface critique, then, we might imagine what dimensions of human experience and the world we inhabit cannot or *should* not be translated or interfaced.

Slabs and clouds

Using this rubric, here I want to examine in brief two case examples.[15] First, consider Urbanscale's Urbanflow system, an 'urban operating system' that would facilitate journey planning and wayfinding (privileging pedestrian travel), service discovery (including locations, reviews, open hours, etc.), access to ambient data (including information on all the signature 'urban informatics' concerns, like air quality and noise pollution) and 'citizen responsiveness' (i.e., encouraging citizens to report problems and make requests for public services).[16] Urbanflow, they claimed, would offer a 'dedicated platform where the city and its citizens can meet'. Their detailed proposal for the city of Helsinki envisioned larger-than-human-scale slabs positioned throughout the city.[17] These screens would detect motion, 'wake up' when you walk by and 'hail' you to interact, and they would immediately place you in the middle of a map – 'You Are Here' – situated at your current coordinates, oriented to reflect the cardinal direction you are facing.

Urbanscale and their partners, Nordkapp, paid more attention than most smart city developers to interface design and human–computer

Interfacing urban intelligence 55

interaction-driven understandings of user experience, while also allowing for serendipitous discovery *and* evincing a keen aesthetic sensibility. The design team claimed that, with Urbanflow, 'the city itself becomes ... easier to navigate for visitors, and more serendipitous for locals. City officials and municipal governments would be provided with a completely new way to connect with citizens and visitors.' Still, we must wonder about the politics of the interface's egocentric framing: the fact that you, the user, are always at the centre. What urban imaginaries and realities are 'toggled off' when your own navigational, informational and service needs are always front and centre?

Second, the 'Cloud' is an interfacial monolith at superscale.[18] Bringing together a massive global team of designers, engineers, artists and organisations (including Arup, Google and MIT), the Cloud was to be an observation deck for the 2012 Olympic Games. Its tall, spiral ramp would carry pedestrians and cyclists high up to a cluster of transparent inflatable spheres and observation decks, where visitors could walk 'amongst the clouds'. The inflatable structure was to be itself a substrate for data visualisation; it would allow for the geolocation of information about medal winners and attendance at the Olympic events, energy use, transportation patterns, mobile phone activity, even historical information about the region. And it would display some of that data via augmented-reality interfaces, which would 'layer' information on top of the landscape visible below. The Cloud would also generate data by collecting rainwater, harnessing wind and providing a unique sensory experience for visitors to be *in* the weather – in the ubiquitous London clouds while in the Cloud. As explained by Dan Hill (2009), then an Arup representative on the design team, the Cloud would 'take aggregate individual patterns and reveal them at civic scale, thus binding the city's activity together via a gentle ambient drizzle of data'.

Pie-in-the-sky it may have been, but the embodied interactive experience is worth considering as a model for urban interfaces. The Cloud proposed a macro-scale view that approximated the scale of modern information networks, *literalising* the metaphor of the data cloud. Participants would have assumed the position of 'aggregators' by walking around the space and kinaesthetically, choreographically, tying together various threads of data.[19] Its primary public would have been the visitors to Olympic Park – but because the monumental structure would be widely publicised on television and the Internet, its 'audience' would have been global. That audience could have posted their own relevant content on social media, which might have then made its way to one of the screens inside the Cloud, for folks on-scene to see.

But we do not know how that data would have been made perceptible. We see no representation of the embedded screens or their interfaces in the team's renderings, and we have no indication of what other sensory outputs might have been engaged. The renderings emphasise visitors' elevated point of view and kinaesthetic experience, which do indeed allow for a novel 'embodiment' of urban data. But I wonder: by transforming surveillance and aggregation

56 *Shannon Mattern*

into an immersive display, a fair attraction, without addressing the power and privilege associated with those perspectives and roles, would the Cloud have 'destroy[ed] the ... divide between audience and spectacle', or would it have turned its subjects, and their data, *into* spectacle?

Breaking the frame

In his critique of financial interfaces, economist and philosopher Georgios Papadopoulos (2013) acknowledges the potential of the interface to function disruptively (such a shame that this term has been spoiled by Silicon Valley!), unmasking the norms and limitations of the financial system it models, and offering a 'transparent' look at its underlying ideologies. Galloway (2012: 94) similarly calls for a 'counter-cartography' – which might be realised through the urban interface – that reveals and tests the protocols of our 'informatic imagination'. It is not enough merely to 'intervene at the level of "content"' – for instance, to use a flow chart or PowerPoint or Google Map to trace networks of power. We have to test the 'prohibitions' of our plat- forms' forms and materialities and affordances, too; we need to experiment with 'new data types, new "if-then" statements, new network diagrams, new syllogisms' (Galloway 2012: 97).

Can we create a formal or structural parallel between the urban structures we desire and the interfaces we create to mediate those cities? Are we sure, Hill (2013) wonders, that core civic values – serendipity and productive inef- ficiency, personal and civic responsibility, 'meaningful activity from citizens and government, the city as public good, and ... diversity and regard for the *affective* dimensions of urban experience – are part of the smart city vision?' Furthermore, he asks, 'are our governance cultures and tools in the right shape to genuinely react to the promise of the network?' Are these same values embodied *formally* in our smart city interfaces? Could governments use these tools to 'boldly prototyp[e] new versions' of themselves? Could citizens use these same tools to investigate urban power structures and access to resources? We should be using our urban interfaces to afford our publics a peek 'down the urban stack', to the invisible infrastructures that make the city work; to call attention to the unrepresented populations and urban problems that are filtered out of our whitewashed and abstracted city render- ings; to highlight opportunities for improvement, and the roles that everyday people could play in effecting that change. We could be using our urban interfaces to educate our publics about the nature of government and the expanding 'science' of urban management – about the methodologies of data gathering and analysis, the politics of visualisation, the algorithms behind the 'urban operating system' and the servers and wires and waves that make it all possible.

Consciously and critically designing our urban interfaces could compel us to ask questions about what kind of cities we want, and what kind of citizens we want to be. The creation of a *better* interface – an interface that reflects

Interfacing urban intelligence 57

the ethics and politics that we want our cities to embody – is necessarily a collaborative process, one drawing on the skills of designers of all stripes, technicians, engineers, logisticians, cultural critics and theorists, artists, bus drivers and sanitation workers, politicians and political scientists, economists, policy-makers and myriad others (including women and people of colour, who have been egregiously underrepresented in relevant debates). If our interfaces are to reflect and embody the values of *our* city, the conception and creation of those interfaces should be *ours*, too – not Cisco's, not the administrators', certainly not *mine* or *yours*. But ours.

Acknowledgement

This chapter is an abridged and modified version of an essay of the same title that I published in *Places Journal* in April 2014. Please visit https://placesjournal.org/article/interfacing-urban-intelligence/ for the expanded, richly illustrated essay.

Notes

1 There is a rendering of the dashboard in Mattern (2014a).
2 See Intel Collaborative Research Institute (2012).
3 Consider the workshop *Interfacing with the City* at the 2011 FutureEverything festival in Manchester; participants explored the city and documented the 'bleed points' where the physical and virtual world connected: CCTV cameras, Wi-Fi routers, digital art, etc. They used this documentation to discuss 'how digital layers are visible or hidden and how their presence is mediated through the city' (Strutz 2011).
4 See Mattern (2014b) for a more thorough discussion of the various ways of *theorising* interfaces.
5 See also Hookway (2014).
6 See also Wikipedia (2015).
7 Of course, some cities of the world are more concerned with providing basic urban services – like adequate housing – than designing flashy interactive facades. In most of these developing areas, according to Anthony Townsend (2013), despite all the attention paid over the past decade to cheap laptops, smartphones are 'destined to be the true face of ubiquitous computing', a model of 'everyware' computing that is central to visions of the smart city, on the global scale. Mobile phones 'have spread the fastest and have become the single most transformative tool for development' – and via SMS, they can deliver text-based data to residents in less richly wired parts of the globe (Christine Zhen-Wei Qiang, quoted in Townsend 2013: 178). Some international development organisations have designed rugged public kiosks to deliver urban informatics in these regions, too (Fabian 2011; see also Rekow 2013 for the widespread use of SMS messaging systems).
8 For a discussion of the long history of the 'city-as-machine' metaphor, and of conceptualising the city through computational models, see Mattern (2013b).
9 Other metropolitan areas are creating a 'city protocol', an 'urban innovation model' dedicated to the creation of 'reports, standards, certification systems, services definition, best practices and recommendations to turn cities into more innovative and sustainable environments' (quotes here and above in Living PlanIT (n.d.)). Also, in Cisco's press release: 'In the same way as the Internet Protocol shaped

58 *Shannon Mattern*

the original development of the Internet, the City Protocol will be discussed and developed internationally, setting up an evolutive protocol based on the agreement of a global community. It will deliver benefits within and between cities, by addressing urban development in an integrated systemic way' (Cisco 2012). Such projects are predicated on the assumption that cities from Kenya to Canada to Cambodia operate on a standardised system of rules, regardless of local history, culture, geography, climate, etc.

10 Anthony Townsend (2013: 288) argues that 'community-owned broadband is one of the best investments a smart city can make'; which not only allows citizens ready access to Web-based content, but also 'puts the city in control of its own nervous system, giving it tremendous bargaining power over any private company that wants to sell smart services to the city government or its businesses or residents'.

11 See *Melbourne Smart City*, available at http://www.cityofsound.com/files/c40_melbourne_report_final_email.pdf [accessed 26 November 2015]; for more on ambient interfaces, see McCullough (2013).

12 Townsend suggests that we need 'a new social code to bring meaning to and exert control over the technological code of urban operating systems'. Part of that social code is an ethic of technical development – a commitment to creating 'simple, modular and open source' urban software and an 'organically evolved set of open standards'; to documenting and archiving our data streams; and to 'modelling transparently' – to 'exposing the algorithms of smart city software', most of which are guarded by government and industry (Townsend 2013: 284, 287, 290, 295).

13 Anthropologist Dorien Zandbergen (2013) writes about her involvement in an interdisciplinary team that designed an air-quality reading device. She found that compromises and contradictions in the design pointed to 'different types of futures, and, by extension, to different ways in which the ideal of this alleged smart city can be realised'. While the device's hardware was open source, its software was commercial, which meant that its full features were available only to paying customers. Furthermore, when the device was ultimately enclosed in a shiny, user-friendly casing – thus blackboxing the critical issues debated throughout the design process – the device 'stopped facilitating discussions about the actual meaning and reliability of the data, and instead adopted marketing language, selling "transparency", "efficiency", and above all, a Plus account with helpdesk facility'. She suggests that, in smart cities, 'user-friendliness' should apply not to its 'flashy interfaces and shiny casings', but to 'discussions of power and value that go into the production of our everyday technologies'.

14 While the original post has been inexplicably redacted, the ideas it contains are still of great value.

15 In the longer version of this article (Mattern 2014a), I offer a number of other case studies plus illustrations related to the two examples discussed here.

16 See Urbanscale (n.d.).

17 See Nordkapp and Urbanscale (2011).

18 See http://www.raisethecloud.org/ [accessed 19 August 2015].

19 See the brochure for the Cloud http://web.mit.edu/giodn/Public/theCLOUD_texts.pdf [accessed 1st April 2014].

References

Bratton, B. (forthcoming 2016) *The Stack: On Software and Sovereignty*, Cambridge, MA: MIT Press.

Bruno, G. (2002) *Atlas of Emotions: Journeys in Art, Architecture and Film*, New York: Verso.

Interfacing urban intelligence 59

Cisco, (2012) 'Barcelona, GDF SUEZ and Cisco announce the launch of the city protocol', 28 August 28 2012, available from http://newsroom.cisco.com/release/998539/Barcelona-GDF-SUEZ-and-Cisco-announce-the-launch-of-the-City-Protocol [accessed 19 August 2015].

Dourish, P. (2001) *Where the Action Is: The Foundations of Embodied Interaction*, Cambridge, MA: MIT Press.

Drucker, J. (2011) 'Humanities approaches to interface theory', *Culture Machine*, 12, available from http://www.culturemachine.net/index.php/cm/article/viewArticle/434 [accessed 17 November 2015].

Drucker, J. (2013) 'Performative materiality and theoretical approaches to interface', *Digital Humanities Quarterly*, 7(1), available from http://www.digitalhumanities.org/dhq/vol/7/1/000143/000143.html [accessed 17 November 2015].

Fabian, C. (2011) 'Spaces around digital access: kiosks in sub-Saharan Africa', *Libraries, Archives and Databases*, 11 April 2011, available from http://www.wordsinspace.net/lib-arch-data/wordpress_libarchdata/?p=279 [accessed 19 August 2015].

Galloway, A.R. (2012) *The Interface Effect*, Malden, MA: Polity.

Greenfield, A. (2012) 'The city is here for you to use: 100 easy pieces', 3 December 2012, available from http://speedbird.wordpress.com/2012/12/03/the-city-is-here-for-you-to-use-100-easy-pieces/ [accessed 15 August 2015].

Haffner, J. (2013) *The View from Above: The Science of Social Space*, Cambridge, MA: MIT Press.

Hill, D. (2009) 'Sketchbook: The Cloud', *City of Sound*, 11 November 2009, available from http://www.cityofsound.com/blog/2009/11/the-cloud.html [accessed 19 August 2015].

Hill, D. (2013) 'On the smart city; or, a "manifesto" for smart citizens instead', *City Of Sound*, 1 February 2013, available from http://www.cityofsound.com/blog/2013/02/on-the-smart-city-a-call-for-smart-citizens-instead.html [accessed 19 August 2015].

Homecker, E. and Buur, J. (2006) 'Getting a grip on tangible interaction: a framework on physical space and social interaction', *Proceedings of ACM CHI 2006 Conference on Human Factors in Computing Systems*, 437–46.

Hookway, B. (2011) *The Interface*, PhD thesis, Princeton University.

Hookway, B. (2014) *Interface*, Cambridge, MA: MIT Press.

Huhtamo, E. (2013) *Illusions in Motion: Media Archaeology of the Moving Panorama and Related Spectacles*, Cambridge, MA: MIT Press.

Intel Collaborative Research Institute (2012) *Sustainable Connected Cities*, available from http://www.cities.io/ [accessed 17 November 2015].

Kurgan, L. (2013) *Close Up at a Distance: Mapping, Technology, and Politics*, Brooklyn: Zone Books.

Johnson, S. (1997) *Interface Culture: How New Technology Transforms the Way We Create and Communicate*, New York: Harper Edge.

Lefebvre, H. (1996) *The Urban Revolution*, Minneapolis: University of Minnesota Press.

Lefebvre, H. (2003) *Writings on Cities*, New York: Oxford University Press.

Living PlanIT (n.d.) *What is Living PlanIT?*, available from http://www.living-planit.com/what_is_living_planit.htm [accessed 28 August 2012].

McCullough, M. (2013) *Ambient Commons: Attention in the Age of Embodied Information*, Cambridge, MA: MIT Press.

60 Shannon Mattern

Mattern, S. (2013a) 'Infrastructural tourism', *Places*, July 2013, available from https://placesjournal.org/article/infrastructural-tourism [accessed 19 August 2015].

Mattern, S. (2013b) 'Methodolatry and the art of measure', *Places*, November 2013, available from https://placesjournal.org/article/methodolatry-and-the-art-of-measure [accessed 19 August 2015].

Mattern, S. (2014a) 'Interfacing urban intelligence', *Places*, available from https://placesjournal.org/article/interfacing-urban-intelligence [accessed 17 November 2015].

Mattern, S. (2014b) 'Interface critique, revisited', *Words in Space*, 22 January 2014, available from http://www.wordsinspace.net/wordpress/2014/01/22/interface-critique-revisited-thinking-about-archival-interfaces/ [accessed 19 August 2015].

Nordkapp and Urbanscale (2011) *Urbanflow Helsinki*, available from http://helsinki.urbanflow.io/ [accessed 19 August 2015].

Papadopoulos, G. (2013) 'Digital money, the end of privacy, and the preconditions of post-digital resistance', *Post-Digital-Research*, available from http://post-digital.projects.cavi.dk/?p=569 [accessed 19 August 2015].

Parks, L. (2012) 'Zeroing in: overhead imagery, infrastructure ruins and datalands in Afghanistan and Iraq', in J. Packer and S.B.C. Wiley (eds) *Communication Matters: Materialist Approaches to Media, Mobility and Networks*, New York: Routledge.

Rekow, L. (2013) 'Including informality in the smart citizen conversation', in D. Hemment and A. Townsend (eds) *Smart Citizens*, Manchester: Future Everything Publications, 35–8.

San Juan, R.M. (2001) *Rome: A City Out of Print*, Minneapolis: University of Minnesota Press.

Singer, N. (2012) 'Mission control, built for cities', *New York Times*, 3 March 2012.

Solomon, R. (2013) 'Last in, first out: network archaeology of/as the stack', *Amodern 2: Network Archaeology*, available from http://amodern.net/article/last-in-first-out/ [accessed 19 August 2015].

Strutz, E. (2011) 'FutureEverything 2011', *YOUrban*, 25 May 2011, available from http://yourban.no/2011/05/25/futureeverything-2011/ [accessed 19 August 2015].

Tironi, M., Criado, T.M. and Musiani, F. (2014) 'Opening up the urban interface: the smart city and other experimental forms of "infrastructural politics"', *Society for Social Studies of Sciences Annual Conference*, 20–23 August 2014, Buenos Aires, Argentina.

Townsend, A. (2013) *Smart Cities: Big Data, Civic Hackers, and the Quest for a New Utopia*, New York: W.W. Norton and Co.

Urbanscale (n.d.) *Urbanflow*, available from http://urbanscale.org/projects/urban-flow/ [accessed 19 August 2015].

Vidler, A. (2011) 'Photourbanism: planning the city from above and from below', in *The Scenes of the Street and Other Essays*, New York: Monacelli, 317–28.

Wikipedia (2015) *Protocol Stack*, available from http://en.wikipedia.org/wiki/Protocol_stack [accessed 18 August 2015].

Wilson, B. (2005) *The World in Venice: Print, the City, and Early Modern Identity*, Buffalo: University of Toronto Press.

Zandbergen, D. (2013) 'Real smart cities are not user-friendly', *Leiden Anthropology Blog*, 18 December 2013, available from http://www.leidenanthropologyblog.nl/articles/real-smart-cities-are-not-user-friendly, [accessed 19 August 2015].

5 Abstract urbanism

Matthew Fuller and Graham Harwood

Introduction

One of the first computational models of a city was set out in Thomas Schelling's paper *Models of Segregation* (1969). In this and related papers, he attempted to provide a logical model of the dynamics of racial segregation in North American cities and laid groundwork for what later became known as agent-based modelling (Schelling 1969). Although *Models of Segregation* did not at first use a computer, it sets up some of the basic characteristics and problems of the field. Such work is also expressed contemporarily, for instance in the work of J. M. Epstein (2002) and others in the area of computational social modelling.[1] We use this work as a starting point to think about the relationship between urban morphologies and the politics of models and with the increasing and multiform kinds of merger between computational systems, models and city forms, what it means to inhabit different scales of abstract structure. It is in this juncture that abstract urbanism arises.

This chapter examines the ways in which logical forms are positioned in relation to urban life as a means of discussing the relations between the city and software and will develop a discussion of such logics in relation to questions of abstraction, reduction and empiricism. By working with the materiality of computational systems, especially as they unfold into the urban – and the urban in a full sense, as something involving complex comings into being of desire, imagination, technologies and forms of power – we can at the same time recognise an art of working with the tendency to reductionism through which modes of abstraction may operate and also work with the highly and complexly empirical. As social simulations are increasingly embedded in, or cleave close to, lived social forms, the texture and reality-forming capacities of these logics and the fantasies they inspire and live by need to be examined.

Development of simulation as a scientific practice

One attractive aspect of modelling as a means of experimental understanding is that it offers a science of behaviours rather than of essences. It is peculiar,

62 Matthew Fuller and Graham Harwood

therefore, that one of the earliest examples of social simulation derives from a highly essentialist ontology. Perhaps this might be seen as an example of a new epistemic form emerging out of a prior set of commitments that it has yet to break. *Models of Segregation* builds on the game theory established by Morgenstern and von Neumann (1947). Schelling's (1960) earlier game-theoretic book, *The Strategy of Conflict*, can be seen as a presiding spirit in *Models of Segregation*'s attempt (Schelling 1969) to map and rationalise options in the decisions around actions in the schematised space of non-zero-sum conflict.[2] The opening stages of the paper set up segregation as a fundamental axiom of great applicability. Schelling mentions men and women, Catholics and Protestants, boys and girls, and officers and enlisted men in an army. Not all types of segregation necessarily tend towards dichotomous formation. People are also sorted by 'sex, age, income, language, colour, taste, comparative advantage and the accidents of historical location', amongst other factors. It is assumed that the sorting behaviour for each of these is the same.

In the model, a two-dimensional line is drawn (it is important to note that this is a line, not a grid) with equal divisions of space along its axis. The line is populated with an equal number of 'black's and 'white's. While the distribution looks even on the macroscopic level, at the microscopic level it is uneven. Maybe three blacks are conjunct with one white, then a black and then three whites. If the whites and blacks are content with a 50% split between the colour of their neighbours then those who have a white neighbour on one side and a black neighbour on the other reach the contentment threshold and stand still if the neighbourhood to be considered has a radius of one. Those with 'too many' black neighbours or white neighbours will move in order to achieve contentment. In a neighbourhood with a radius of one, the line **BBBWBWWW** would, several iterations later, become **BWBWBWBW**. If the neighbourhood extends to two houses, then the B and W in the middle of **BBBWBWWW** would be looking for new neighbourhoods. To summarise, in Schelling's model, each agent is 'black' or 'white' and aims to reside in a neighbourhood where the fraction of blacks or whites is above a prede-fined tolerance. Schelling's algorithm for determining the pattern of residence either creates complete integration or complete segregation.

Curiously, there is no reflection on the constitution of racial sorting even in excusatory fig-leaf terms. Like the stories of house-hunting amongst 'professors and their wives' that Schelling (1971; 1978: Chapter 4) describes elsewhere, the specific categories upon and through which segregation operates are described as if natural, not even worthy of equivocation as to their relation to social structure. The racism of the work is both that it operates by means of racial demarcation as an autocatalytic ideological given and second that it provides a means of organising racial division at a higher level of abstraction. To say that Schelling operates within an ideologically racialised frame is not to claim either way as to whether Schelling as a person is or was consciously racist, but that, in these papers, racial division is an uncontested,

Abstract urbanism 63

'obvious' social phenomenon that can be *reduced* in terms of its operation to a precise set of identifiers and operations. Goldberg's formulation of the problem of racism is useful here:

> The mark of racist expression or belief, then, is not simply the claim of inferiority of the racially different. It is more broadly that racial difference warrants exclusion of those so characterized from elevation into the realm of protection, privilege, property, or profit. Racism, in short, is about exclusion through depreciation, intrinsic or instrumental, timeless or time-bound.
>
> (Goldberg 2009: 5)

The naturalisation of such a situation of depreciation by at-a-distance means in which entities kindly self-organise into ghettos out of their own otherwise unlimited choice must have been a marvellous boon to someone. What these papers offer is the construction of a machine for the operation of binary categorisation that in turn becomes an engine for spatial organisation, of preference-based segregation, as if the provision of housing in the form of a market is entirely smooth and demand driven, as if there are no variations in housing kinds and qualities, geographical features, cultural variations in population, of wealth, and so on.

What Schelling's work allows for is an operation of governance beyond that of direct sorting and selection, the direct command and control of populations, but rather by eliciting and installing an action grammar in which people 'spontaneously' recognise, in the words of Nina Simone's *Mississippi Goddam* (1964), 'I don't belong here, I don't belong there'.

Schelling offers the image of urban form being operated upon by an 'invisible hand', emerging at a higher level in social and material channelling. There is a tension, then, between the figure of this invisible hand and the view of the agent. The hand operates in an ostensibly emergent or natural way, arising out of the conditions of the situation as they are, beyond how they are seen by individual actants.

Abstraction as urbanism

Schelling's abstract machine is one for the bipolar reduction of variation. One of the advantages of such an abstraction is that it requires no specific material form, simply logical equivalence. As recounted in a glowing festschrift chapter, Schelling initially used pennies, heads or tails up, on a draughts board to simulate, 'what sort of segregation patterns develop given various types of preferences and alternative definitions of neighbourhood' (Zeckhauser 2006: x). The scale of the board becomes the limit factor of the diagrams published in a later paper, *Dynamic Models of Segregation* (Schelling 1971). One can imagine a media-archaeological analysis of the history of simulation starting with such boards. John Conway, in developing

64   Matthew Fuller and Graham Harwood

the *Game of Life*, famously extended his to cover most surfaces of his office (Gardner 1970). Equally, only having four significant neighbours, termed 'Neumann neighbours',[3] draws a simplifying factor from the board, the constraints of which may in turn be surpassed by the volume of processing offered by electronic computing.

Indeed, a media analysis of the field can divulge a number of aspects of its material practice that are often rendered conceptually and procedurally invisible. One such is that models tend to be bound by the temporal constraints of 'turns' in which all agents shift at the same time. Most models need to have all variables change at the same time – but models of sociality need to vary the periodicity of change for individual agents. Equally, in the model's interaction with hardware, the need to represent data to human users renders the allocation of CPU cycles to drawing graphical representations something of an interference when compared with how many agents could be processed instead.

A few years after Schelling's work was published, Ted Nelson (1987: 149) stated in *Computer Lib* that simulation is always political.[4] Computers, as an abstract machine for the integration of all symbol systems – those operated upon by discrete values, or values that can be rendered as digital – provide a great degree of plasticity in the social forms they might potentiate: hence the significance of Nelson's formulation. But the specific kind of politics simulated is also articulated by the qualities of the mathematical structures they come into composition with (rule sets; systems of four or eight neighbours; bounded, unlimited or wrapping grids; and so on). It is a rare case in which there is a direct correlation between the various scales of model, media, mathematics, the social form modelled, the ideological commitments specified as politics in such simulations and the actual politics of the material operations of such systems in use. Each of these scales is active.

Diagram city

Epstein and Axtell's (1994) *Growing Artificial Societies: Social Science from the Bottom Up* drew on *Models of Segregation* and from Conway's *Game of Life*. In Conway's cellular automata and Schelling's space of segregation, the environment has no active properties, something that has consequences when these models carry over into urban planning and cityscape modelling. Epstein and Axtell's innovation was to place agents in an active environment and to programme them to explore for simple codifications of basic resources to keep their metabolisms alive. Agents and environment have internal states and behavioural rules that are fixed at the start or that can inherit change in interaction with each other. This is a model as a form of regression analysis, or rather of using regression as a form of proposition-making mechanism, where the relations between entities are fixed but variable. The environment is a lattice of resource-bearing sites in a medium that is separate from the agents, but on which they operate and with which they interact.[5]

Abstract urbanism 65

Epstein has produced a body of work discussing the ethics around agent-based modelling that seek to affect US governmental policy by creating explicit models that can be used to explain social phenomena; something he is careful to distinguish from prediction. In *Why Model?*, Epstein (2008) challenges the assumption that scientific theories are created from the study of data. He asserts that without a good theory, it is not clear what data should be collected. Modelling requires theorisation and so creates enquiring habits of mind that he posits as essential to freedom.

By contrast, agent-based models have been eagerly taken up as objective explanations of conflictual social forms. The capacity to express forms of emergence, with the invisible hand effectively rationalising commonsensical observations of the inevitability of such phenomena as racial segregation excites dreams of implementation. As such, this aspect of this work evinces a fascination with finding fundamental laws of social aggregation, rhetorically building on those found in natural sciences, in turn afforded by those historically associated with mathematics. Such kinds of model and associated discourse still act in a representational mode, rather than one of enquiry.

Simulations now operate in a wide range of cases and kinds. They act as a form of prognosis and forecasting, of pre-emption and the maintenance of irresolvability as well as having the ability to formulate an explanation with empirical traction without having to be true. Simulations also develop specific kinds of techniques and vocabularies, as well as the software to handle and interpret them – object-oriented programming being one such example (see Fuller and Goffey 2014). Object-oriented programming is fundamental to how agent-based modelling conceives of itself, as it allows objects to hold data and functions in internal states. The object exports a limited set of methods with which to interact with it – and the data, rather than being globally accessible, are held privately to the object. This is why the behaviour of objects comes to the surface – rather than the data that underlie them. Functions or methods are the agents' rules of behaviour.

One novelty in this kind of work is the way particular forms of computational abstraction themselves become operative elements in social and urban formations. Computation becomes folded into the operations of societies, and social forms become computational problems. As the programmable city begins to incorporate models, such systems become more than representational. Here, there is a correlation between formulations, such as those of Epstein and Schelling (and those that followed in developing simulated societies), and the social sorting by software described by Steven Graham (2005) in his noted article *Software-Sorted Geographies*. In agent-based modelling, by contrast, there is an interplay between the schema of sorting and the actions of individuals and social formations, without engaging with the level of implementation. Where there is a difference is that Graham describes a disciplinary sorting *on* the social. There are kinds of sorting occurring, but these are more adequately expressed as a multiscalar, multivariable sorting enacted by agents bearing seemingly lucid and operable preference lists arrayed in

66   Matthew Fuller and Graham Harwood

relation to the behaviour and imagined preferences of others, apparently reducible to hard and fast organisation. A particularly interesting moment to watch for is when the two merge to some extent, either in actual implementation, or in the seductive idea that such reductions are fully adequate explanations of specific slices of reality.

In the case of the racism of Schelling's *Models of Segregation*, the categories pre-exist the machine. The machine is there to sort them, to anticipate their actualisation, to provide a degree of abstraction in which they can be reckoned, and by which the abstraction too can be worked up into an actor of a kind in itself. This operation of abstraction is crucial to understanding software as a cultural, city-making force.

Logics

The use of computers implies the interrelation of different forms of logic, at the levels, for instance, of programming the machine to perform calculations and of regulating the behaviour of users in pushing around mice and navigating menu systems to produce desired results. One way to think about how the mass adoption of these forms of logic effects society is in the mode Foucault described as discipline, one that analyses and breaks down a phenomenon through modelling it to produce a kind of remote control. Computation disciplines the way a phenomenon is approached and analysed so that when it becomes visible again from within the computer it makes the phenomenon materially available for comparison and modification. As users participate in the flows of power created by the comparison of information, they become normalised to its process and are themselves enrolled in the interrelation of logics.

Computational forms of normalisation establish the configuration of logics needed to make the materiality of the phenomenon available for modification via abstraction, verification and reward. The repeated construction and use of these forms of logic provides a form of progressive training for those that model, feed, collect, process and react to such logics, as well as those objects that are the subject of its calculations. Logics decompose processes and the entities, including people, that are aggregate with them. The routine processing of or interaction with such models provides a collective logic to be applied to all areas of society and the natural world. The move beyond discipline, however, is characterised by the absence, further withdrawal or multiplicity and duplicity of the ultimately reliable, central control that discipline implies as a structuring principle.

Logic gates

Part of the legacy of Schelling's and Epstein's work is in the police, academic and intelligence projects aiming to predict riots via sentiment analysis. 'Negative words', 'hate speech', 'positivity' and expressions of anger stand

Abstract urbanism   67

in for a population of shifting emotional registers, moving from stable states to those that can be used to require the maintenance of policing budgets, harsher policies and sudden rashes of inflamed and excited research budgets. The operators of such machines sell their technical fixes as providing a neutral oversight, in which the free expression of populations and individuals can be mapped and cross-checked for 'naughtiness'. What happens is rather more complex; social forms are interwoven with those of the state, which itself attempts to follow too many filiations and clusterings. In the meantime, academic chancers position themselves as dubious mediators, able to appear to delve into the firehouse of text produced by a population mapped according to weightings assigned to strings of characters. We enter into a condition of a generalised politics of experimental control without controlled experiment.

Claus Pias suggests that recent theories such as actor–network theory and radical constructivism come from the same stock of ideas as simulation, since for both:

> Their knowledge is consciously – and as a matter of course – furnished with a hypothetical index, they admit to their fictional components, they position themselves within their conceptual frame of reference, they thematize their performance, they are aware of their problematic genesis, and they specify their limited application.
>
> (Pias 2011: 54)

A useful provocation following such a proposition is to be found in Latour and Lépinay's reading of Tarde (2009: 19): 'If you really want to quantify – which is after all the foundation of all sciences – you should try to find all the available types of quantum, instead of just using one to analyse all the others.' This premise underlies some of the enthusiasm for big data analysis at present. It also perhaps implies that social reality is a simplified model of more adequately complex modelling schema. But we can also suggest that William Bunge's (1971) later mode of maximalist empiricism coupled with high degrees of statistical abstraction is of great relevance here. The proposition is that to study is to become actively involved, to observe is to change, but also to recognise, that though such change may be reciprocal, it may not be symmetrical and equivalent. These, now, are the stakes of watching and participating, since in the city understood as a platform for self-organisation, algorithms, rule sets, data structures, interfaces and procedures have highly and perhaps questionably promising agency (Chopra 2014). The recent scandal of researchers from Facebook and the Universities of California and Cornell using Facebook's news feed to operate and experiment on whether people responded to the filtering of what appeared in their news feed on the basis of whether it was associated with emotional 'negativity' or 'positivity' should be seen as a part of this tendency. The researchers note that Facebook constantly experiments with the algorithm to fine-tune this aspect of their

68 *Matthew Fuller and Graham Harwood*

'product' (Kramer, Guillory and Hancock 2014). It is this state of perpetual experiment, linking different scales of realities, that is characteristic of the condition of abstract urbanism and the kinds of operation that the integration of modelling with cities encourages.

This operation of the city as open experiment is, of course, one subject to the analysis of power. For Epstein and Axtell, agent-based modelling enforces habits of mind that are essential to intellectual and democratic freedom. An agent-based model must be explicit and open and be able to be examined and doubted, reconfigured and rerun. Epstein aligns agent-based modelling to scientific modes of inquiry that he sees as antithetical to established discursive intellectual systems. Agent-based modelling provides a freedom to doubt large monolithic and deductive forms of knowledge. Epstein and Axtell propose that we are on the edge of a new enlightenment based on the ubiquity of computing. One in which, for Epstein (2008), 'intellectuals have a solemn duty to doubt, and to teach doubt. Education, in its truest sense, is not about "a saleable skill set". It is about freedom, from inherited prejudice and argument by authority.' The question of whether the enlightenment can be fully called upon in this way is in turn open to doubt, but there is something here that suggests some possibilities in that it is a science that explicitly calls subjects into being.

This proposed new mode of science of active abstractions involves cities and social forms in what Stuart Kauffman calls (2000) 'the physics of semantics', logics that have effects in the organisation of conjunction, calculation, control and communication. Such a physics of semantics can be seen, at other scales, in the way that the agent-based model is involved in the specific forms of hardware and software development that conjoin both meaning-making scaffolds and physical properties. Object orientation in programming is seen as a cogent worldview, capable of answering difficult questions about behaviour that emerge from complex subjects in the social or in economics, where, '[it] facilitates essentially any interaction structure (social network) and activation regime' (Axtell 2003). In contemporary accounts, agent-based modelling also links its ambition to the growth of CPU processing and the availability of hard-disk space and network processors assumed under Moore's law. The 'promising' nature of abstract cities is thus also woven into multiple scales of their materiality.

This suggests that there is the possibility for a mode of experimentation, and of experimental politics and urban living that moves from the logics of theorems or axioms to an abstract empiricism. Historically, software-based simulations essentially replaced the kinds of hardware-based simulations or analogues of biological, cognitive and social systems developed in places such as Heinz von Foerster's Biological Computer Laboratory in Illinois (Müller and Müller 2007). The questions posed change in this transition, becoming allied less with the philosophical concerns characteristic of the Biological Computer Laboratory, with its emphasis on epistemology and the question of abstraction and reduction from material empirical conditions. We are now

Abstract urbanism 69

well into another similar transition where, instead of moving from hardware to software (with hardware becoming less experimental and idiosyncratic as it is rendered in the form of commodity electronics), social and urban forms become places of computational interoperation and experiment.

Urban space is increasingly produced in the production, circulation and analysis of large volumes of structured and unstructured data. Models and modelisations are being integrated into the design of such spatial forms as stadia, streets and stations at conceptual and pre-emptive stages for the purposes of safety, transit design and revenue protection. In such cases, agents become active as urban entities installed and active in the symbolic and material orders of the city.

Just as computational forms structure reality, so do other kinds of model. Abstract urbanism is hypothetical, fictional, maximally empirical and, of course, abstract. This means that the way in which abstractions become materially operative has to operate through these conditions, and also – under certain regimes of rhetoric – to shield them, as simply fact-based extrapolations. To recognise that they are imaginary, as models, without being merely false or simple reifications, is part of the art of abstract urbanism. To see agent-based modelling in such a way is to recognise that models are also partial cities operating like partial objects, formalised slivers of an urban configuration taken for a whole and working their drives into active diagrams. Such a condition, in which the possibilities of social fractures being triggered in the models and then implemented are manifest, cannot but add an ambiguous potency to the operations such an art promises. To work abstract urbanism in the condition of models becoming cities then is also to open the possibility of operating with a maximalist empiricism. It is to operate with delicacy and attentiveness in the design of models, but also to the arguments, spaces and politics that they bear, that they determine and into which they are smuggled, driven and suffused, and which in turn they rely on to sustain themselves. It is to saturate models with variables, and to open abstraction to social disruption rather than to prepare the abstract retrenchment of urban injustice.

But to recognise abstract urbanism is not solely to postulate an interesting set of potential political practice, but more, to come to terms with a fundamental change in the consistency of cities today – they are suffused with logics. This is not simply to say that streets are data structures, people are variables and the city is a grid laced with numerical nutrients, which in their interaction produce an adequate if simplified mimicry of urban life; but that the city, the exemplary space of modernity in all its complexity of desire, violence, multiscalar layering, imagination, invention and struggle is also a place of experiment with modes of composition and of self-emergence at multiple scales of abstraction. Such a space is one where fantasies of control, of understanding, of ordering, of establishing implicit and explicit coordination and pre-emption coexist with their enactment, their failure, their use as excuse, and as a space where logic coexists with the surprise of the unforeseen.

70 *Matthew Fuller and Graham Harwood*

Agent-based modelling provides a means for the phantasmatic appearance of logics as an always present compliment of logic itself in that it mobilises means by which things occur in and for themselves in the mode of emergence, and for a space for arranging the coming into being of ideas of the city that are beyond the habitual means of interrogating existing coordinates. Here, in the state of being promising, logics both pre-empt surprise and rely upon it to provide a gateway to emergence understood as the self-constitution of reality; a reality that is, on the one hand, seemingly unblemished by mess, or, on the other, one forged in the full ongoing complications of the cityscape in which it becomes manifest. This is a deeply ambivalent position. The physics of semantics in which such emergence is made is therefore worthy of attention with all the precision and inventiveness that can be mustered, as it too becomes a space in which the city occurs.

Notes

1 Exemplary of work building on Epstein's model includes Casilli and Tubaro (2011) and Davies *et al.* (2013).
2 The paper is revised in Schelling (1978).
3 Edward F. Moore gives his name to systems of eight neighbours, expanded to include those at the corners in a rectilinear grid.
4 'All simulation is political. Every simulation program, and thus every simulation, has a point of view. Just like a statement in words about the world, it is a model of how things are, with its own implicit emphases: it highlights some things, omits others and always simplifies.' (Nelson 1987: 149).
5 See Axtell and Epstein's *Sugarscape* software.

References

Axtell, R. (2003) 'Economics as distributed computation', in T. Terano, H. Deguchi and K. Takadama (eds) *Meeting the Challenge of Social Problems via Agent-Based Simulation*, Heidelberg: Springer, pp. 3–23.
Bunge, W. (1971) *Fitzgerald: Geography of a Revolution*, Cambridge, MA: Schenkman Press, reprint University of Georgia Press, 2011.
Casilli, A.A. and Tubaro, P. (2011) 'Why net censorship in times of political unrest results in more violent uprisings: a social simulation experiment on the UK riots', *Social Science Research Network*, available from http://papers.ssrn.com/sol3/papers.cfm?abstract_id=1909467 [accessed 18 November 2015].
Chopra, S. (2014) 'Computer programs are people too', *The Nation*, 29 May 2014, available from http://www.thenation.com/article/computer-programs-are-people-too/ [accessed 29 August 2015].
Davies, T.P., Fry, H.M., Wilson, A.G. and Bishop, S.R. (2013) 'A mathematical model of the London riots and their policing', *Scientific Reports*, 3(1303): 1–9.
Epstein, J.M. (2002) 'Modeling civil violence: an agent-based computational approach', *Proceedings of the National Academy of Sciences*, 99(Supplement 3): 7243–50.
Epstein, J.M. (2008) 'Why model?', *Journal of Artificial Societies and Social Simulation*, 11(4): 12.

Epstein, J.M. and Axtell, R. (1994) *Growing Artificial Societies: Social Science from the Bottom Up*, Cambridge, MA: MIT Press.

Fuller, M. and Goffey, A. (2014) 'The unknown objects of object orientation', in P. Harvey, E.C. Casella, G. Evans, H. Knox, C. McLean, E.B. Silva, N. Thoburn and K. Woodward (eds) *Objects and Materials*, London: Routledge.

Gardner, M. (1970) 'The fantastic combinations of John Conway's new solitaire game "life"', *Scientific American*, no 223, October 1970: 120–3.

Goldberg, D.T. (2009) *The Threat of Race: Reflections on Racial Neoliberalism*, Oxford: Wiley Blackwell.

Graham, S.D.M. (2005) 'Software-sorted geographies', *Progress in Human Geography*, 29(5): 562–80.

Kauffman, S. (2000) *Investigations*, Oxford: Oxford University Press.

Kramer, A.D.I, Guillory, J.E. and Hancock, J.T. (2014) 'Experimental evidence of massive-scale emotional contagion through social networks', *Proceedings of the National Academy of Sciences of the United States of America*, 111(24): 8788–90.

Latour, B. and Lépinay, V. (2009) *The Science of Passionate Interests: An Introduction to Gabriel Tarde's Economic Anthropology*, Chicago: Prickly Paradigm Press.

Morgenstern, O. and von Neumann, J. (1947) *A Theory of Games and Economic Behaviour*, Princeton: Princeton University Press.

Müller, A. and Müller, K.H. (eds) (2007) *An Unfinished Revolution, Heinz von Foerster and the Biological Computer Laboratory (BCL) 1958–1976*, Vienna: Edition Echoraum.

Nelson, T. (1987) *Computer Lib: Dream Machines*, 2nd edn, Redmond: Tempus Books of Microsoft.

Pias, C. (2011) 'On the epistemology of computer simulation', *Zeitschrift für Medien- und Kulturforschung*, 1: 29–54.

Schelling, T. (1960) *The Strategy of Conflict*, Cambridge, MA: Harvard University Press, 2nd edn, 1980.

Schelling, T. (1969) 'Models of segregation', *The American Economic Review*, 59(2): 488–93.

Schelling, T. (1971) 'Dynamic models of segregation', *Journal of Mathematical Sociology*, 1: 143–86.

Schelling, T. (1978) *Micromotives and Macrobehaviour*, New York: W.W. Norton and Co.

Simone, N. (1964) 'Mississippi Goddam', in *Nina Simone in Concert*, Eindhoven: Philips.

Zeckhauser, R. (2006) 'Thomas Schelling, ricochet thinker', in R. Dodge (ed.) *The Strategist: The Life and Times of Thomas Schelling*, Hollis, NH: Hollis Publishing.

6 Code traffic
Code repositories, crowds and urban life

Adrian Mackenzie

Introduction

> The initial step can be made through the venerable geographical act of mapping the expanding realm of machinekind, clearly part of the remaining *terra incognita*.
>
> (Horvath 1974: 188)

In what frame and at what levels of abstraction does the density and plurality of code in the city become legible or even enumerable? Writing in 2002, Nigel Thrift and Shaun French addressed a version of these questions: 'Is there any way of making a more general assessment of software in the city?' (Thrift and French 2002: 314). They sketched some possibilities, ranging from hegemony to haunting:

> It would be easy at this point to fall back on some familiar notions to describe software's grip on spaces like cities. One would be hegemony. But that notion suggests a purposeful project, whilst software consists of numerous projects cycling through and continually being rewritten in code. Another notion would be haunting. But again the notion is not quite the right one. Ghosts are ethereal presences, phantoms that are only half-there, which usually obtain their effects by stirring up emotions – of fear, angst, regret, and the like
>
> (Thrift and French 2002: 311–12)

In their review of different understandings of software in the city, they affirm something quite elementary: 'numerous projects [... are] continually being rewritten in code'. The rest of this chapter could be seen as an update on that observation from 2002. What has happened to the cycling through and rewriting of code?[1] Thrift and French go on to describe three geographies that were cycling – or as I would prefer to say, trafficking – code through cities: a geography of *writing code*, a geography of *power and control* and a geography of *indeterminancy*.

Code traffic 73

The first of these geographies is the most obvious, the large and complex geography of the writing of software – of the production of lines of code – a geography that takes in many different locations and many different languages and which has been built up progressively since the invention of programming in the 1940s.

(Thrift and French 2002: 323)

According to Thrift and French, the geography of software writing clusters around key places and regions: Silicon Valley, New York, London and a number of auxiliary software mass production zones (often concentrating on such tasks as consulting, testing and support) in countries like Ireland and India. China, Russia and Brazil are not mentioned. As we will see, this geographical centring still matters, but in a somewhat reconfigured form: code cycles through platforms that tremendously redistribute the production of lines of code.

A second, less concentrated, geography of power, conceived in Foucauldian terms as the conduct of conduct, or massive proliferation of corporeally practised rules, was also unfurling through software: 'In essence, we can say that it [software] consists of rules of conduct able to be applied to determinate situations,' (Thrift and French 2002: 325). Through this power geography, software increasingly interlinks rather than compartmentalises urban processes. In many ways, the app economy, the virtualisation of computing into the Cloud and containerised infrastructures, and the spectacular growth of social media platforms or, indeed, the Internet of sensor-equipped Things attests to an intensified application of rules to determinate situations. Again, coding itself, the process of specifying, configuring and propagating these rules of conduct, has not been exempt from the conduct of conduct. Coding has been powerfully recoded in recent years.

Thrift and French (2002: 328) envisaged a final more open and less localised geography in which abundance produces indeterminacy and lack of closure:

The general profusion of software, its increasing complexity and consequent emergent properties, all count as means of producing playful idioms that have not been captured by dominant orders. Software's very indeterminacy and lack of closure provide a means of creating new kinds of order.

(Thrift and French 2002: 328)

In this geography, 'profusion' and 'increasing complexity' generate less orderly or regulated idioms. These playful idioms are largely irreducible to the geographical centres of coding or power-generated control practices, and therefore take on singular forms, arise in unexpected locations and articulate non-representational processes. Thrift and French attributed this generative aspect of software to the phenomenality of code as a form of *traffic*:

74   *Adrian Mackenzie*

> Software is more like a kind of traffic between beings, wherein one sees,
> so to speak, the effects of the relationship. What transpires becomes
> reified in actions, body stances, general anticipations. We would argue,
> then, that software is best thought of as a kind of absorption, an expecta-
> tion of what will turn up in the everyday world.
>
> (Thrift and French 2002: 312)

The 'traffic between beings' they refer to here, the reification of 'general
anticipations', the curiously contrasting descriptions of software as absorption *and* expectation, could be seen as implicitly urban. They concern 'traffic'
in everyday worlds. In this third geography, the traffic between beings, we
might see processes of composition that not only generate much code traffic,
but assemble compositions of people and things that turn up new things.

More than a decade later, these geographies remain in play. Code work
is concentrated in more or less the same places; and the coded conduct of
conduct certainly continues. But when we think about code in terms of traffic, what has happened to it? What kinds of new order have eventuated?[2] As
I will suggest, a complicated set of reorderings of code traffic have occurred.
The centred geographies of code production have been somewhat decentred
through a much more multilateral or networked flow of code. At the same
time, the very arrangements that have dislocated the centres of software
production have themselves become the platform for new platform-based
centres or hubs for code. In turn, these centres attract and generate saturated
streams of coding traffic that bring new indeterminacies, diverse distributions, encounters and adaptations into play.

We could give the code traffic a Deleuzean or a Tardean formulation.
Deleuze and Guattari write:

> Assemblages are passional, they are compositions of desire. Desire has
> nothing to do with a natural or spontaneous determination; there is no
> desire but assembling, assembled desire. The rationality, the efficiency, of
> an assemblage does not exist without the passions the assemblages bring
> into play, without the desires that constitute it as much as it constitutes
> them.
>
> (Guattari and Deleuze 1988: 399)

Deleuze and Guattari's notion of assembling as passional composition or
putting together suggests one way of thinking about what is generated in
code traffic. The 'traffic between beings' moves through paths by processes
that we might understand, drawing on crowd sociologists such as Gabriele
Tarde and Robert E. Park, as *imitation*. For both Tarde, the microsociologist
of crowds, and Park, the urban sociologist, imitation powerfully yet unpre-
dictably effects repetition and invention, and generates new urban forms of
various kinds (Borch 2005). In particular, Tarde speaks of a 'coadaptation
of imitative fluxes, a cooperation, even in an individual brain, but always a

multitude of agents social and infinitesimal, and their ordinary ideas' (Tarde 1902: 270). While there is much to discuss here (for instance, Tarde's political conservatism and anachronism poses analytical problems), the 'coadaptation' of imitations between a multitude of infinitesimal agents, beneath and around individuals, suggests a way of thinking of what happens in code traffic. Understood either as passional compositions or coadapting imitative fluxes, we might come closer to a concrete understanding of how the transient coagulations and diffusions of code traffic may play out in control structures, in architectures, in matters of concern, etc. Examining patterns of imitation in code moves the emphasis away from code-shaping-cities to code-as-crowd. In the code-crowd, mutually shaping imitative fluxes run between people and machines in places.[3]

To treat *code traffic*, in terms of Tardean crowd sociology, as a coadaptation of imitative fluxes is not to deny the production and power geographies of code. It is not to say that code does not still act on cities, on space, on public and private practices. High-profile and much discussed changes taking place in computational platforms (mobile devices, virtualisation and containerisation in the Cloud, etc.) and in algorithmic processes (machine learning) intricately reorganise urban life. What transpires there is rapidly reified in actions, body stances, etc. But it might also be worth seeing how code has become a mixing process, reconfiguring the architectures, logistics and diffuse circulation of individuals in cities. We would, from this standpoint, no longer concentrate on following how software emanates from global production centres as hierarchical or supervisory control structures reorganising cities. Furthermore, we would no longer focus on isolated pieces of software, systems or applications but on the transverse flows that change how code itself moves and takes shape. We would apprehend coding itself as something closer to pedestrian and vehicle movements in a busy street, in which branching, merging, starting, turning and stopping compose transient multiplicities adapted to particular problems and situations. That is to say, we might attempt to see code as noisy and crowded, propagating aggregates in which juxtapositions, proximities and patterns of imitation multiply through each other.

`git` as code traffic: dangerous coagulation or regularised order?

The study of code traffic poses some empirical problems, but we can glimpse some of the traffic in code via increasingly aggregated code repositories. A huge number of code repositories (possibly around 50 million) are now hosted publicly online at a few code repository sites, such as GitHub.com, Bitbucket.com, code.google.com and SourceForge.net. Focusing on one of these repository hosting platforms – GitHub.com, allegedly the 'largest code repository on planet' – might be a way to see traffic in code, and to track how coadaptive, infinitesimal fluxes flow.[4] Code moves in and out of these repositories in many different ways. This movement is not logistically or hierarchically controlled. It constitutes a vast, complex reticular movement.

76   *Adrian Mackenzie*

Much of the flow of source code passes through a single piece of software called `git`. 'Git', an English word for a person who acts foolishly or annoyingly (often in a crowd), was chosen by Linus Torvalds in 2005 as the name for a new concurrent versioning system for source code. In 2002, Torvald's work on GNU/Linux epitomised for many people the emergent power of open source collaboration – 'crowdsourcing' – on the Internet to build things outside the geographies of the software industry. (Even then, as Thrift and French observed, Linux was a quite centralised hierarchically and industry-supported software project.) In turn, `git`, a revision control system for code, allows incremental changes to code made by many people working a common software project to merge with or diverge from each other. Today, `git` is probably the most widely used revision control system for code (followed by the interestingly named `subversion`).

What should we make of the control of revisions to code in terms of code traffic? In practice, a whole series of converging and diverging movements of cloning, forking, pulling, pushing, requesting, branching and merging pass through `git`. Often used on the command-line, commands such as `git clone`, `git commit`, `git push`, `git stash`, `git pull`, `git branch` and `git merge` suggest some of the elementary movements that generate code traffic in and out of nodes in `git`-connected bodies of code. For instance, some `git` commands replicate whole bodies of code, while others simply add, remove or alter small bits of code. These scale-variations, I would suggest, matter to the flows of imitation that occur. Movements of code can take place very incrementally, as small bits of code move around, or on a large scale, as whole bodies of code travel between different bits of software. As a contemporary site of coding, `git` merits much more empirical description than this, but for the present purposes `git` instantiates a much more distributed and granular cycling and rewriting traffic in code. These broadened and differentiated movements, while certainly not unique or unprecedented in the history of inscriptive techniques, record-keeping systems or archives, have become chained and interlinked in recent coding cultures in ways that generate the rapid transformations associated with many millions of code projects. Different bodies of code clone and branch off from each other, and occasionally, but not necessarily, merge again. The geography of coding would become less aligned to individual developers in specific times places and times, and more open to a range of different styles of code movement, ranging from an uncontrollably fluxing miasma of microscale projects through to vast hierarchical code architectures (such as the `linux` kernel). They in turn modify the mode of movement of code itself by removing some of the checkpoints, barriers and thresholds between production and deployment, between design and use.

Torvalds did not reckon with social media. Since late 2007, GitHub has provided a hosting platform for many `git` repositories, and now attracts the largest share of code traffic of any code repository. From the perspective of the `git` software, GitHub is just another remote code repository. But given that many, in fact around 13 million, local `git` repositories have GitHub.com as their remote repository, then GitHub becomes a hub for `git`. The network and code traffic that now runs through GitHub is on the scale of a medium-size social media platform. That is, with 13 million repositories, 6 million developers, and around 250 million events in the public event stream (at the end of 2014), GitHub itself is a kind of code terminus, whose functioning, architecture and machinery symptomatically enunciate contemporary code traffic more generally. In relying on `git`, GitHub.com promotes a radically decentred patterning of code traffic. But this `git`-like mobility of code stands in tension with GitHub's own existence as a platform, a platform for 'social coding'.

Making Github into a `git` terminus

Several hundred GitHub staff ('hubbernauts') are scattered across a dozen or so countries, a somewhat dispersed geography for a relatively specialised software company that started in 2007 in San Francisco. GitHub work life is also putatively non-hierarchical, with no management hierarchy, only a `git`-like structure of fluid teams working on projects.[5] In principle, GitHub itself therefore makes itself into something like a terminus for code traffic, and is, itself, constructed and maintained via just such traffic. The geography of work on GitHub is still very much centred in San Francisco (followed by Portland, Chicago, Seattle, Boulder, etc.), despite claims of decentralisation.[6] As Thrift and French (2002) argued, geographical localities still matter greatly to code. But this largely localised traffic in and around GitHub is perhaps less important than the kind of movement of code traffic it seeks to operationalise. The hubness or centrality of GitHub is something to be produced or made via a combination of geography, rules of conduct and new forms of order flowing through code.

If GitHub itself has been produced using `git`, does it epitomise the kind of code traffic I am attributing to `git`? In some ways it does. If we look at the code generated by the staff listed as the GitHub team (233 at the time of writing), there is some evidence of their `git`-like activity as they write the code that constructs, augments, reshapes or expands GitHub as a platform. Figure 6.1 offers a view of what happens as the several hundred hubbernauts work on GitHub as a platform.[7] It is important to note that only some of the GitHub code appears here. The anchoring repository `github/github`, the repository that contains the code for whatever GitHub becomes, remains private.

The events shown in Figure 6.1 roughly summarise some of the code traffic associated with GitHub's own code during the last few years. We see this traffic in the form of events, social coded repackagings of rawer or somewhat more elementary `git` movements. The mix of different event types still, however, suggests something of the `git` flow of code. While PushEvents embody code writing and ForkEvents imply copying (and hence imitation),

78   Adrian Mackenzie

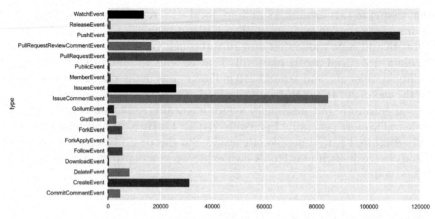

Figure 6.1 Event counts for the GitHub team

many other events, including IssueCommentEvents, PullRequestEvents, IssueEvents and WatchEvents, point to different kinds of traffic in code. In some ways, the variety of event categories shown in the figure already highlights some of the analytical instabilities in tracking code traffic. The events mix git-related practices, such as pushing or forking, with GitHub-specific devices such as pull-request or follow that seek to socialise or 'hubify' the movements of code. 'Social' events outweigh technical events, and disentangling what belongs to git from what GitHub has added becomes difficult (although not impossible since GitHub must preserve all git movements even as it recodes them as 'social'). GitHub as a terminus for code traffic rechannels and reshapes much of the traffic that passes through it. To the ongoing capillary flow of code it adds all the social media-style baggage of followers and watchers, comments, liking and tagging. This socialisation of code traffic, as we see next, generates its own kinds of traffic.

GitHub as collective meta-git

How would a social media platform affect the traffic between beings or the cycling–rewriting practices of coding? Hubbernauts such as defunkt, mojombo or technoweenie have thousands of followers and hundreds of repos (i.e., repositories) to their names. While the GitHub team has participated in some 17,000 public repositories in some way (including just watching), they work much more heavily on several hundred of these (see Figure 6.2).

The top repositories display some important features of GitHub as a platform seeking to social reorganise the flow of code traffic. Many of these repositories relate to the building out of GitHub as a massive git instance, a kind of meta-git. It is hardly surprising that hubbernauts contribute to the git project itself or reimplementations of git such as libgit2, objective-git, rugged, hub (a 'wrapper' for git) or many-branch-repo. All of these

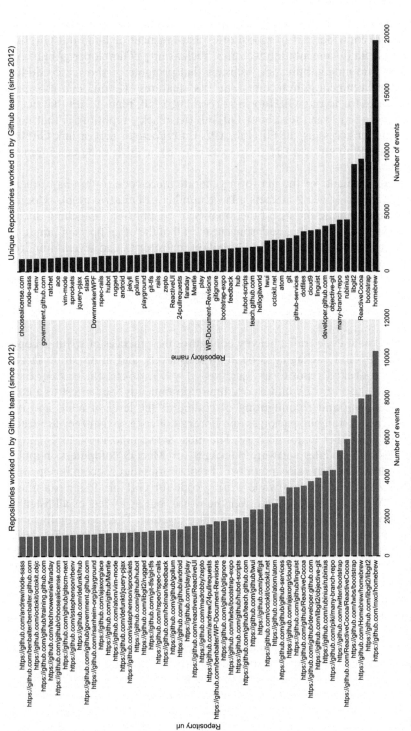

Figure 6.2 Repositories worked on by the GitHub team

80 *Adrian Mackenzie*

projects are imitations, reimplementations or variations on `git`. Hubbernauts also make contributions to repositories that augment or build out GitHub, ranging from documentation websites, such as https://developer.github.com or https://training.github.com, websites that promote or showcase GitHub (https://government.github.com/) or its features (`24pullrequests`), repositories for testing GitHub (`hellogitworld`), repositories that act as question-and-answer sites about GitHub (feedback), repositories that contain code for accessing the GitHub APIs (http://octokit.net) or link GitHub with other Web services (`github-services`) or other code development platforms (`git-tfs`).

Certain elements of the platform generate more code traffic than others. For instance, `libgit2` attracts a large number of imitative events (cloning or forking) because the `git` functionality of committing, branching, merging, forking, cloning, etc., underpins nearly all of the other flows of imitation associated with the growth of 13.2 million repositories and several hundred million events. Typically of such entities, `libgit2` migrates throughout the software development ecosystem so that 'bindings' to `libgit2` have been made in almost any programming language imaginable, from Delphi to Lua, as well as to database back-ends such as `MySQL`, `redis`, `memcache` or the ubiquitous `sqlite`.

Hubbernaut code traffic heavily configures the practices of writing, copying, viewing and packaging code at various levels, and in disparate facets. Heavily trafficked repositories, such as `cloud9`, `dotfiles`, `gitignore`, `vimmode`, `rbenv`, `ace` and `atom`, figure prominently, and attest to a constant retooling and reconfiguring of coding at the level of hand and eye movements. Arranging packages and libraries of code so that they are ready to hand is another major activity. The most active repository, `homebrew`, manages and updates software packages for MacOS computers, popular with coders. There are also a number of repositories that concern how people sit down and keep coding while writing code for GitHub. `Play` is a music server: 'We have employees all over the world, but `Play` lets us all listen to the same music as if we were all in the office together. This has actually made a big impact on our culture,' (https://github.com/github/play). Similarly, `Hubot` and `Hubot-scripts` are part of a software robot system that the GitHub team use extensively to maintain the GitHub platform, run the many online chatrooms they use as they work with each other, continuously deploy the changes they make on the master branch of `github/github` onto their production servers (the servers that actually run the code that makes up GitHub) and send updates to various social media platforms. One Hubot runs the whole of GitHub. Finally, many repositories listed here concern the infrastructure of GitHub as a software platform. Some are language-specific environments heavily used at GitHub, such as `rubinius`, an implementation of the Ruby programming language. Some, such as `rails`, are libraries that provide much of the dynamic infrastructure that holds GitHub as a collection of servers and databases together as a platform. Other repositories, such as `choosealicence` or `linguist`, implement GitHub features concerned with licensing or tagging repositories by programming language. Since GitHub repositories can also function as webpages, blogs or wikis, other repositories, such as `jekyll` and `gollum`, provide code for that. Other heavily used repositories, such as `bootstrap`, `zepto` and `twui`, provide elements of the graphic layout, colours, styles, fonts and icons that comprise the visual appearance and interactive features of GitHub pages (and I return to this kind of software later).

The fabric of GitHub as a platform is constructed and connected along many edges. It folds in many different elements on various scales, ranging from almost microscopically perceptual configurations, such as editor settings, through to large infrastructural developments, such as `elasticsearch`. GitHub comprises programming language implementations, server infrastructures, deployment mechanisms, Web-frontend frameworks, various social media formats (wiki, blog), Javascript page and graphic elements, as well as the code versioning system of `git`, robots that automate chatrooms and servers that streams music to developers at different places and times. All of these together recursively construct the platform, with varying degrees of coherence and visibility, ranging from the vital `github/github` repository through to the many public-facing repositories that hubbernauts either release to the world or participate in publicly. The broader point here is that code traffic in and around GitHub is itself constantly transformed, modified and intensified by the flows of imitation that hubbernauts themselves semi-consciously generate as they assemble the platform. Music, robots, editors, libraries, databases and webpages intersect with each other as the small-crowd teams of GitHub work and, in the object of their mimetic immersion, with GitHub itself. The flow of elements comprising GitHub is, I suggest, typical of the ways in which code traffic concatenates things today. The mixing of different things in code traffic generates the forms, the changes in scale, the new modes of distribution, partitioning or localisations associated with contemporary life. The platform GitHub, in this case, itself a platform in principle oriented to the multiplication of code traffic, is a deeply passional assemblage, not a rationally ordered technology.

The panoply of code repositories frequented by the GitHub staff suggests something more general about the flow of code traffic. The recursive work of hubbernauts on GitHub can be seen as projected over the three urban-code geographies described by Thrift and French. We can now see that the urban centring of software writing still largely applies, but subject to some significant transformations in how it relates to such settings. The `git` version control processes open centres to more distributed and mutable collectives. The widely scattered geography of the GitHub team suggests something of this. The second geography of power and control (conduct of conduct) no doubt runs through much of what hubbernauts make (and here we could think, for instance, of the social coding of `git` traffic as events, or farther afield, the many DMCA takedown notices posted at https://github.com/github/dmca,

82   Adrian Mackenzie

or the recent denial-of-service attacks on GitHub attributed to the Chinese government, or the repo `choosealicence`, which seeks to regulate flows of code according to legal licence). This power geography, however, does not completely supplant the geography of indeterminacy or the 'new forms of order' that GitHub itself as an assemblage exemplifies, even as it builds out the GitHub platform as a hub for widely dispersed and somewhat vagabond flows of code.

Github as convolutional process

The 'social coding' apparatus that is the visible face of GitHub – watchers, followers, stars, showcases, search facilities, along with their attempts to render code flow more like public spaces (see the 'showcases' at http://github.com/explore for examples of this public-making) – does not completely corral or control the imitative fluxes on GitHub. The primary `git` fluxes are more networked than the social media apparatus that GitHub assembles because they are not dependent on the formats and facades supplied by the GitHub platform, but instead mix people and things together. In other words, these *convolutional* fluxes animate the more crowd-like aspects of code traffic, and they criss-cross geographies, cities, feeding into and overloading GitHub geography in key respects.

How would we characterise something of these relatively pre-social imitative fluxes in the GitHub traffic?[8] Some analytical purchase on the convolution of people and things in code traffic can be gained by looking at the full names of repositories on GitHub. Note that these names are not coded by GitHub. Repository names on GitHub are lightly formatted. The first part of a repository name refers to a person or organisation ('mojombo', 'wycats', etc.) and the second to the specific code repository (`grit`, `merb-core`). Both parts of the full repository name are interesting, but the name as a whole points to an intersection between groups and people and things, between coders and code. The constant variations of these names bear the traces of the complicated enmeshing of people and things, between coders and code that looms large in code traffic.

For present purposes, however, the second part of the name is more symptomatic since it refers more directly to the code. A simple comparison between repositories on GitHub in early 2007 and in 2014 suggests something of the tension between the efforts to socially code the fluxes and code traffic more generally. Early repositories on GitHub suggest a rather orderly and sensible traffic in beings. Table 6.1 (column 1), which shows the first 20 repositories on GitHub, dating from 2007–2008, lists repositories created and worked on mainly by GitHub hubbernauts themselves and a few others. These are the repositories that somewhat recursively host the code from which GitHub was being made. In the early days of GitHub, these names are largely comprehensible in terms of the GitHub platform itself. Repository names like `grit`, a Ruby-language version of `git`, `git-wiki` or `merb-core` (a Ruby

Code traffic 83

Table 6.1 20 early and recent repositories on Github.com

2007	2014
mojombo/grit	2m1tsu3/practice
wycats/merb-core	tylerdmace/ledomme
rubinius/rubinius	yehiaelghaly/xssya
mojombo/god	istvan-antal/commandjs
vanpelt/jsawesome	JohnKrigbjorn/ObjectOne
wycats/jspec	chenx/Ci35_1
defunkt/exception_logger	mohsenbezanj/AI_Project
defunkt/ambition	Dineshkarthik/blogengine
labria/restful-authentication	sapanbhuta/Sapari
technoweenie/	gwoodroof/chat-gwoodroof
restful-authentication	
technoweenie/attachment_fu	tryuichi/Hello-World
topfunky/bong	prateek0020/NepTravelMate
anotherjesse/s3	discoverfly/discoverfly.
	github.io
anotherjesse/taboo	evan-007/ng-wikiful
mojombo/glowstick	sanemat/zipcode-jp
wycats/merb-more	donreamey/PJKiller
macournoyer/thin	discoverfly/discover
jamesgolick/resource_controller	jkkorean/MIUI-KK
defunkt/cache_fu	rtofacks1/ionic-app
bmizerany/sinatra	jkkorean/MIUI-JB

Web-development framework) nearly all relate to various aspects of GitHub as a platform under development. Other platforms and concerns are already present (`sinatra`) but they are somewhat marginal to the work of developing a platform to host `git` repositories.

A similar list from seven years later in 2014 reveals many complications (see column 2 of Table 6.1). The names of coders have become increasingly unrecognisable, even allowing for the internationalisation of GitHub use that quickly developed between 2007 and 2014. The coder names in GitHub become more and more like random patterns of key presses, as if coders have become less individual, more crowd-like in their identities. (Indeed, thousands of repository and actor names comprise key sequences such as `qwerty`, `asdf`, `poiu`, `lkjh` or `1234`, all of which derive from the keyboard layouts.) Something similar happens to the repository names. Only a few components from the early days are recognisable in type (that is, things like a `blogengine` or `footer-fixed-bootstrap`, and, as we will soon see, the `bootstrap` Web-development framework is almost a fixation for GitHubbers, since it provides the look and feel of GitHub itself). Many other git elements of this stream are also recognisable and proliferate widely on GitHub: `practice`, `Hello-World`, `testing` and `temp` repositories occur in huge numbers on GitHub (of the order of millions or more). These trivial fluxes are like people starting to edge into a crowd, to form part of

84 *Adrian Mackenzie*

Table 6.2 Most-forked repositories on GitHub in January 2013

Forks	Repository
1478	`bootstrap`
1276	`Spoon-Knife`
763	`dotfiles`
504	`rails`
426	`html5-boilerplate`
410	`jquery`
375	`homebrew`
345	`linux`
343	`android`
291	`phonegap-plugins`
280	`node`

a mass on the move. Broad swathes of generic imitation surface here too. We can also see here the appearance of quite disparate matters of concern: `game-cho-android` and `AI_Project` may have some similarities, but at first appearance they lie quite a long distance apart from each other. It is very hard to see any flux of imitation here. Like the many repositories named using convenient patterns of keystrokes, these repositories seem almost like code-noise. This might support a sense of code traffic as transient and somewhat disorderly multiplicity, but it hardly seems to reflect the coadaptation of imitative fluxes that, following crowd sociologists such as Tarde and Park, we might see as materialising code in the city.

If we start counting imitative events, things look a little different. For instance, in January 2013, around 200,000 repositories were forked (or copied). Forking, as suggested previously, is a basic imitative event in `git`-like practices. The most-forked repositories have a now familiar look (see Table 6.2). This list is reasonably familiar since it has major platforms like `linux`, `android` and `node`, as well as a popular test repository on GitHub called `Spoon-Knife`. But even the most-forked repository in this list, `bootstrap`, is not a single or homogeneous imitative flux. Look at what else was forked heavily in January 2013 relating to `bootstrap`, listed in Table 6.3.

While it was copied more often than any other repository in that month, the `bootstrap` repository itself is accompanied by many variational imitations. The total count of `bootstrap`-related forks during January 2013 is, for instance, 3074, almost twice the number of the forks of `bootstrap` itself (1478). Widening the frame slightly, we can see (Figure 6.3) that since 2012, `bootstrap` has been an important imitative flux running through GitHub, and has been the most highly 'starred' code repository on GitHub for several years.

The stackplot of ForkEvents (or their equivalent and underlying `git clone` operations) associated with the `twitter/bootstrap` repository shows a more differentiated flux of imitation. The imitation varies over time, as we

Table 6.3 Most-forked bootstrap-related repositories during January 2013

Forks	Repository
1478	bootstrap
109	bootstrap-datepicker
84	jekyll-bootstrap
60	bootstrap-wysihtml5
54	bootstrap-tour
48	Twitter-bootstrap-rails
48	bootstrap-sass
46	bootstrap-datetimepicker
43	jquery-ui-bootstrap
42	bootstrap-modal
40	wordpress-bootstrap
36	bootstrap-daterangepicker
31	sass-Twitter-bootstrap
31	Bootstrap-Image-Gallery
26	rails3-bootstrap-devise-cancan
26	bootstrapwp-Twitter-Bootstrap-for-WordPress
24	metro-bootstrap
24	bootstrap-timepicker
23	bootstrap-toggle-buttons
23	MopaBootstrapBundle
19	twitter.bootstrap.mvc
16	CodeIgniter-Bootstrap

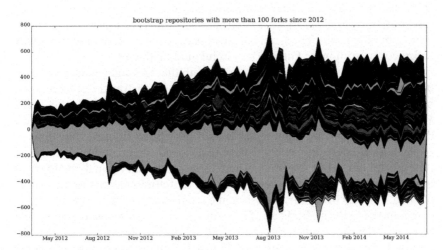

Figure 6.3 Bootstrap repositories with more than 100 forks since 2012

would expect, but the patterns of imitation are heavily interconnected with each other through repositories that juxtapose or merge different repositories with each other. The several thousand bootstrap-related repositories are much more diverse than bootstrap itself. They combine variously with

86 *Adrian Mackenzie*

mobile devices (Android, iOS), with Web browser software (IE6), with various Web-development infrastructures (django, rails, ASP, PHP), with media platforms (WordPress, Google, CodeIgniter) and server management systems (sinatra). They respond to events in the main `bootstrap` repository, but also have a life apart from that repository that relates to other platforms and other software projects. Here, something like the coadaptation of imitative flux begins to come into view. Each of the devices, platforms or systems in these variations has its own code traffic, its own crowds of coders and code, that begin to mix here with `bootstrap`. In this copying, varying, merging and diverging, there is more than simple imitation, but encounters between different things taking shape in aggregate form. This convolutional change is not captured or controlled by the GitHub platform and its social coding devices. It is perhaps true, however, that GitHub, for almost the first time, allows these collective dispositions, expressed in confused and transient pluralities, to be tabulated.

Conclusion

Code deeply shapes infrastructures, devices, services, protocols and many mundane capillary orderings in cities. Or does it? Might not code itself be patterned by the urban, by dynamics and transients, by diagrams and vectors that code itself expresses and enunciates without fully controlling? I have been suggesting that any response to such questions has to grapple with the changing character of code traffic. That traffic has many different facets, some of which can be architecturally reorganised and enclosed, others of which remain subtly diffuse and imprecise. The simple contrast between `git` traffic and its socially coded concentration on GitHub is a useful guiding thread.

There are many other dynamics on GitHub that we might analyse in terms of coadaptation of imitative fluxes. The very crude tracking of imitation based on forking and repository names could be refined in various ways. We could ask, for instance, what are the most-forked repositories, and how do changes in copying practices help us think about different directions of movement of code and coders. I have mentioned the profusion of `dotfile` repositories in the last few years. These repositories can be analysed in terms of micro-gestural and micro-perceptual differentiations at work in the writing of code. Choices of colour, font size, line separation, shortcuts for keystroke commands and the multiplicity of configurations for code development could be used to develop a much richer account of how people move through code, almost like a 'gait analysis' for code. Similarly, the metrics of the name space could, at a very different end of infrastructural dimensioning of code help us see how, for instance, the contemporary rescaling of computational infrastructures through 'Cloud' computing or virtualisation ripple across code-as-crowd. In all of these settings, the mergers, coalescences, branching and replication of bodies of code suggest that there is no single operational level at which code governs cities.

Regardless of these possible directions of analysis, the broader point here is that software today is less like a machine, a system or even an assemblage, and more like a crowd. That is, it has a fluxing, flowing and somewhat disordered existence that generates powerful flashes and movements, that creates atmospherics and densely woven patches of order, but remains unstable and dynamic.

Notes

1 Thrift and French's empirical response to their own question begins with the Y2K bug, and the long lists of software potentially affected by it: keypad locks, pagers, solar panels, smoke detectors, camcorders, video cassette recorders, elevators. Although these lists now look dated, when a similar listing would include many things that did not exist in 2002, Thrift and French's (2002) description of the effect of software development on urban space remains recognisable: 'We will exist in a broadband world in which the Internet will be a permanently available "Cloud" of information able to be called up through a number of appliances scattered through the environment. These appliances will be something more than portals for information. Rather, like many other devices which will not have Internet connections, they will be "practice-aware"' (315) and 'will, through a process of cultural absorption into practices, sink down from the representational into the non-representational world, so becoming a part of a taken-for-granted set of passions and skills' (318). The fact that these developments more than a decade later are still very much in train suggests that there is something quite predictable about the development of software and coding in organising urban life and spaces.
2 Writing in 2014, Thrift again addressed coded cities: 'Take just the case of coded cities understood as a whole' (Thrift 2014: 13), and then proceeded to offer a sixfold topography of the code city – as externalisation of capitalist power, as prescribed matter of concern, as care-laden responses to the demand for resilience, as projected-retrojected dream life, as navigational geometry and as materialised visualisation. He finally suggested that something links this diversity: the possibility for 'these entities to learn [...] to transform themselves'. Echoing the 2002 discussion of the geography of indeterminacy, he attributed this possibility to 'emergent tendencies arising out of complexity' or 'through simple happenstance which places them in unexpected situations which require adaptation' (13). The sixfold evocation of the coded city somewhat complicates the geographies of software in the city, but it reiterates the transformative capacity of indeterminacy. The 2002 formulations on indeterminacy and 'traffic between beings' grow into forms of novel encounter in 'unexpected situations'. (While urban sociology has long understood cities in terms of encounters between strangers, Thrift's account shifts the emphasis to unexpected encounters between other beings.) Coded cities' 'capacity to learn' transpires, according to this account, in elementary forms of movement understood as *code traffic*. If this is the case, the 'authoring', the 'learning' and the transformations should not only be traceable in code, but coding itself matters greatly as a process where externalisations, matters of concern, geometries, projections, visualisations, resilience-care, etc., come together and affect each other. The volume and composition of the traffic of coding itself as a cycling and recycling might be an important trace of more general transformations.
3 This, I should note, is a departure from most crowd theory, crowd psychology and crowd sociology. In most crowd theory, things hardly figure at all. As I will sketch, points of identification occur between systems, platforms, protocols and patterns just as much as between individuals or groups.

88 *Adrian Mackenzie*

4 The GitHub team takes a strong interest in bootstrap, a set of components such as buttons, forms, progress bars, tables, typographic elements and colour themes for Web front end development. These visual elements figure heavily in the visual appearance of GitHub as a social media platform; hence, bootstrap already matters to the social coding of code that GitHub itself does.

5 The only problem with this is that the GitHub co-founder, Tom Preston-Werner (aka mojombo, id = '1' in the GitHub user list – in other words, the first hubbernaut ever) has recently had to step down as CEO after much publicised allegations of sexist and discriminatory language and behaviour in the workplace (Newman 2014). I largely leave the workplace dynamics of GitHub aside here, but they are symptomatic.

6 This geography refers to the 'hubbernauts' themselves, not to GitHub users, who are much more dispersed.

7 We can see some of what the GitHub team has been doing in GitHub repositories by running queries against the GitHub API (application programmer interface) or using the archived datastream of GitHub activity at GithubArchive.org. All of the numerical data in this paper result from queries run against the GithubArchive.org record of GitHub traffic. In the case of Figure 6.1, the query process went: find all the public repositories on which the named 'actor' works, and count the different actions they perform on those repositories. If we run this query for all hubbernauts (233 at the time of writing), as well as mojombo, something of the network of work done on GitHub itself begins to appear. I am assuming that the coding of GitHub can be seen in git traffic.

8 Tracking imitative fluxes means engaging with things that inherently lack any full formatting or clear outline. I focus here on the names of repositories and the names of actors. I have argued elsewhere that naming practices and code name spaces offer a rich resource for thinking about recursive and imitative processes in software culture (Mackenzie 2014).

References

Borch, C. (2005) 'Urban imitations: Tarde's sociology revisited', *Theory Culture & Society* 22(3), 81–100.

Guattari, F. and Deleuze, G. (1988) *A Thousand Plateaus: Capitalism and Schizophrenia*, London: Athlone.

Horvath, R.J. (1974) 'Machine Space', *Geographical Review*, 64(2): 167–88.

Mackenzie, A. (2014) 'useR!: aggression, alterity and unbound affects in statistical programming', in O. Goriunova (ed.) *Fun and Software: Exploring Pleasure, Paradox and Pain in Computing*, New York: Bloomsbury Academic.

Newman, L.H. (2014) 'The results of GitHub's harassment investigation are vague', *Slate*, 21 April 2014, available from http://www.slate.com/blogs/future_tense/2014/04/21/github_ceo_tom_preston_werner_is_cleared_but_still_resigns_over_harassment.html [accessed 24 August 2015].

Tarde, G. (1902) *Psychologie Économique*, Paris: F. Alcan.

Thrift, N. (2014) 'The "sentient" city and what it may portend', *Big Data and Society*, 1(1): 1–21.

Thrift, N. and French, S. (2002) 'The automatic production of space', *Transactions of the Institute of British Geographers*, 27(3): 309–35.

Part II

Locative social media and mobile computing

7 Digital social interactions in the city

Reflecting on location-based social networks

Luigina Ciolfi and Gabriela Avram

Introduction

Digital interactions are increasingly interwoven with spaces and places in urban settings, with such interactions mediated by and in turn shaping the technologies that facilitate them. In this chapter, we focus on understanding these interactions using location-based social media (particularly Foursquare) as a way to reflect on the technological support of human activities, and on the relationship between code, digital agency, and the physical world. Our perspective is that of human-centred computing, particularly Computer-Supported Cooperative Work – a multidisciplinary field studying collaborative practices in socio-technical systems, with a focus on unearthing and detailing the mediational role of technology in human cooperation, coordination and social interaction.

Whether purposely built for mobile devices and with a focus on location (e.g., Foursquare; Swarm), or simply featuring in other platforms that rely on location data such as Facebook Places or Twitter, various LBSNs increasingly mediate social and interpersonal interactions in urban settings. The essential technological infrastructure enabling such interaction is the possibility of linking data to particular places by means of mobile devices capable of detecting their own location through GPS or other mechanisms. Within different apps, location-based social media user activity takes different forms: from 'checking in' (e.g., users register their presence at a venue), to linking location data to digital content for sharing, to gameplay associated with occupying a location and performing certain activities at that site. The means of socially sharing these activities with contacts and other users is also constrained by the platform, for example a photograph with location information, or presence at a location with associated content, or a map of movements and check-ins.

Such practices become coded into the platform back-end system, capturing both the log and content of social interactions, as well as the location to which they relate. Therefore, a digital 'cloud' of social interactions becomes embedded into the physical reality of a city, of its neighbourhoods, public places, cafés, transportation hubs and any other locations identified by social media users (by user-initiated check-ins or by the content that is generated, such as

92   Luigina Ciolfi and Gabriela Avram

photographs or textual recommendations and tips), and by the tools they use (for example, through automatic geotagging). Conversely, the code determining a platform's interaction and functionality is continuously changed to reflect user activities and feedback, and to implement design decisions on how LBSN services work.

Amongst others, two sets of issues with respect to LBSNs are emerging that we wish to investigate further. First, how such localised interactions in physical spaces are triggering and feeding back into the software: how are various location-based social media platforms framing people's perceptions and identifications of locations? How is code both facilitating and scaffolding a set of social interactions relating to various spatial configurations in physical spaces? Second, how such a cloud of interactions is rematerialised in the physical world: how are physical spaces and places affected by their digital counterparts and by people's activities on LBSNs? There are already occurrences of rematerialisation of digital presence and interactions in the physical world: for example, venue owners displaying badges on their premises that inform customers of their online presence (e.g., TripAdvisor, Booking.com). Could LBSN interactions in relation to a venue be made somehow more perceivable or tangible in the physical world by the way in which certain environments are designed? Could the presence and interactions that are encoded in LBSN software shape more distinctively the physicality and materiality of places? For example, should new approaches to urban planning and environmental design become concerned with accommodating and facilitating LBSN interactions, as they do so for in-presence, analogue ones?

In the following sections we define and discuss these issues concerning LBSN, both drawing from and consolidating the findings of human-centred computing literature on physical or digital interactions using location-based social media, and from empirical studies of LBSN use that we have conducted in two cities.

Location-based social media: identifying interactions

Since the introduction of LBSN commercial platforms in the mid-2000s, a number of studies have been conducted within human-centred and social computing to examine how they are being used by various groups of users (Eagle and Pentland 2005; Barkhuus *et al.* 2008). One of the main foci of such work has been Foursquare: a mobile app launched in 2009 and now with over 50 million registered users worldwide, approximately 50% of whom are based within the USA.[1]

While the core interaction offered by the service remains that of linking digital activities to a particular place or commercial venue, the Foursquare interface, services and how it operates have changed significantly since its public launch. Users register their presence at a venue by "checking in". Photographs can also be uploaded when checking in, and comments and tips added to a venue. Initially, Foursquare incorporated a game-like element,

Digital social interactions in the city 93

where users would gain points whenever they checked in and could become 'mayor' of a certain place by checking in repeatedly over time, and could also gain 'badges' by achieving a certain number of check-ins or by completing particular tasks (e.g., checking in at movie screenings). Users' check-in performances would be compared with those of their contacts, although users could compete for a mayorship against any other Foursquare user. Both badges and point scoring features were partly phased out in 2014 as part of a major redevelopment of the platform. The remaining supported activities were split into two separate apps, a redesigned Foursquare and a new app called Swarm. Foursquare now functions as a venue-finding and recommendation app only – it helps users locate places of interest near them in various categories (food, shopping, etc.), lets them 'like' a place thus marking it as a favourite, and read and add tips and recommendations about a place. The platform can also be used by owners of registered businesses for promotions and marketing. Conversely, all the interactions relating to broadcasting one's location to contacts and gaining recognition for doing so are now supported by Swarm, an app where users interact only with direct contacts, gaining certain rewards for repeated check-ins. Swarm supports some new activities, such as planning outings to particular venues involving contacts, and profile personalisation through digital 'stickers' that can be freely added. On Swarm it is not possible for users to see who else is checked in at a venue, unless it is one of their contacts. Activity on both Foursquare and Swarm can also be shared on other social networks.

While usage of Foursquare and Swarm is yet to be studied in depth as we write, researchers have explored the previous incarnations of the app for a number of years. Such studies have extended earlier work examining practices and motivations around social location sharing (Barkhuus *et al.* 2008), and have focused on various aspects of Foursquare, notably which interactions people perform on the app, how users manage their visibility, reputation and privacy, and how they explore physical spaces through the app.

In their empirical study of checking in behaviour, Lindquist *et al.* (2011) identified a set of motivations as to why people decide not only to interact with the app at a venue (e.g., finding the venue on Foursquare, reading content about it), but also to broadcast their presence to followers. People check in not only for social motivations, but also for personal ones, such as keeping an account of their own movements, of the places they visit and how often. However, the social motivations are more frequent and more articulate. One set relates to communication and coordination with friends and family: the desire to share personal information at a distance with contacts, and in return to see where friends have been. Often, Foursquare is used as a way to coordinate meetings and other activities with friends. Another set of motivations relates to the wider Foursquare community: people enjoy discovering new people frequenting similar venues to themselves, and reading their recommendations. In some cases people check in at a venue just before they leave for safety reasons – leaving a 'false trail' to avoid potential stalkers.

94　*Luigina Ciolfi and Gabriela Avram*

As for deciding which places to check in at, people make distinctions between routine and non-routine places: some decide not to check in at routine places because they are seen as uninteresting, and instead check in at places that are seen as special or exciting (e.g., large events, entertainment venues). Others check in at routine places either to gain Foursquare points or because they were bored and checked in for something to do. Other considerations are made by users when deciding to check in at private places, such as a private residence or their own homes: there are privacy concerns regarding revealing such locations, and people often refrain from checking in at somebody's home in order to keep its location private. Checking in at one's own home is often done as a way to tell friends that one is home safely, or is available for calls or visits. Interestingly, privacy concerns also come into play when deciding not to check in at certain public venues, such as at the doctor's, the bank, etc. Moreover, impression management concerns emerge in these decisions as well, for example, deciding not to check in at a fast food restaurant because it might create a bad impression for others (Lindquist *et al.* 2011).

Cramer *et al.* (2011) further explored aspects of privacy and self-presentation focusing on the performative effects of checking in. They identified instances of *purpose-driven* (Tang *et al.* 2010) motivations (similar to those detailed in Scellato *et al.* 2011), such as obtaining discounts, discovering new places, gaming (gaining mayorships), as personal bookmarks, and for amusement when bored. Instances of *social-driven* (Tang *et al.* 2010) check-ins were motivated by networking with friends or recommending a venue, but also by wanting to learn about the people frequenting a venue who were unknown to them otherwise.

However, Cramer *et al.* (2011) observe how LBSN activity goes beyond the two categories of *purpose-driven* and *social-driven*. Their data shows instances driven by self-presentation, lifestyle choices and identity. Self-presentation requires a finer understanding of the audience that a check-in will be shared with. Furthermore, Cramer *et al.* examine the perspective of the check-ins audience: people saw check-ins from friends as a way to obtain recommendations on things to do and places to visit, or as a motivation to attend an event or place. They were also annoyed by friends who checked in too frequently (thus sending repeated notifications) or without a clear motivation. Cramer *et al.* (2011) found that motivations can change for every instance of checking in (and for each venue), and that certain motivations can sometimes conflict with others, for example, wanting to check in for the purpose of gaining gaming points might contrast with not wanting to annoy others with too many notifications.

Guha and Birnholtz (2013) have further explored the ways people think about location sharing and how impressions are formed and managed. They identify a blurring between public and private spheres of life when sharing a location and viewing a check-in: for example, one's presence at certain places is kept private (e.g., the gym) although such places are, strictly speaking, public. Conversely, certain places are private (e.g., a friend's home); however, people decide to check in there and to reveal their location (e.g., when there is a party going on). Such decisions are usually made depending on how visible the user thinks the check-in will be: people are careful about how certain contacts might perceive their behaviour, and about how certain check-ins might create tensions within their network. An example of this is checking in to a restaurant to claim a discount, but at the same time broadcasting being out to the social circle at a time when it could be inappropriate. Tensions might also arise when sharing one's location could be perceived in different ways by different contacts (e.g. a friend vs a parent).

Guha and Birnholtz (2013) have also detailed certain tricks that people employ when sharing their locations, such as checking in at locations where they are not in order to make a better impression. They call one phenomenon 'check-in transience', linked to the fact that Foursquare's newsfeed to users only displays the latest location where their contacts have checked in. People who do not want their 'real' last check-in displayed for too long on their contacts' newsfeed will check in somewhere else immediately so that the friends will see that latter check-in. Participants in this study admitted to making judgements on people they did not know well in real life based on their check-ins (e.g., which café they visited, etc.), and therefore were very sensitive about how they presented themselves to and were perceived by their contacts.

All these studies have highlighted the many privacy concerns surrounding LBSN interactions. Users tend to be aware of them, particularly regarding residential privacy (Jin *et al.* 2012), and decide to risk exposure only in particular circumstances. Foursquare public data has also been used for other developments, for example recommendation systems, such as algorithms for predicting which tips attract more attention on Foursquare and for supporting the creation of marketing strategies on LBSNs (Vasconcelos *et al.* 2014), and models combining cellular data and LBSN activity to infer types of activities in neighbourhoods and urban centres and to aid urban planning and management (Noulas *et al.* 2013).

The findings of this small but in-depth set of studies reveal much about people's use of LBSN and their motivations and strategies. In relation to the issues we focus on in the remainder of this chapter, we have already seen instances of the complex relationship between the system (its code and other components, such as the database logging user-generated content) and people's interactions, and how the two shape one another. One example of this is users being careful about the last location they check in at because the software will keep displaying it until a new one is shared. However, much remains to be studied. The playful and game-like aspects of LBSNs and their connection to real-world spaces are yet unexplored, although other location-based social gaming practices have been studied in depth (O'Hara 2008). More crucial to overcome, in our opinion, is the limited attention paid to the way in which LBSNs contribute to the way places are made, lived and reconfigured. While other technological platforms have been investigated in terms of how they mediate understanding of and attachment to real-world environments (Farnham *et al.* 2009; Scellato *et al.* 2011), existing human-centred computing work on LBSNs focuses mainly on individual practices, often without focusing on the actual locales in relation to which they occur.

It is important to pay attention to the way venues, neighbourhoods and cities are lived in and perceived by virtue of the cloud of digital interactions and data that are tied to them: do LBSN activities impact on place attachment? Or on the way an area is discovered, explored and navigated? We have addressed some of these issues in two small-scale studies of LBSN interactions via Foursquare in Limerick and Sheffield. We now describe our empirical explorations and the main findings arising from them.

Studying Foursquare use in two cities

The existing studies of Foursquare discussed in the previous section employed a methodology consisting of surveys and interviews. For our study, we have combined a series of interviews with online observations of interactions on Foursquare. The most extensive part of our study (comprising online observations and interviews) has been focused on Limerick, a regional city in the midwest of Ireland. A second part of the study consists of online observations only, and focused on Sheffield, a regional city in South Yorkshire (UK).

We conducted online observations of 15 Limerick venues – every month since October 2012 – and of ten Sheffield venues every month since December 2012. We chose similar venues for observation in both cities to compare online activity at locations holding similar purposes. The venues included: public markets, museums, train and bus stations, public parks, university buildings, cafés, shopping malls, pubs and restaurants, cinemas, theatres and sporting venues. The observations consisted of monitoring mayorships and check-ins and the addition of content (photos, tips, etc.) for each venue. These data were documented through notes and screenshots. The semi-structured interviews of the Limerick Foursquare users were conducted between October 2012 and May 2013 and involved 12 local participants. We combined the interviews with online observation of the accounts of the participants for 2-week periods.

In their check-ins, our participants expressed support for a new business, shared Wi-Fi access details at venues and provided information on hidden gems in the city. Check-ins were also used to signal personal availability ('I am at work', 'I am in town', 'I am out of town'). People checked in at certain venues for one-off or particularly significant happenings (performances, conferences, sport events), similarly to what has been observed in previous work. However, many users we observed checked in regularly at a familiar place, where the purpose of checking in was not only to broadcast an exceptional or exciting occurrence (e.g., an unexpected meeting), but also to describe the day's mood or ongoing activities.

Motivations for using Foursquare that emerged echo to a large extent the findings from previous studies: there are personal motivations as well as social motivations underlying the decision to check in and provide content. As the respondents to our interviews included business people in the 40–60-year-old bracket (whereas the participants in previous studies were mostly younger university students), we saw motivations connected to professional activities, not only to socialisation and lifestyle. For example, people checked in to endorse a venue for business meetings. Another example is checking in at home to signal one's unavailability for work matters. An additional motivation that we noted is civic activism: people check in to broadcast that they are doing something good for their city, encouraging others to join. In answer to our interview questions, participants thus explained their motivations to check in: *'going to places so that I feel I own them'*; *'when I do check in – I spot people that I know'*; *'tell someone I'm up, tell someone I'm moving'*.

Our online observations gave us insights on how spaces and places become represented on LBSNs in a way that previous work had not highlighted. Activities associated with venues can be surprising, or provide insights that are not obvious by looking at the venue description or visiting that physical location. For example, in Limerick, the Stella Ballroom is classified on Foursquare as a historic site and not simply as an entertainment venue (it is now used as a bingo hall), and many check-ins refer to the exhibition held there on the history of Limerick ballrooms. In Sheffield, many check-ins and tips at the train station refer to socialising, as one of Sheffield's most popular pubs is located there and many people check in at the station, rather than at the pub venue (Figure 7.1).

Popular venues attract many check-ins and user-generated content. Their representation on Foursquare depicts their busy atmosphere: the Milk Market in Limerick is a hub of LBSN activity on Saturdays (the day the full market is held), where people check in as it is 'the place to be' and where friends also tend to converge. In this case, checking in is also a way to see if other friends have arrived. Foursquare activity at this location peaks at weekends, thus the venue's cloud of interactions fluctuates significantly on different days. A similar example in Sheffield, albeit within a different temporal frame, is the Crucible Theatre: while attracting a steady flow of LBSN interactions throughout the year by theatre enthusiasts, it becomes a veritable hub during April when the World Snooker Championship is held there. Indeed, the majority of tips left by users are updated during that period and refer to the tournament, rather than to the regular theatrical season (Figure 7.2).

Foursquare venues used to collect a trail of banter and 'private' messages between people in the form of a venue tip, for example, between regular frequenters battling for a mayorship. In this case, the tips were used not to provide information for the larger community, but to foster the connection between particular users (Figure 7.3). The gaming aspect also gave rise to a proliferation of Foursquare venues: users could create new venues – increasing venue granularity in places where sublocations can be identified

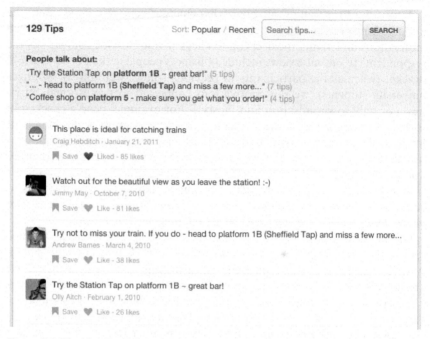

Figure 7.1 Tips for Sheffield train station
Source: Foursquare http://4sq.com/574TDX, 25 April 2014

Figure 7.2 Tips for the Crucible Theatre, Sheffield
Source: Foursquare http://4sq.com/aw3G01, 25 April 2014

Digital social interactions in the city 99

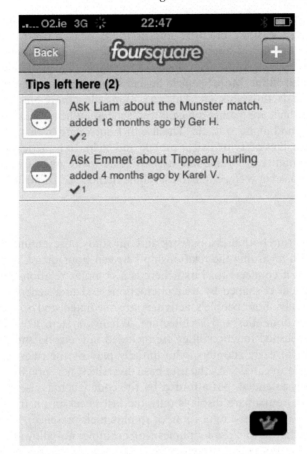

Figure 7.3 Tips used as private banter at a Limerick pub
Source: Foursquare http://4sq.com/9J9NOn, 9 June 2013

(for example, a platform at the train station) – to be first to check in and obtain points.

Our online observations also gave us insights on the content that users create for particular venues. Photos have a variety of subjects and purposes: for example, photos uploaded to a popular hotel in Limerick illustrate events taking place there (conferences, business meetings, etc.), recommended food at the hotel restaurant (a function similar to that of tips), or various corners of the building and the view from it. This content represents a place from multiple points of view: structural characteristics, but also activities taking place there and people frequenting it.

Our study looked at two cities and we were thus able to compare Foursquare interactions in both settings. While there were many similarities between them, some differences could also be noted. Probably as a result of the significant difference in geographical size and size of population between the two cities, in Sheffield (the larger of the two), the Foursquare user group is much larger than in Limerick; however, there appear to be weaker ties between users overall (e.g., number of interactions between users), with some tight 'packs' of friends interacting with each other on Foursquare, but probably knowing each other well offline. More Sheffield businesses use LBSN, with venues offering special deals, discounts, etc. This goes alongside a more lifestyle-oriented use of tips, which are mainly directed to a general audience with recommendations for good nights out, etc. The use of Foursquare in this case is more similar to the likes of TripAdvisor mobile and Yelp. In Limerick, the overall smaller community of Foursquare users translates into more frequent informal interactions between people (both offline friends and strangers).

Discussion

The insights from both previous work and our study pose a number of issues for discussion regarding the relationship between Foursquare, its users and the locations it connects to. First, there is a complex relationship between how the system is shaped by user interactions and user-generated content and, conversely, how people's activities are mediated and shaped by the system's functionalities and architecture. When a system like Foursquare is released, selected functionalities are included in the code and they shape the practices of early adopters, who initially play by the rules to see what the new platform can do. As the user base diversifies, new practices appear – not originally intended, but afforded by the code (such as users exploiting the fact that Foursquare displays only the last check-in on friends' newsfeeds either to emphasise a location, or to hide their presence). The system's owners can choose to close loopholes (for example, not allowing check-ins at faraway locations) or to support the new practices by including them in the next release. Very often, innovations introduced from the top down via new versions of the code are met with resistance by frequent users, as their current practices are disrupted. As a consequence, users have to go through a whole new sense-making cycle and appropriate the new version by altering their practices.

Not only the activities that the code enables but how they are enacted is another aspect that reciprocally shapes interactions: the code is designed for a specific context and so are the ways of content production. For example, textual contributions are called 'tips'; however, as Foursquare is trying to move into the market occupied by Yelp, it becomes obvious that Foursquare's tips are not actual reviews and could not be used as such. Users leave tips, such as the amount in coins you need for parking in a specific place, or recommendations, such as 'Try the chowder' which are not actual reviews. The field name 'tips' instilled a specific behaviour – this illustrates how the design choices influence the content contributed by users.

From a different perspective, Foursquare makes the content generated by its user base available for new uses through the Foursquare APIs. All kinds of mash-ups have been created to take advantage of such data, by extending the Foursquare code. Therefore, there is an interesting tension between the possibilities and the constraints offered by the platform, from the point of view of regulated use and of appropriation. There are also important issues to flag regarding the relationship between people and specific places that is now mediated by LBSNs. The LBSNs extend some of the possibilities that real-world locations offer people to link to others, to take advantage of what a place offers or to find privacy and quiet. The relationship between a person and a place is made more visible by the encoding of LBSN interactions on a platform such as Foursquare. Furthermore, such a relationship is also extended by the possibility of novel forms of digital interaction, such as sharing recommendations amongst strangers. The platform also makes visible community relationships to a place, and their importance in an urban environment: examples of this are the Milk Market on a Saturday (Figure 7.4), a rugby game in Thomond Park stadium for Limerick, the World Snooker Championship in April and the December Christmas Village at the Peace Gardens for Sheffield.

While other researchers emphasised the potential for coordination created by check-ins, our findings show that awareness of who else is (or was) in the same place is an important element and is interpreted as a recommendation for the place itself. Moreover, the digital buzz around a venue (many check-ins, many tips and photographs) is an endorsement of that place's importance

Figure 7.4 User photographs of Limerick's Milk Market
Source: Foursquare https://foursquare.com/v/the-milkmarket/4bc03935920eb71309b4182c/photos, 9 June 2013

102 *Luigina Ciolfi and Gabriela Avram*

for the community. Users get a glimpse into their contacts' favourite places and their trajectories. Awareness of events is another interesting element that is a sort of side-product of Foursquare.

Through these visible clouds of interaction, Foursquare and other LBSNs make navigating an unknown neighbourhood or area less daunting. The Foursquare venues in a city constitute a crowdsourced map of places that, most of the time, is very different from an official one. The users' check-in preferences shape each city's list of venues that both users and non-users can consult for finding good places for specific purposes: coffee, Wi-Fi access, etc. This connects to the issue of 'rematerialisation' – of whether the digital interactions enabled by the code can be made visible or perceivable in real-world places, either for LBSN non-users or for users by means others than the app. There are already instances where a venue's connection to an LBSN is made visible, for example, by displaying Foursquare membership badges in the physical space. However, much more happens in digital form that is only available to the app users: being able to see photos, tips and comments, as well as which Foursquare friends have checked in there. Check-ins by friends, tips and photos make a new place feel familiar, allow users to see how it looked on certain occasions or when a specific event occurred. We think it is important for human-centred computing researchers to further explore whether technologies such as ambient or tangible media could be employed to enable some of these interactions in a way that is less confined to a device (the mobile phone) and more embedded into the materiality of the environment. This is connected to issues of physicality and performativity in interaction. The practice of checking in when arriving at a venue is often frowned upon by some people – as well as being considered socially unacceptable in certain locations or circumstances. Some people's refined planning in order to make the check-in performance acceptable or discreet is linked also to their awareness of the visibility of this action to a general audience. Making check-ins and other interactions available in novel ways would require careful consideration of the social visibility and acceptability of such practices.

Conclusions

This chapter reflected on people's interactions with the popular location-based social media platform Foursquare and on how they are entwined with the code that enables them, with other users, and with the real-world spaces and places that they link to. We presented a summary of findings emerging from human-centred computing research on Foursquare, and we integrated these with the results from studies of Foursquare use that we have conducted in two cities. In our studies, we wished to characterise further the relationship between LBSN interactions and the places in which they occur, to extend previous work and to address a gap in human-centred computing research that has only been partially filled (Silva *et al.* 2013). Finally, we highlighted some issues for further discussion, particularly on the relationship between the Cloud of LBSN interactions and the real-world places in which they occur, and on how code enables, shapes and is in turn shaped by users' activities and instances of system appropriation. In-depth studies of other location-based digital activities, such as turfing (Chang and Goodman, 2004) and geocaching (Neustaedter *et al.*, 2013) and their ties with the materiality of the city have shed light on how such certain digital practices can be better supported: a deeper understanding of such dynamics in LBSN can lead to novel contributions in this respect.

Note

1 (Foursquare 2015)

References

Barkhuus, L., Brown, B., Bell, M., Sherwood, S., Hall, M. and Chalmers, M. (2008) 'From awareness to repartee: sharing location within social groups', *Proceedings of CHI 2008*, New York: ACM Press, 497–506.

Chang, M. and Goodman, E. (2004) 'FIASCO: game interface for location-based play', *Proceedings of DIS 2004*, New York: ACM Press, 329–32.

Cramer, H., Rost, M. and Holmquist, L.E. (2011) 'Performing a check-in: emerging practices, norms and "conflicts" in location-sharing using Foursquare', *Proceedings of MobileHCI 2011*, New York: ACM Press, 57–66.

Eagle, N. and Pentland, A. (2005) 'Social serendipity: mobilizing social software', *IEEE Pervasive Computing*, 4(2): 28–34.

Farnham, S.D., McCarthy, J.F., Patel, Y., Ahuja, S., Norman, D., Hazlewood, W.R. and Lind, J. (2009) 'Measuring the impact of third place attachment on the adoption of a place-based community technology', *Proceedings of CHI 2009*, New York: ACM Press, 2153–6.

Foursquare (2015) *Foursquare*, available from https://foursquare.com/about [accessed 19 November 2015].

Guha, S. and Birnholtz, J. (2013) 'Can you see me now? Location, visibility and the management of impressions on Foursquare', *Proceedings of Mobile HCI 2013*, New York: ACM Press, 183–92.

Jin, L., Long, X. and Joshi, J.B.D. (2012), 'Towards understanding residential privacy by analyzing users' activities in Foursquare', *Proceedings of BADGERS'12*, New York: ACM Press, 25–32.

Lindquist, J., Cranshaw, J., Wiese, J., Hong, J. and Zimmerman, J. (2011) 'I'm the mayor of my house: examining why people use Foursquare – a social-driven location sharing application', *Proceedings of CHI 2011*, New York: ACM Press, 2409–18.

Neustaedter, C., Tang, A. and Judge, T.K. (2013), 'Creating scalable location-based games: lessons from geocaching', *Personal and Ubiquitous Computing* 17(2): 335–49.

Noulas, A., Mascolo, C. and Frias-Martinez, E. (2013) 'Exploiting Foursquare and cellular data to infer user activity in urban environments', *Proceedings of MDM 2013, IEEE 14th Int. Conference on Mobile Data Management*, 1–10.

104 *Luigina Ciolfi and Gabriela Avram*

O'Hara, K. (2008), 'Understanding geocaching practices and motivations', *Proceedings of CHI 2008*, New York: ACM Press, 1177–86.

Scellato, S., Noulas, A., Lambiotte, R. and Mascolo, C. (2011) 'Socio-spatial properties of online location-based social networks', *Proceedings of ICWSM'11*, 1–10.

Silva, T.H., Vaz de Melo, P.O.S., Almeida, J.M., Salles, J. and Loureiro, A.A.F. (2013) 'A comparison of Foursquare and Instagram to the study of city dynamics and urban social behavior', *Proceedings of UrbComp 2013*, Article no 4, 1–8.

Tang, K., Lin, J., Hong, J., Siewiorek, D. and Sadeh, N. (2010) 'Rethinking location sharing: exploring the implications of social-driven vs. purpose-driven location sharing', *Proceedings of UbiComp'10*, New York: ACM Press, 85–94.

Vasconcelos, M., Almeida, J. and Conçalves (2014) 'What makes your opinion popular? Predicting the popularity of micro-reviews in Foursquare', *Proceedings of SAC 2014*, New York: ACM Press, 598–603.

8 Feeling place in the city
Strange ontologies and location-based social media

Leighton Evans

Introduction

Modern cities are infused with code, and the operations of systems and governance are dependent upon code. Kitchin and Dodge (2011: 22) describe the operations of software as bound up in, contributing to and altering the conditions through which society, space, time and spatiality are produced. The view of the city as a site of urban informatics (Thrift 2014: 1263) is the logical outcome of a view of the city as not only constituted by coexisting software and code, but also of a city that is made up of sensors and devices designed to relay governance through operations of algorithms and code (see Greenfield 2013; Batty 2013). However, accounts of urban governance rarely focus on the everyday mundane nature of technology, code and software (Thrift 2014: 1264). Nonetheless, people adopt technology as part of their everyday practices and adapt to it. Moreover, digital computational technologies operate largely beyond the circumspection of their users.

This 'withdrawal' of the functioning of code can be understood as a 'vicarious causation' (Berry 2011: 153) that encapsulates the way in which the world is presented through devices. The process of understanding the world is vicarious in the way that digital devices are continually emerging and withdrawing from circumspection given their internal hidden computational state. However, while code is withdrawn from conscious experience, it nonetheless plays a part in the co-creation between individual and technology in producing an understanding the world. For example, smartphone applications, such as LBSNs, involve an interaction with code that shapes the experience of place in the modern city. Berry (2011: 146) thus argues that new digital technological devices are becoming embedded in our way-of-being, such that a computational mode of being emerges. Consequently, new social ontologies and computational social epistemologies become dependent on and mutually constituted through code (Berry 2012: 381). Berry (2011: 152) uses the term 'computational image' to describe the cultural techniques used to select, store, process and produce data to computationally process the world, which is then presented back to the user. This process must necessarily involve a translation from the physical to the computational (what

106   Leighton Evans

Kitchin and Dodge (2011) term transduction) and a translation from code to interface.

Understanding code in this way is important because of the rise in ubiquitous computational technologies for mediated interaction with the physical environment. This embodied interaction with computers centres around 'the creation, manipulation and sharing of meaning through engaged interaction with artefacts' (Dourish 2001). Tangible computing is allied to social computing (social networking) and location-based services embedded in devices. Using these devices results in the production of an embodied agent, an intelligent agent that interacts with the environment through a physical or virtual body in that environment. Mackenzie (2010) develops a similar line of thinking in discussing the phenomenon of wirelessness, arguing that the continual engagement with computational devices and gadgets leads to a tendency to seek and make continuous network connections. This tendency is an embodiment of an attunement to living in a world with a proliferation of networked computational devices. Mackenzie's work links a phenomenological approach, with studies and theories of urban space that emphasise how computational devices alter and mediate the experience of space. For example, Kitchin and Dodge (2011) emphasise the importance of computer code in the transduction of urban spaces; Shepard (2011) argues that the 'dataclouds of the twenty-first century' increasingly shape experiences of the city; and de Souza e Silva and Gordon (2011) use the concept of 'networked locality' to show how particular usage of networked devices, and the information they can provide from delocalised storage, can increase nearness to places rather than increase distance in a phenomenological sense.

Other work has explored the use of LBSNs from an explicitly phenomenological position (see Evans 2015). Following notions that the mobile computational devices that we carry (e.g., smartphones, tablets) are involved in both embodied and hermeneutic relations with the user (Ihde 1990), and are also in a position of alterity with regards to their functioning and execution of code (see Evans (2014) for a discussion of the execution of code in LBSN), this chapter conceptualises what role code plays in shaping understandings of place. The partially immaterial and withdrawn collection of instructions, algorithms and commands, it is argued, is critical to how users experience the world, yet users move in and out of contact with code and enjoy a relationship with code that is vicarious and beyond circumspection.

By engaging Peter Sloterdijk's theory of spheres (1998; 1999; 2004) to conceptualise the presence of code in the modern city, the chapter contributes to the debate on the interaction between code and its users. A framework for explaining both the presence of code in the city, and its importance in gaining understanding and sociality in the city, will be drawn from an exposition of Sloterdijk's *Sphären*. This framework will be exemplified using ethnographic data from a critical case study on the LBSN Foursquare. The examples used are indicative of users engaging with devices, code, data and social media to establish a familiarity and phenomenological feeling of place in novel

Feeling place in the city 107

environments. The 'worlding' (Heidegger 1962) of users by code, accessible through devices, is therefore positioned as a key element in understanding place and as a critical aspect of the post-phenomenology of being in the smart city.

Sloterdijk: spheres, bubbles, foam and code

Sloterdijk's *Sphären* project can be seen as a trilogy of works that answers the question 'Where is man?' rather than 'What is man?' (Schinkel and Noordegraaf-Eelens 2011: 11). This is an engagement in a Heideggerian project concerning the nature of being in relation to place rather than time (Elden and Mendieta 2009: 6). Like Heidegger, Sloterdijk makes much of the thrownness of man into the world (Sloterdijk 1998: 275). This thrownness or not being comfortable in the world makes man a restless creature who is always remaking worlds, fashioning dwellings and dwelling as a phenomenological being-in-the-world through connection with the other (Elden and Mendieta 2009: 7). Essentially, man is always looking to normalise his spatial existence and find comfort (van Tuinen 2009: 299). Sloterdijk's project establishes being-in-the-world as being-in-spheres, in that being is always spatial and social (in that it is always being-with). The concept of the sphere refers to the *da* of Heidegger's *Dasein* in that it refers to 'there'. For Sloterdijk, spheres are the original product of human being-together, in other words shared spaces of perception and experience. Sloterdijk's project moves from microspheres (or bubbles), which are the most intimate spheres of coexistence, such as the intra-uteral relationship between unborn child and mother, to the macrosphere level of globes, and to the globalised level of foam. It is the last type of spherical relationship, foam, which is of interest when considering the worlding of human beings using code, but understanding foam is dependent upon an understanding of the spheres that historically precede it.

A sphere is a shared psycho spatial immunological edifice (Schinkel and Noordegraaf-Eelens 2011: 13): a shared, lived-in space. This is a way to conceptualise social life as consisting of the continual building up and leaving of spatial connectives, from the basic dyad to complex swarms of people. Sloterdijk's historical project traces the development of these spheres from the microscopic level of the interpersonal, to the macroscopic level of the globe and terrestrial conquest, to the multiplicity of simultaneous connections that overcome spatial and temporal barriers in the globalised, 'foam' sphere. The 'where' conceptualised is a protective sphere that can be virtual, but is nevertheless always meaningful and reassuring as a place distinguished from the infinite and fragmentary world (Schinkel and Noordegraaf-Eelens 2011: 22). Societies themselves consist of these 'turbulent and asymmetrical associations of space-multiplicities' or spheres (Sloterdijk 2004: 57).

The spheres are, therefore, what being-in-the-world structurally is, in that the sphere *is being-with*. Foam as a sphere of being is 'an interlocking

108   *Leighton Evans*

and multiple set of cells' that are representative of connection and relation. Klausner (in Elden 2012: 8) identifies four attributes of foam: it is made up of variable shapes and sizes; it lacks a clear centre; it is both fragile and interconnected; and it is part of a process of creation. Foam, then, is a metaphorical attempt to conceptualise the ever-changing places of being-in-the-world, from the smaller, more intimate, to the networked and globalised. Foam is not centred on the person; it is a place that is characterised by particular connections. These connections are not just fragile in that they are impermanent, but necessarily fragile as the sphere is creative and old connections (and therefore old bubbles) are constantly being replaced by the new in foam. Elden (2012: 8) draws parallels between this view and Deleuze and Guattari's concept of the rhizome but, unlike the rhizome, foams are loosely structured and not reducible to complex arrangements and networks. Foams are made of bubbles that are connected but always separate. Sloterdijk's bubbles, therefore, enter a process of osmotic integration with other bubbles, and this multitude of bubbles (enabled by networked communications as well as physical proximity) makes up foam. Importantly, the bubbles are both connected and isolated. This vicarious connection indicates that while the bubble is connected to others it is not reducible to its connections, and, therefore, is not just a node brought into being by virtue of a network of connections and extinguished accordingly at the dissolution of that network.

The *Mitsein* (being-with) that is a bubble is always being-amongst-others or a dwelling amongst others. Like Heidegger's concept of dwelling as a freedom from the world of *das Man* and a technologically enframed mode of being, Sloterdijk's dwelling is a bringing-forth of the world rather than a standing-forth or technological mode of being that is forced upon man. As Morin (2009: 58) argues, this is an attempt to theorise contemporary society through a reworking of Heidegger's existential analytic of *Dasein*, and draws on a detailed narrative of the historical development of humankind and human society to reach this aim. Sloterdijk interprets the development of humanity as a development of different forms of spatiality and understanding space. The move from microsphere to plural-sphere is a move that is from strong, close relationships to weaker, looser, distant relationships facilitated by technology that allows for such ties to exist. The stage of foam goes beyond Heidegger's own analysis of technology as *Gestell* or standing reserve. The third phase of foam addresses the global reach and information saturation associated with networked society (Morin 2009: 59).

To understand the relevance of Sloterdijk to understanding place through LBSNs, it is necessary to trace what kinds of world-forming praxis 'global foams' allow for and allow to be conceived (Morin 2009: 60). Foams are processes that lend themselves to stability and inclusiveness (Sloterdijk 2004: 50). With regards to the social, the basic component of the social is the dyadic sphere, and the social itself is composed of intersubjective relations between autonomous subjects. The human being never exists alone, but only in the world of co-subjectivity, where the human being is animated by the presence

Feeling place in the city   109

and gaze of others (Laermans 2011: 115). The possibility and realisation of this coexistence is possible through the communication networks that link people to known and unknown others (Laermans 2011: 116). With regards to everyday praxis, one can consider the use of media and computational devices as praxis of world making and sphere creation. Traditional broadcast media produce a constantly renewed and fleeting cohesion-effect through the production of common news themes and common interests (Laermans 2011: 117). Mass media communications arouse temporary interests that produce an affective involvement in the topic, and which are therefore responsible for the construction of spheres. Thus, media produces instant cohesion through a bombarding of the 'foam' bubbles that make up contemporary society (Laermans 2011: 118). This mass media information is not stored, but simultaneously produced and used up in its reception, and while there is a surplus of information in modern society, there is still a process of making and reproducing to attract and sustain attention (Laermans 2011: 120).

The mass media has power through the centralised position and ability to synchronise the attention of many individuals and other 'ego-spheres' (Laermans 2011: 126), thus creating a common sphere of interest or attention. However, the digital and social media environment lacks this cohesion. Merrin (2014) contextualises the presence of digital computational devices or gadgets within a rise of hyperludic media – hyperfunctional gadgets that produce media streams centred on the individual. This kind of media produces a highly personal media experience that is dependent on the execution of code and contributes to the subjective experience of the world of the user. When considering social media, the common sphere is the medium (device or platform), but the messages on platforms such as Twitter are more numerous, diverse, personalised and fragmentary than on any broadcast medium and are reliant on code to function. In considering the impact of social media and LBSNs, it is attentiveness or mindfulness that is critical. The media messages (posts, tips, tweets) that create attention in the user create a 'bubble' of attention from the 'foam' of messages carried through digital media. In the praxis of social media use, place and location act as determiners of attention that allow for receiving and engaging with particular media messages provided by other users. Through the execution of code, LBSNs can harness social gazetteers, location information and personally relevant data for users in a location to represent the world in a particular manner. That is place as *place* – a meaningful location where meaning is co-created by code, user and device. To exemplify this, the notion of place-specific messages being critical to forming Sloterdijk's bubbles of dwelling in foam will now be explored with reference to the use of the LBSN Foursquare.

Code in praxis: Foursquare and understanding place

The following analysis draws on an ethnographic study – conducted in 2011 and 2012 using mixed methods, including online surveys and face-to-face,

110 *Leighton Evans*

Skype and e-mail interviews – of 65 users of the LBSN Foursquare. The purpose for this ethnography was to investigate what Foursquare was being used for and what effect on the understanding of place practices of Foursquare use have for users. A hermeneutic phenomenological analysis (van Manen 1997) as a derivative analytic method from critical discourse analysis (Fairclough 1995) was employed to analyse the data with regards to how usage affected an understanding of place for the user. Some brief excerpts are used here to exemplify the formation of world-revealing bubbles in the use of the LBSN.

Foursquare allows users to make check-ins to places within its database of places, create check-in spots and explore comments on places made by other users. The following is an example of familiarising oneself with an unfamiliar place through the application:

> In specific circumstances, the service has made me aware of places around me. The majority of check-ins I make are for places I already know, but there are a few times when I have used Foursquare to find new places. In York, I used Foursquare to find a pub that was showing a football match I wanted to see by looking for pubs and tips, and then using the map facility. When in places that I don't know, unquestionably Foursquare has helped make me more aware of places.
>
> 'James', Foursquare user

'James' used the LBSN to find a place, and to locate himself relative to that place. The definition of place being used here, in conjunction with Sloterdijk's concept of the bubble, is somewhere that is meaningful for the user as he or she dwells in that place. Here, 'James' is employing the LBSN to locate and ground himself in that locale. This transforms the meaningless space of unfamiliarity into a place of familiarity based on the function of code to provide hyperlocal information. The user creates a 'bubble' from the information available through Foursquare and then inhabits the place created.

There is evidence that the device can, through the provision of data on places in the databanks of the LBSN, replace learnt processes of finding one's way in the world and navigating places. Being without the device creates a feeling of homelessness or an inability to dwell:

> Being deprived of this extra sense wouldn't affect my desire or ability but would perhaps make me feel 'underpowered', perhaps in a similar way that a heavy cold affects people's senses of taste or smell. It feels an enhancement of my own capabilities, extending my knowledge about my immediate environs. The GPS abilities of my iPhone do indeed feel like an extra sense; perhaps not one as important as seeing or hearing, but definitely on a par with smell or taste.
>
> 'Lars', Foursquare user

Feeling place in the city   111

'Lars' identifies the device as an augmentation of his senses, heightening understanding of the world when used and being conspicuous in absence. The device is an addition to the existing means of collecting information about the world that is the foundation of understanding. In navigating the media-saturated world, if the device is a necessity then the code that allows it to function is too. The device is in effect a gateway to the 'foam' (connections to information and other users) that is necessary to create the 'bubble' of dwelling. The following comment is also useful in this context:

> When I drive down the road with my phone docked, I see that little blue and white dot on the screen. I realise that's me, and I see all the cars around me, and realise they have dots too. I'm just another face in the world. I suppose programs that are aware of where I am have given me a bit of a drive to explore this big world. I have a guide that I can fall back on, and that lets me go out and explore a bit more. I mean, what's that strange landmark on Foursquare called Stabber's Alley? Just how dark and foreboding is it? Better go see during the day.
>
> 'Kirk', Foursquare user

'Kirk' identifies with the denotation of the device on the digital map (the 'blue dot') as *himself*, so the distinction between user and device withdraws in use (as per Heidegger's tool analysis; Heidegger 1962: 406–412). The device, which is doing the work of locating oneself in the world in this instance, is not considered separately as an entity. In the Sloterdijk-influenced analysis proposed here, the device and user coexist in the bubble that is the experience of place. The experience of the device as one with the user – withdrawn when used as a tool – is one of absence, but as the device is continually updating, representing the world as one moves through the world physically, it is becoming present, demanding attention and thinking. The device links with other things (servers, databases, other devices) beyond conscious experience and continually feeds back to the user. Ihde (1990: 86) explains this as a hermeneutic relation between technology and human being, where the technology acts as an immediate referent to something beyond that device. While the focus of the user is on the device and interface, the user's experience is not with the device itself but the world that it is referring to and the landscape suggested by the gazetteers. In this case, the device withdraws (while still performing the work it is tasked with in revealing the world) to become part of the world. This is reinforced by this comment:

> I think my view of the world has changed by using these services – or at least how I view the world. When visiting new places, I used to stick to small areas, which I could achieve familiarity with quite easily, whereas now using location-based services means that I can use the device with confidence to locate myself and familiarise myself with the place. I am aware that there is a contradiction in that, in that I am only familiarising

112 *Leighton Evans*

myself with the representation of the place from the service, and so there is a tension between familiarity with place and service – and in considering how I see the world, I suppose I am seeing it more through the device than through exploring it physically.

'James', Foursquare user

'James' is aware that he familiarises himself with the device, interface and service, and that the result of this is a familiarity with place that is dependent upon the device and software. The real-time information is given unobtrusively and so the device is always ready-to-hand (continuing its presence as a co-constructing element in the understanding and revealing of place) and always operational and ready to disrupt with information. The device is never fully withdrawn as it interacts with the foam that is the code and networked information the device accesses. The co-presence of the code in the 'bubble' shapes this understanding of world.

Continual information given in real time by the device affects understanding of the world, and changes orientation to the world in a practical way for place and location:

Suddenly the ability to ask for directions is lost! In the past I'd often end up wandering around new places relatively aimlessly but it was just as good as going somewhere specific because that kind of wandering can lead to making new discoveries. If you are headed in a very specific direction with a very clear aim, you might risk missing things along the way, which is a shame.

'Joan', Foursquare user

With the device (assuming connectivity is a given), the existential possibility of being lost is reduced, and if the technological conditions are optimal then being lost could be something that is impossible. The chance discovery, the valuable new place found, the orienting oneself in the unfamiliar place that leads to a new familiarity and the creation of an existential locale through orienting oneself to the objects and entities in the new locale are replaced by computational coexistence. The feeling of place is dependent on the device, as being lost or 'placeless' is not a possibility if one uses LBSN as a part of everyday navigating the world. If this has been done, then place as a familiar existential locale is always possible through the use of the device as a co-constructor of the sense of place in the world. As such, the bubbles that we dwell in, according to Sloterdijk, can always be created if one can access that information through code in the 'foam'.

Conclusions

The examples taken from the ethnography of Foursquare users illustrate an understanding of the networked world where code, data and information

Feeling place in the city 113

shape everyday understanding of place. Although this chapter has used a relatively narrow illustration of this, information may come from the plethora of screens in the modern city, other social media platforms or traditional media. 'Dwelling-in-bubbles' in the networked world occurs as applications (through the execution of code in devices and through network connections) provide people with information that is used in the everyday practices of life. Code is an actor in the functioning of these critical elements (application, device); without the functioning of code these bubbles would not exist.

In the modern, networked world code – as a withdrawn actor in the functioning of devices – is necessary to the possibility and actuality of the creation of what Sloterdijk calls 'bubbles'. The feeling of place can be achieved through the use of applications that inform on place: giving information, relative location, and cues and information from others that provides a social dimension to the praxis of use. Code, in this view, acts as a membrane that allows for flows of data, information and social activity through the foam and into bubbles. Code is the membrane that allows for the information that characterises the networked society to flow and influence. The presence of code foregrounds our presence in the modern world, affording the possibilities of dwelling and understanding while being withdrawn and opaque to the users of computational devices.

Heidegger's great fear of technology (1977) was the flattening effect that occurs through the use of modern technology: the erasing of temporal and spatial dimensions of being leading to a worldview, where all entities are seen as a resource to be used. The view of networked behaviour in this paper illustrates a de-distancing (van Tuinen 2009: 111) that comes from the use of code-dependent devices and applications to understand places. Users may pick up information left many years before by users they will never meet, and use this to establish a dwelling in place. The de-distancing that occurs is not seen as a danger but as a condition of the loose and fragile connections of bubbles that make up the plural-spherology of modern life. Place and the feeling of place is, in these examples, a co-constituent between the device, the application and the mood of the user in the bubble that has been created through digital and computational praxis.

Acknowledgement

The research for this paper was conducted under *The Programmable City*, a project funded by a European Research Council Advanced Investigator award (ERC-2012-AdG-323636-SOFTCITY).

References

Batty, M. (2013) *The New Science of Cities*, Cambridge, MA: MIT Press.
Berry, D.M. (2011) *The Philosophy of Software: Code and Mediation in the Digital Age*, London: Palgrave/Macmillan.

114   *Leighton Evans*

Berry, D.M. (2012) 'The social epistemology of software', *Social Epistemology*, 26(3–4): 379–98.

Dourish, P. (2001) *Where the Action Is: The Foundations of Embodied Interaction*, Cambridge, MA: MIT Press.

de Souza e Silva, A. and Gordon, E. (2011) *Net Locality: Why Location Matters in a Networked World*, Chichester: Wiley Blackwell.

Elden, S. (2012) 'Worlds, temperaments, engagements: introducing Peter Sloterdijk' in S. Elden (ed.) *Sloterdijk Now*, Cambridge: Polity.

Elden, S. and Mendieta, E. (2009) 'Being-with as making worlds: the "second coming" of Peter Sloterdijk', *Environment and Planning D: Society and Space*, 27(1):1–11.

Evans, L. (2014) 'Maps as deep: reading the code of location-based social networks', *IEEE Technology and Science Magazine*, 33(1): 73–80.

Evans, L. (2015) 'Being-towards the social: mood and orientation to location-based social media, computational things and applications', *New Media and Society*, 17(6): 845–60.

Fairclough, N. (1995) *Critical Discourse Analysis: The Critical Study of Language*, London: Longman.

Greenfield, A. (2013) *Against the Smart City (The City is Here for You to Use)*, London: Verso.

Heidegger, M. (1962) *Being and Time*, trans. J. Macquarrie and E. Robinson, Oxford: Blackwell.

Heidegger, M. (1977) *The Question Concerning Technology, and Other Essays*, trans. W. Lovitt, New York: Harper Perennial.

Ihde, D. (1990) *Technology and the Lifeworld: From Garden to Earth*, Bloomington: Indiana University Press.

Kitchin, R. and Dodge, M. (2011) *Code/Space: Software and Everyday Life*, Cambridge MA: MIT Press.

Laermans, R. (2011) 'The attention regime: on mass media and the information society', in W. Schinkel and L. Noordegraaf-Eelens (eds) *In Media Res: Peter Sloterdijk's Spherical Poetics of Being*, Amsterdam: Amsterdam University Press.

Mackenzie, A. (2010) *Wirelessness: Radical Empiricism in Networked Cultures*, Cambridge, MA: MIT Press.

Merrin, W. (2014) 'The rise of the gadget and hyperludic me-dia', *Cultural Politics*, 10(1): 1–20.

Morin, M.E. (2009) 'Cohabitating in the globalised world: Peter Sloterdijk's global foams and Bruno Latour's cosmopolitics', *Environment and Planning D: Society and Space*, 27(1): 58–72.

Schinkel, W. and Noordegraaf-Eelens, L. (2011) 'Peter Sloterdijk's spherological acrobatics: an exercise in introduction', in W. Schinkel and L. Noordegraaf-Eelens (eds) *In Media Res: Peter Sloterdijk's Spherical Poetics of Being*, Amsterdam: Amsterdam University Press.

Shepard, M. (2011) *Sentient City: Ubiquitous Computing, Architecture and the Future of Urban Space*, Cambridge, MA: MIT Press.

Sloterdijk, P. (1998) *Sphären I – Blasen, Mikrosphärologie* [Spheres I – Bubbles, microspherology], trans. W. Hoban, Frankfurt am Main: Suhrkamp.

Sloterdijk, P. (1999) *Sphären II – Globen, Makrosphärologie* [Spheres II – Globes, macrospherology], trans. W. Hoban, Frankfurt am Main: Suhrkamp.

Sloterdijk, P. (2004) *Sphären III – Schäume, Plurale Sphärologie* [Spheres III – Bubbles, plural-spherology], trans. W. Hoban, Frankfurt am Main: Suhrkamp.

Thrift, N. (2014) 'The promise of urban informatics: some speculations', *Environment and Planning A*, 46(6): 1263–6.

van Manen, M. (1997) *Researching Lived Experience: Human Science for an Action Sensitive Pedagogy*, 2nd edn, London: Althouse Press.

van Tuinen, S. (2009) 'Air conditioning spaceship earth: Peter Sloterdijk's ethico-aesthetic paradigm', *Environment and Planning D: Society and Space*, 27(1): 105–18.

9 Curating the city

Urban interfaces and locative media as experimental platforms for cultural data

Nanna Verhoeff and Clancy Wilmott

Introduction

> When defining our identity and the identity of others, our sensory abilities are increasingly replaced by networked surveillance and identification technologies. How do we experience the way our body and identity are being 'measured' as functional and controllable products? Can touch based perception play again a role in experiencing the other's identity? [...] Together you compose new, temporary, non-traceable, and non-controllable networked identities.
>
> (Verhoeff and Cooley, 2014)

The local set-up of *Saving Face* by artists Karen Lancel and Herman Maat (2012) comprises a large, public, urban screen and an application with facial recognition software for a smaller screen, housed in a kiosk. The work invites participants to touch and trace their faces and thereby 'paint' themselves on the smaller screen in front of them, thus contributing their image to the database (see Figure 9.1). Meanwhile, the individual's face on the large screen transforms into a composite image of the larger community of participants, past and present, who have traced their faces. Between these various mechanisms, screen-to-screen communication across spaces, databases of tracings and interactive touchscreen technology, software and code work to bring together the urban interface of the artwork, structuring its relations and performativity as they arise. Yet, this interface structure is not accidental – such urban interfaces are coded and designed to experiment with their affordances, bringing to the fore discussions about contemporary public space, networked urban culture and the relationship between code and space. Furthermore, in the intersection between the datafication and the proliferation of digital interfaces for 'culture', artworks like *Saving Face* can help establish theoretical and analytical tools for the critical evaluation of these interfaces of cultural curation.

This article establishes three main arguments centred on these themes. First, we propose that the analysis of media artworks, installations and other locative-based media projects brings different conceptual and theoretical tools to

Figure 9.1 Saving Face installation
Source and copyright: 2013 Ruthe Zuntz, reproduced by permission.

the already growing fields of software studies (Manovich 2013) and the relationship of code and algorithms to cities and the built environment (Kitchin and Dodge 2011). As multiscreen, site-specific, social and participatory ecosystems, which work according to the dual principles of physical touch and, what Verhoeff and Cooley (2014) have called elsewhere, haptic, gestural 'looking', *Saving Face*, specifically, and other artworks, more generally, offer a context for reflecting on the movements of people and the circulation of data and images across platforms, the urban context as living and layered archive, and the activity and gestures that are elicited by a variety of screen-based, cultural interfaces. Because it allows the mobile subject in a public space to engage in the process of creation and dissemination of images, the artwork enables us to consider the specificities of current uses of mobile, interactive and networked media. It presents these as a process, an operation, working with technology, on the one hand, and as a communal, collaborative, public engagement on the other. As such, the work *is* what it *does*, or, if you prefer, it does what it is.

Second, the concerns of software studies and the programmable city are reflected into media artworks themselves, as they offer the potential to test the limitations of affordances, play with possibilities and engage embodiment and performativity at a stage of temporary reflexive impasse – wherein the artwork occupies a theoretical as well as material space. In this way, as a *theoretical object* – or object to 'think with', *Saving Face* can be used to interrogate how urban projects can be understood as (curatorial) laboratories for embodied criticality. It is an allegorical example of design, and an example of theoretical analysis. Indeed, the work is *reflexive*. It proposes itself as embodied thought, not only on interactive screen media, but also on a cultural understanding of the physical or material, as well as networked *connectivity*. It experiments with its technological affordances (Gibson 1979). It conducts such an experiment in that it works to critically expose how these affordances operate in the act of working with them. At the same time, *Saving Face* experiments with ways of addressing the social questions about subjectivity and visibility within a connected and participatory framework raised by the potential of its individual affordances. Thus, *Saving Face* can also be considered as performative and experimental, in the sense that it makes that which it analyses. This performative potential is the 'message', one could say, in McLuhan's terms (1964) – or, arguably: the medium is the method (Verhoeff 2013).[1]

The value of media analysis becomes evident when the relative transparency of these artworks is counterposed by the blackboxing of more pervasive, although no less curated, digital networked systems. As Kitchin and Dodge (2011) have argued, the countervalent nature of code/space is directly linked to urban systems, embedded within the built environment, regulating the flows and rhythms of the city. Furthermore, the proprietary status of many of these algorithms, and the way in which they are shrouded with a peculiar curtain of governmentality (Rouvroy and Stiegler 2015) means that they are often treated with (perhaps, rightful) suspicion because they are impossible to unpack without prior access to behind-the-scenes information. This limits the way in which we can understand these spaces. For example, this blackboxing means that, for the most part, the algorithms and geotracking software that govern space are both protected (copyrighted) and hidden away from scrutiny and criticism. However, rather than attempting to untangle what may well be an impossibly complicated web, it may be possible for artists and critics to grapple with the realities of code/space by using (small-scale) media projects that reconstruct such urban dispositifs and take them as examples to think *with*.

Departing from the specificities of the work *Saving Face*, such media or performance installations allow us as scholars (in the words of the artists) to understand and theorise particular sets of relations, including those of programmability, urban environments and algorithmic cultures. In fact, it is precisely because of their diversity – a diversity common in artistic and innovative design – that such tactical media projects (though in some cases they may be framed as educational projects), which want to positively and creatively embrace those technologies, can be used to help us think through their counterpart contemporary concerns: geolocative tracking and algorithmic power in code found in the digital cartography and database-logic that provides the grid for our urban mobility. While often unclear as to how or to what end these mobile technologies seem to inspire social and critical ambitions to not only call up location-specific data (whether trivia, commercial messages, entertaining or 'educational' content) but also allow for performative and 'awareness' enhancing, participatory forms of civic engagement or agency.

This leads to our third objective. This chapter addresses some theoretical underpinnings of an analytical approach to understanding how location-based media, or urban interfaces, layer urban spaces. It sketches some thoughts about a potentially critical–analytical approach to the 'cultural interfaces' (Manovich 2001) of current urban projects that use location-based media, and it offers an approach to understanding these projects as curatorial machines for cultural data. To do this, we zoom in on efforts such as *Saving Face* to provide access to data and their collections – whether or not instigated by museal and archival institutions or whether more bottom-up civic collaborative projects. These works, as theoretical objects, allow us to investigate layering as a design principle for urban interfaces as navigational laboratories.

These three issues foreground a long-standing interest in the way in which mobility shapes our visual practices: in the way we act, experience and think *with* mobility. This thinking-with is what underlies creativity and experimentation. To be precise: in design we find this thinking-with at the intersection of technology and practice. As such, navigation and mobility entail more than the portability of devices, the principles of ubiquitous computing or the temporality embedded in what we can call performative digital cartography. Mobility and navigation are cultural in the sense that they not only bring forward process as a cultural form, and emphasise not only the experiential and performative but also the philosophical nature of being-in-the-world, but they also shape our thinking in and as a process. This emphasis on thinking-with accompanies an ongoing dialogue with figures that function as tropes: figures or spatiotemporal visualisations which bring together a metaphoric and systemic logic of using and thinking about media – for instance, the navigational as trope of mobility in the visual culture of the moving image. A powerful, pervasive, yet sometimes uncritically used metaphor of layering can be useful to describe the experience of using mobile and location-based screen technologies, but it needs to be specified in analytical terms, in our opinion, in order to become a true concept.

Here, we focus on the logic of layers and layering that we can recognise in our use of and thinking about media technologies as cultural interfaces – interfaces that bring us tools to reflect on culture. In this sense, it means moving beyond systems and relations to explore the performativity of interface technologies, which occurs in the reciprocity of creativity and reflexivity. How does design work with what we can do with technologies and how does this become a thematic in itself: how does design work with, and, by this, also reflect on these affordances? It is the critical implication of questioning by doing in design that we wish to address in the context of the role of code in urban experience: in what way can we embrace code as a critical means to interrogate urban culture?

The curatorial in dispositifs

In the face of fast-paced innovation and transition, it is necessary to develop concepts that may help us to approach the diversity and fugitivity of projects as urban interfaces; to frame them in a coherent conceptual universe in order

120   *Nanna Verhoeff and Clancy Wilmott*

to better grasp the details, their comparative specificity and to assess their historicity.[2] The dispositif – the arrangement that encapsulates technology, subject and image – is particularly useful as a heuristic device that is scalable for the comparative analysis of any systemic or composite object (van den Boomen 2014). It allows us to historicise and situate, synchronically or diachronically, differences and similarities between media forms.

The concept of dispositif is wide-ranging and far-reaching. Michel de Certeau (1980) offered a critique of Foucault's famous 'panoptic' conception of the dispositif as a formation for surveillance and control, and has inspired an approach to dispositif as that which opens up 'possibilities of contact, participation, play, as well as bodily and sensual experiences' (Kessler 2007)[3] This reconsideration of dispositif as a networked arrangement that allows for various forms of agency and performativity is useful for a pragmatic, analytical approach to interactive and locative interfaces.[4] Media dispositifs can thus be understood as the arrangements that establish relations and processes between, and organise spatial and temporal settings of, technologies and practices that produce subjects and shared meanings. We take the location-based projects under discussion, with *Saving Face* as the primary example, as installation-dispositifs that comprise a layered interface – layeredness here understood as the spatiotemporal relations designed in, and organised by, the interface. The notion of layering is designed to be productive for the analysis of hybrid compositions of interfaces, of images and of spatial constructions of navigation, which are produced in the act of interfacing.

Moreover, the concept of the curatorial puts a specific spin on that concept of dispositif; one that begs for an analysis of this layering, and enables us to analytically tease out the relationship established by the installation and the larger urban dispositif that encapsulates the work. Dispositifs, or any kind of spatiotemporal spectatorial and participatory arrangement, entail a form of curatorial design. The curatorial is here understood as a broader conceptual framework for the design of, and programming within, cultural spaces – whether virtual, social, geographical or conceptual – than the more narrow sense of curation as the professional practice of designing museum exhibitions. It constructs a reflexive positioning of elements, it is constituted in its operation (in the vein of curatorial machines) and is embodied in the experience of the possibilities of contact, and of playful and participatory engagement invoked by this design. It is this coming together of thought and experience that is at stake in curatorial design: an embedded and embodied criticality below the surface.

For our understanding of the curatorial, as derived from the word curation used for museum and other exhibition practices, we may bring together the English 'to expose', which includes the meaning of 'laying bare' and the French verb 'exposer' – to display, as well as to argue (Bal 1996: 8). It is this specific combination of analysis and argument, or the analytical and the rhetorical, that we can recognise as main principles of 'the curatorial' across disciplines and in different cultural contexts. Indeed, within our mediatised culture, we speak more and more of curatorial practices outside of institutional walls. The city has been conceptualised as urban, curatorial space, for example. The authors of *Digital_Humanities* define curation in analytical and rhetorical terms in the context of digital, networked culture, as: 'the selection and organisation of materials in an interpretive framework, argument, or exhibit' (Burdick *et al.* 2012: 17).

Whatever the medium, platform or institutional context, curation can be seen as *care* for the constellation of elements – their selection and organisation – and their interpretative framework. Indeed, as Burdick *et al.* (2012: 18) continue: 'Rather than being viewed as autonomous or self-evident, artefacts can be seen being shaped by and shaping complex networks of influence, production, dissemination, and reception, animated by multilayered debates and historical forces.' To curate, then, is: 'to filter, organise, craft, and, ultimately, care for a story composed out of – even rescued from – the infinite array of potential tales, relics, and voices' (Burdick *et al.* 2012: 34). Or, in the concise summary by Marc James Leger, curation is 'a practice that creates a space for discourse and critique' (Leger 2013: 12) – a space-making, discursive, and critical endeavour. When we speak of interactive and networked installations or systems, this discursive and framing aspect of curation is part of the design of creative engagement between artefact and public in interaction. This performative potential of media-based dispositifs involves curatorial design.

Interestingly, a similarity with media has inspired work on museums and exhibition practices as well. For example, Kossmann *et al.* (2012) have a symmetrically opposite perspective and argue for an understanding of museum exhibitions as media in a McLuhanian sense, including their essential 'transforming potential'. The authors point out how the 'open, associative nature of the format' fits the cultural moment (Kossmann *et al.* 2012: 33). They consider the exhibition as an 'interface with a critical function, directing the view and transforming the message into a manifest interpretation'. For an interest in interactive mobile or location-based media, the analogy with exhibitions as spatial media through a concept of interface is inspiring for the development of a critical approach to these practices. In this comparison, we would include tours (audio tours, mapped tours, GPS-based, augmented-reality applications, etc.) as mobile forms of exhibition.[5] A necessary step in this comparison of curation of museum exhibitions and curation in media projects is to discern the distinction between curation by the project itself – the curatorial at work, so to speak – and the institutionally embedded practice of curation of these projects within, for example, a collection, a museum, or an archive.

Taking the curatorial as a heuristic concept, we can move from the technical principles of exhibition and programming practices in institutional contexts, and focus in our analysis of the underlying curatorial logic within dispositifs of public, urban installations or media projects in the broadest sense. This can contribute to a conceptualisation of a notion of cultural curation that brings together the multiple levels on which the curatorial logic is at work.

Dispositifs as curatorial machines

Within a culture that so privileges innovation, urban interfaces are much like 'laboratories for experimentation', to borrow a term from science and technology studies. An experimental system, a laboratory can be conceived of as: 'a heterogeneous constellation of theories, objects, instruments and practices redefining each other constantly and whereby this redefining is the result of a play with possibilities and, ultimately, a form of problematisation' (Keilbach and Strauff 2012: 83). Indeed, these urban interfaces explore and question their own possibilities. While we creatively invest in these projects and herald them as new interfaces for civic engagement, playful learning and participatory culture, we need to develop tools for analysis, comparison and criticism.[6] However, traditional evaluative criticism struggles in understanding qualities that are also, precisely, inherent vulnerabilities of urban interfaces. When it comes to concerns about meaning and sustainability, our thinking about innovative and experimental interfaces must take into account the fact that such interfaces are inherently short-lived, that they enable but also require participatory engagement, and that they have a transformative potential that may or not be effectively deployed.

So, let us start with the specificity of urban, location-specific media 'projects'. We consider these *as* dispositifs, in the sense of spatiotemporal situations or assemblages that bind together the image, the interface and the interfacing subject. We make a distinction, here, between the *interface* such as the device, installation, or screen as the site of input and output (when we speak of what we see and use) and the *apparatus* when we refer to the wider machinic assemblage of which it is part, which comprises, for example, also software, network protocols, GPS, online connectivity, etc. We speak of *dispositif* when we are concerned with the arrangement or relational system of interface and subject. This entails a perspective on the performativity of urban interfaces characterised by connectivity, participation and navigation, and brings to the fore the transformative, and thus, inherently critical potential of urban interfaces. This transformative potential is the locus of experience and meaning and, hence, cultural significance of design.

Central to this argument, and what we will consider here, is a concern with what we understand as critical and how curatorial ambitions of criticality and care can be analysed in the context of these urban projects. This concern is augmented by often uncritical interpretations of criticality – ones which assume a simple deconstructionist approach or are pseudo-political yet do not allow us to theorise and reconceptualise its foundations. Central, then, in this context, is the concept of dispositif, for it allows us to consider both the specificity of arrangements or assemblages – the design of elements and set-up that includes a participatory subject – and a critical perspective for how this subject is encapsulated and constructed by this design.

Many use the term 'critical' often but what do they mean by it? How does it work? What does it do? In the case of performative, interactive, participatory

Curating the city 123

urban media interventions, it is perhaps productive to approach this as an embedded and embodied criticality. Criticality, in Irit Rogoff's (2006) terminology, refers to a performative function of critique, which is experienced in encounter, which 'takes places' at the interface:

> [...] in a reflective shift, from the analytical to the *performative* function of observation and of *participation*, we can agree that meaning is not excavated for, but rather, that it 'takes place' in the present. The latter exemplifies not just the dynamics of learning from, of looking at and of interacting with, works of art in exhibitions and in public spaces, but echoes also the modes by which we have inhabited the critical and the theoretical over the recent past. It seems to me that within the space of a relatively short period we have been able to move from *criticism* to *critique*, and to what I am calling at present *criticality*. That is that we have moved [...] to criticality which is operating from an uncertain ground of actual *embeddedness*.
>
> (Rogoff 2006: 2; emphasis added)

It is there, outside the regime of representation and in the realm of performativity, that, according to Rogoff, active and critical participants are produced. Indeed, interactive media design often explicitly addresses the connection between thinking and doing. By bringing together the creative, experimental and critical, philosophical underpinnings of the social-political ambition of design, this reflection underscores the way in which design works with a layering of urban space – a layering that allows for a participatory and critical engagement with urban culture; a layering that is designed and curated. As such, it is possible to approach urban interfaces, or location-specific 'media projects', as curatorial machines; they are designed as techno-social assemblages that practise curation – the verb 'practise' understood here to indicate process, rather than product – as they filter, select, order, shape content and meaning, and position the public as spectator or participant.

Saving Face as a curatorial machine

Let us now sketch two sets of aspects that we can develop in the analysis of curation: the earlier coupled analytical and rhetorical aspect of curatorial design (curatorial vision), and the overarching mission of care and critical potential (criticality) inherent in what we can call cultural curation: the care for and critical investment in the relationship between these three levels of curation. We do this by looking at the way *Saving Face*, in a reflexive gesture, demonstrates, questions, and, as such, critiques these aspects.

As a laboratory for experimentation, this work thematises the way in which its design establishes new connections, allows for forms of interaction

124   *Nanna Verhoeff and Clancy Wilmott*

and encourages forms of haptic and participatory engagement. It asks for a critical–analytical perspective on its status: to make visible and to question the project as a form of design that, itself, makes statements about its own inherent critical potential, its criticality, that stems from the reciprocity of analysis and argument.

Saving Face explicitly addresses three aspects of the layered and location-based interface that are brought together within a dispositif of urban interfaces: the participatory agency of the individual in the act of interfacing, the installation as public event, and the questioning of traceability of the image in the composite, networked collection or database. There lies its performativity.[7] Significant about *Saving Face* is the centrality of the face in this layering – as the central image on the urban screen, in the intimacy of the participant's gesture of stroking one's own face in order to conjure up the screen image as a networked composition: a collage of the different faces of other, earlier participants. The title of the work with the double entendre of recording one's face and not losing face in front of (or facing) a public, brings to the fore the question of individuality and public identity. The face as quintessential communicative element in interaction provokes us to probe the notion of 'interface' as central to curatorial design.

The interface of the installation works with the principle of touch and a haptic and material form of looking as a gesture of making, saving and tracing the image, and, as such, seems to comment on several issues at stake in our argument. As an artwork, it puts technology and connectivity between the hand, the screens, and the archive, database or network centre stage. It is an interface *par excellence* and literalised by visualising the way it functions as technological arrangement and the touch of the user that activates its operation. On the one hand, the artwork reminds its participants that they are being seen; that to be in urban, public space means to be visible. On the other hand, it endeavours to intervene in how visibility operates, how visibility – the public face – signifies. The gesture of touching one's own face in order to visualise one's self in relation to others points to the processual character of navigational gesture in the context of location-aware technologies. In this way, it harkens back to a long history in which photography (art) and policing (governance) are mutually informing. The artists themselves acknowledge this connection:

> In a visual, poetic way *Saving Face* shows our emotional and social encounter with trust, visibility, privacy in our 'smart' cities. When defining our identity and the identity of others, our sensory abilities are increasingly replaced by networked surveillance and identification technologies. How do we experience the way our body and identity are being 'measured' as functional and controllable products? Can touch based perception play again a role in experiencing the other's identity?
>
> (Lancel and Maat, 2012)[8]

Curating the city 125

As the artists indicate, *Saving Face* counters the abstraction we frequently encounter in public places. It gives significance to an activity – navigation and its gesture – that is routine, everyday and, presumably, inconsequential. By returning the 'face' to 'interface', the project raises questions about presence, subjectivity, visibility and the anonymity often attributed to being in public. The work is highly personal, yet combines the private intimacy of auto-touch – a gestural selfie – with a highly public and collaborative, yet very temporary, visibility on screen.

The collage of different faces displayed on screen is a tracing – as well as a tracking – of multiple actions by multiple participants accumulating and metamorphosing across multiple moments. A composite image, it speaks symbolically to the multiplicity of subjectivity and to the temporal layering of various individual presences. The processuality of the navigational gesture does leave a trace – albeit an untraceable one. An iconic image of individual faces – fractured and reassembled into a new whole – it says: 'we were here' rather than who we are. The image testifies to past gestures, the image's morphing evolution inviting further interaction and gesturing. At the same time, each live update of this visualisation keeps record of – or tracks – the to-be-future traces (uploaded in a Flickr stream). The installation bears witness to and renders visible the processual layering that is the semiotic process of the navigational gesture: a trace of the act of tracing.

The way in which the urban, public context is a layer in the design that requires curating, becomes clear when we consider the way this installation – like so many locative media or artworks – travels. Its location specificity is one that is, paradoxically, flexible. Elsewhere, Verhoeff (2012) has spoken about the ambulant locatedness of mobile media; here, migrating locatedness may be more appropriate. Indeed, each location-specific installation entails curatorial design, as not every public place is the same. While both are urban spaces, on a well-known square in Amsterdam, the work functions differently from, say, within the walls of a museum.

For example, a different version of *Saving Face*, named *Master Touch* (Lancel and Maat 2013), was set up in the then-newly opened Rijksmuseum for the special occasion of the Museum Night in 2013. There, the images of participants merged with faces of paintings. The similarity between the two installations allows us to consider what makes them different. If we depart from an analysis of dispositif, this comparison between both works hinges, we would say, very much on both the level of the location specificity of the spatial context and the level of its networked connectivity – in the second case, comprising a dataset of images from the museum collection rather than other participants from other locations or other moments.

The description the artists give highlights some interestingly different keywords: '*Master Touch* is an engaging and innovative way to open up data from the digital museum collection for the audience' (Lancel and Maat 2013). This mission sounds different from the earlier cited descriptor of *Saving Face*: 'In a visual, poetic way, *Saving Face* shows our emotional and social

126   *Nanna Verhoeff and Clancy Wilmott*

encounter with trust, visibility, privacy in our 'smart' cities'. We do not have space to go further into the specificity of these differences in vision and mission – nor into the theoretical question about whether and how to consider these as either different installations or different instalments of the same installation – but the juxtaposition of their similarities and differences hopefully demonstrates our point about the levels of the curatorial design of layered interfaces of networked, locative dispositifs.

The design of the interface can be considered a form of curation-at-work, as it makes visible the layers of curation as process. It reflects on the layering of the cultural dispositif that comprises the *in-situ* installation, the local urban and public context and the spatiotemporal interlocal network it is embedded in. Curation on this level entails the design of the possible interaction with technology to generate images, to contribute them to a collection, to create compositions, to disseminate for an engaging, local public. It is curation of curation – so to speak – an embodied self-reflexivity. By *working* with these principles, the installation demonstrates its principles. This opens up to the critical potential inherent in the curatorial.

Conclusion: care and criticality

But what of the curatorial ambition of care? Let us remind ourselves that curation comes from the verb 'to care'. This may seem like a detour from the concept of the curatorial and of software, code and the built environment, but in fact, care is indispensable in all times and places to allow life to be sustained, including the life of social ensembles we call cultures. But care is necessary in many respects, not just in the sense of sustainability. The need to care for objects includes what is usually called conservation in the context of collections, but also the quality of their presentation. It includes the inter-relations amongst objects and the enhanced meanings that may generate in their dialogue.

Moreover, care is needed for the objects' dialogue with the public, including but not limited to physical interactivity. All this may seem to suggest that we must hold the objects' hand, in an affective relationship. But rather than such a chaperone model, curation can also be thought of as the design of a laboratory. Then, it is not so much in relation to this more nostalgic notion of care in conservation, but rather as care for the arrangement of possibilities and experimentation.

Let us conclude with some thoughts about the implications of the model of curating as an analytical framing concept and frame the features, potential and consequences for a broader notion of cultural curating. Through the notion of curating, we can reflect on urban media with the question about what we may take as the consequences of performativity as central to dispositifs of networked, location-based, interactive technologies: the question of care and criticality in design. The curation of culture is the agency and creativity that connects the making with the dissemination of images.

Curating the city 127

The agency is, then, thought of in terms of affordances and responsibilities; the creativity as productive, personal and critical; making, contributing and assessing.[9]

This conclusion is also a proposal to think of design in terms of care. In what way can we embrace and make use of those technologies that potentially change (or have changed) the status of the image? Our key word, care, can be seen to be embodied, or practised, in the installation *Saving Face*. There, the central and intimate act of stroking one's face becomes a contribution to a shared collage, or composite image. This gesture is literally, as well as figuratively, care-ful: the visibility of the subject being on a public screen, adding to the community, underscores the personal and hence responsible nature of the act of participating. One becomes visually part of the image, adding one's face to the otherwise anonymous image.

Networked culture and technological innovation demand changing the principles and the philosophy of the design of public engagement. New platforms outside of the institutions provide new curatorial spaces, and technologies offer new tools for public interventions. Moreover, curation in and of urban space necessarily involves multiple levels of (spatiotemporal) design: of the dispositif of the location-based project, of the urban dispositif, as well as the more distributed and interlocal networked dispositif. The principles of current networked, urban culture and our fast-changing media technologies not only demand critical thinking about, or better, within design, but also offer the tools to change practices of engaging publics. Indeed, transformation and change require and enable a fundamentally critical stance: not a critique outside of it, but a criticality embedded or embodied within design. Changing technologies demands not only for critical reflection on design but, perhaps more urgently, a criticality within design – a design of the interaction with technology that allows for a closer experience of the processes of its framing as a poetic act. As interactive projects, or curatorial machines such as *Saving Face* exemplify, it is by being in touch with the work that we participate in its examination, by tracing its criticality below the surface.

Notes

1 Elsewhere, Verhoeff (2013) has invoked McLuhan's (1964) famous dictum in the title of an essay on the performative nature of interactive technologies and the agency involved in using interfaces for navigation.
2 Lev Manovich's (2001) conception of cultural interfaces is a dialogue of software operation and human activity in their operation, in a working together of cultural, technological and 'human' registers.
3 See Kessler (2007). Kessler is specifically referring here to a special issue of *Hermès* (no 25, 1999).
4 Inspired by similar questions is a more 'science–technology–society' approach to networks that focuses on processes in which human and non-human actors operate. Similar is the network-based thinking, but in contrast with perspectives of 'science–technology–society' or 'actor–network theory', dispositif analysis is more concerned with questions of subjectivity, discourse and power.

128 *Nanna Verhoeff and Clancy Wilmott*

5 But then, exhibitions are already inherently mobile, if we consider their performativity as I have unpacked it at the beginning of this chapter. The spectator, visitor or participant is, after all, mobile in the exhibition. The tour, then, is only a geographically wider net to capture what is at stake in exhibition.
6 Civic learning can be considered 'a form of engagement that combines participation with the act of reflection'. See Gordon and Baldwin-Philippi (2014).
7 As argued elsewhere, the notion of 'layering' is meant to be productive for the analysis of hybrid compositions of interfaces, images and spatial constructions of navigation, as a product of interfacing (Verhoeff 2012).
8 For moving images of *Saving Face* see Lancel and Maat (2011).
9 Others have made a plea for the connection between critique and analysis, and the making of images. Laura Marks (2002), for example, has developed a notion of haptic visuality to conceptualise a more intimate form of critique, and Kember and Zylinska (2012: xvii) speak of media production and enactment and plead for a form of *doing* media studies – a creative mediation – that is critique 'accompanied by the work of participation and invention'.

References

Bal, M. (1996) *Double Exposures: The Practice of Cultural Analysis*, London: Routledge.
Burdick, A. Drucker, J. Lunenfeld, P. Presner, T. and Schnapp, J. (2012) *Digital_ Humanities*, Cambridge MA: MIT Press.
de Certeau, M. (1980) *L'Invention du Quotidien, 1: Arts de Faire*, Paris: Éditions du Cerf.
Gibson, J. (1979) *The Ecological Approach to Visual Perception*, Boston: Houghton Mifflin.
Gordon, E. and Baldwin-Philippi, J. (2014) 'Playful civic learning: enabling reflection and lateral trust in game-based public participation', *International Journal of Communication*, 8: 759–86.
Keilbach, J. and Strauff, M. (2012) 'When old media never stopped being new: television's history as an ongoing experiment', in M. de Valck and J. Teurlings (eds) *After the Break: Television Theory Today*, Amsterdam: Amsterdam University Press.
Kember, S. and Zylinksa, J. (2012) *Life after New Media: Mediation as a Vital Process*, Cambridge, MA: MIT Press.
Kessler, F. (2007) 'Notes on *dispositif*', *Utrecht Media Research Seminar*, available from http://www.hum.uu.nl/medewerkers/f.e.kessler/Dispositif%20Notes11-2007.pdf [accessed 25 August 2015].
Kitchin, R. and Dodge, M. (2011) *Code/Space: Software and Everyday Life*, Cambridge MA: MIT Press.
Kossmann, H., Mulder, S. and den Oudsten, F. (2012) *Narrative Spaces: On the Art of Exhibiting*, Rotterdam: 101 Publishers.
Lancel, K. and Maat, H. (2011) *Saving Face*, available from https://vimeo.com/28499178 [accessed 24 November 2015].
Lancel, K. and Maat, H. (2012) *Saving Face*, available from www.lancelmaat.nl/work/saving-face/ [accessed 17 May 2015].
Lancel, K. and Maat, H. (2013) *Master Touch*, available from www.lancelmaat.nl/work/master-touch [accessed 20 November 2015].
Leger, M.J. (2013) 'Homo academicus curatorius: millet matrix as intercultural paradigm', *On Curating*, 19(June 2013): 14–22.

McLuhan, M. (1964) *The Medium Is the Message*, Cambridge MA: MIT Press.

Manovich, L. (2001) *The Language of New Media*, Cambridge, MA: MIT Press.

Manovich, L. (2013) *Software Takes Command*, New York: Bloomsbury Academic.

Marks, L. (2002) *Touch: Sensuous Theory and Multisensory Media*, Minneapolis: University of Minnesota Press.

Rogoff, I. (2006) *'Smuggling'* – *An Embodied Criticality*, available from http://curatorial.net/resources/Rogoff_Smuggling.pdf [accessed 25 August 2015].

Rouvroy, A. and Stiegler, B. (2015) 'Le régime de vérité numérique: de la gouvernementalité algorithmique à un nouvel État de droit', *Socio*, 4: 113–40, available from https://socio.revues.org/1251 [accessed 25 August 2015].

van den Boomen, M. (2014) *Transcoding the Digital: How Metaphors Matter in New Media*, Amsterdam: Institute of Network Cultures.

Verhoeff, N. (2012) *Mobile Screens: The Visual Regime of Navigation*, Amsterdam: Amsterdam University Press.

Verhoeff, N. (2013) 'The medium is the method: locative media for digital archives', in J. Eckel, B. Leiendecker, D. Olek and C. Piepiorka (eds) *(Dis)Orienting Media and Narrative Mazes*, Bielefeld: Transcript.

Verhoeff, N. and Cooley, H. (2014) 'The navigational gesture: traces and tracings at the mobile touchscreen interface', *Necsus #5: Traces*, available from http://www.necsus-ejms.org/navigational-gesture-traces-tracings-mobile-touchscreen-interface/ [accessed 25 August 2015].

10 Moving applications

A multilayered approach to mobile computing

James Merricks White

Introduction

Smartphone applications (or apps) are a relatively recent but already near-ubiquitous media for engaging with the city, particularly in the global north. A search for 'Dublin' on Apple's App Store and Google Play reveals a rich marketplace of apps for, amongst other things: catching up on local news, monitoring flight arrivals, navigating tourist attractions, negotiating bus timetables, finding bicycle or car hire services, paying for parking, discovering events and finding the right restaurant. Smartphone applications are a common, everyday way of exploring the city. For an urban geographer interested in the intersection of code and the city, smartphone applications offer a rich seam of research, but one that is not without its challenges. On the surface, applications offer a quite simple representation of information about a particular subject. But to perform this task they rely on a vast network of interlocking technologies with a complex spatial topology. This chapter offers a multilayered model, to open the black box, and provide a heuristic for critically examining mobile applications. The aim of this model is clear enough to be readily graspable, but not so reductive as to limit empirical engagement.

This chapter is organised in three parts. I begin by looking at different approaches to computational technology in the city from within the discipline of geography. I make the argument that previous research has tended to focus on one particular layer of what I am calling the socio-technical stack and so fetishise that layer at the expense of others. I next present a multilayered model and chart its conceptual origin within media studies and science and technology studies. This is then used to think through two apps, Hailo and Moves, with particular attention given to their points of intersection with urban politics. This discussion is based on my own experience with the applications, on informal discussions with friends and colleagues, and on encounters with people using the applications in Dublin. I will – not unproblematically – refer to a 'normal use' of Hailo and Moves. I conclude by touching on what a multilayered approach might mean for geographical enquiry into code and the city, and by highlighting some of the literature that might prove useful in developing a more fully conceived ontology.

Moving applications   131

The geography of mobile computing

While geographers have theorised the spatialities of hardware (Graham and Marvin 2001), software (Kinsley 2014) and data (Wilson 2011), there remains little concerted effort within the discipline to explore mobile computing as a socio-technical system that incorporates all of these aspects.

In their development of the concept of splintering urbanism, Graham and Marvin (2001) emphasise the control that private and publicly listed companies increasingly have over networked infrastructure. They contend that the liberalisation and privatisation of the welfare state has led to an unbundling and stratification of utility provision and an overshadowing of its role within everyday life. While their exploration of the politics of infrastructure has motivated proper attention to the materialities of technology in the city, Graham and Marvin focus on political economic forces. As a result, they leave unexplored two questions important to a study of mobile computing. How do networked devices move? And how can computationally enabled agency be properly accounted for?

The geography of software offers some ways to begin to address these questions. For Thrift and French (2002), software is both a hybrid human-object network and a performative textuality. In the first instance, the modelling of algorithms after biological systems has imbued in software a semi-artificial life. Software is understood as a non-human actor, capable of its own agency but contingent upon its contextual relations. In the second instance, software is presented as a way of doing by writing; 'a new kind of cultural memory' (Thrift and French 2002: 310). Code is thus able to write new geographies, of which Thrift and French draw attention to geographies of software production, geographies of power and geographies of play. While making an important theoretical contribution, Thrift and French tend to elide the very real spatial inequalities within which software is produced and in turn reproduces.

Stephen Graham (2005) addresses the politics of computation in the city by introducing the concept of software-sorted geographies. A software-sorted geography is any space that has been produced through automated analysis and regulation. Graham focuses on three kinds of geography: (1) urban access and mobility, controlled by automated traffic and transportation systems; (2) planning and construction, mediated through the use of geographical information and geodemographic systems; and (3) the use of algorithmic closed circuit television systems to record, and then sort, order and classify people and objects in the city. The concealment of the decision making processes that produce such geographies leads Graham to argue that software must be understood as thoroughly political.

Through the introduction of the concept of code/space, Kitchin and Dodge (2011) have endeavoured to show how software and space are mutually constituted. A code/space is a processual transduction of space produced to solve a specific problem – one example they give is of the code/space produced in an airport when one seeks to check in; if the computers are not working, then the

132   *James Merricks White*

space is not transduced as intended and instead acts as a waiting room. Code/ spaces owe their existence to correctly functioning software; if the software program crashes or encounters fatal errors, the code/space cannot be formed or sustained. This allows Kitchin and Dodge to illustrate that the experience of everyday life in the city is determined by software (which is, itself, dependent on a coming together of contested technologies, subjectivities and practices) acting in a range of capacities and across a variety of scales.

Taking up the theoretical work of Kitchin and Dodge, Wilson (2011) argues that data, through processes of standardisation and objectification, have both material form and significance. Data, metadata and their storage in databases are standardised as methods of organising, storing, transporting and retrieving information. Held together by geographically situated practices, a data set might then be understood as an assemblage of different actors and institutions, contingent but distinct from software: a data infrastructure (Lauriault 2012; Kitchin 2014).

While geographies of software and more recent work on data infrastructures help account for the mobility and secondary agency of mobile computing, these approaches often downplay the contested materialities of computer hardware. There is, in effect, a collapsing of the actual into the virtual (Kinsley 2014). If researchers are to properly examine the ways in which computation is articulated through its normal use, it will be necessary, as Gabrys has argued (2014: 39), to consider the way in which software is interwoven with other material aspects of the computational apparatus. To this end, I will now offer a model of interdependent technologies, what might be called a socio-technical stack, for the examination of mobile computing (Losey 2014). By giving hardware, data(bases) and media interfaces an equivalent ontological attention to software, I hope to reveal previously unaccounted for intersections of computation and the city.

The hardware–code–data(base)–interface stack

The production of computation is generated, I contend, through four interlocking and hierarchically organised components: hardware, code, data(base) and media interfaces (see the right-hand part of Figure 10.1).[1] This is not presented as a realist conceptualisation of smartphone applications, but rather in the hope that it might serve as a useful heuristic in critical examinations of mobile computing systems. Before applying these concepts to the apps Hailo and Moves, I will outline the origin of the stack model within media studies, and science and technology studies.

Legal scholar Yochai Benkler offers a model of the Internet (see the left-hand part of Figure 10.1) composed of three discrete layers (2006: 391–392): physical, logical and content. The physical layer consists of the material infrastructure, which connects people together. The content layer includes both the meaningful representations, which people use to communicate, and the mechanisms by which people filter, accredit and interpret that content.

Moving applications 133

Finally, the logical layer connects the physical and content layers through codified algorithms, standards and protocols of interaction. All three layers are necessary for communication and all three layers form the locus of distinct policy debates.

Jonathan Zittrain (2008) adapts Benkler's model, to explore the generative nature of communicative computational technologies. His model (see the centre part of Figure 10.1) is best represented as a technological layer (which is itself composed of physical (material) and protocol (translative) layers), an application layer, and then more tentatively asserted content and social layers (Zittrain 2008: 67). The physical layer includes the wires or airwaves through which data move. Above that is the application layer, which encompasses all of the various and multifaceted work performed by people with computation. Between these two layers is a mediating protocol layer. Zittrain likens the protocol to the neck of an hourglass through which everything flows. As counterpoint to the underdeveloped content and social layers (which consist of the information exchanged in a network and the embodied practices enabled by the model respectively), I propose that the technological and the application layers might better be understood as embedded sociotechnical assemblages, which are continually being produced in a citational manner by human and non-human actors operating at diverse capacities and scales. Such a framing repositions the protocol as open to contestation, but also acknowledges the role it plays within a larger computational apparatus as an instrument of governance.

While the models developed by Zittrain and Benkler suitably emphasise the fixing of mobile computing's various components into hierarchies of technological interdependence, their concepts fail to align with those experienced by, and co-productive of, normal use. In her deconstruction of popular social media platforms, media and communications scholar José van Dijck (2013) weds science and technology studies with a critical approach to political economy. Drawing on the aims of actor–network theory 'to map relations between technologies and people and [...] to explain how these relations are

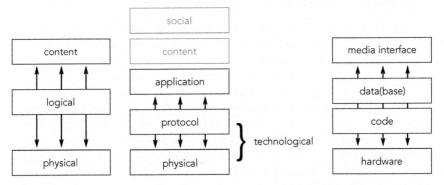

Figure 10.1 From left to right: Benkler's model, Zittrain's model and the proposed model

134 *James Merricks White*

both material and semiotic' (2013: 26), van Dijck proposes five concepts to trace the socio-technological relations of online social networking platforms. These are: meta(data), algorithms, protocols, interfaces and defaults. Data are the quantitative and qualitative information used for computation and metadata the information used to order and understand those data. An algorithm is a list of instructions a computer follows to produce a certain output from a specific input. Protocols are codified behaviours and norms of computational interaction. Interfaces, both internal and customer-facing, mediate interaction, effectively translating the desires of the user to code and vice versa. Finally, defaults are settings that are automatically assigned within a piece of software. This framework is specific enough to examine the materialities and power networks of mobile computing, and it refrains from reducing the social to an effect of the technological. By not focusing on hardware, however, it uproots computational technology from its material geography. While this may allow van Dijck to examine social media as a global and globalising technology, it renders the model unsuitable for analyses where the local is significant.

By focusing on hardware and restricting interfaces to media interfaces (see the right-hand part of Figure 10.1), I am attempting to allow for the way in which the flows of code and data are, in the first instance, reliant upon geographically distributed technology and, in the second, reterritorialised at the point of their consumption. Rather than include all of van Dijck's concepts, I reposition protocols and defaults as supporting scripts, which intertwine with the four layers of the model and enable them to come together. It is my hope that the hardware–code–data(base)–interface model allows not only for the mobility of mobile computing, but also the way in which it is processually articulated in specific and situated ways. In the next sections, I present two examples of how the model can be used to make sense of the taxi service application, Hailo, and the personal life-logging application, Moves.

Hailo and the externalisation of fixed capital

Hailo is the market-leading smartphone taxi app in Ireland. Launched in July 2012, the service is currently used by around half of Dublin's 12,000 taxi drivers. In this section, I use the proposed socio-technical stack to explore how Hailo does work in the world and argue that its business model is dependent upon infrastructure that is external to its operating costs.

When using the Hailo app (Figure 10.2), the immediate and most obvious hardware that a person interacts with is the piece in their hand. The smartphone is an instantly recognisable artefact, at once a cohesive, singular object and an assemblage of specific (and often rare) materials and digital components. Just as the smartphone blackboxes its workings from a user, so too does its consumable form distance the user from the work contributing to its design, sourcing and production. While the compact form of the smartphone

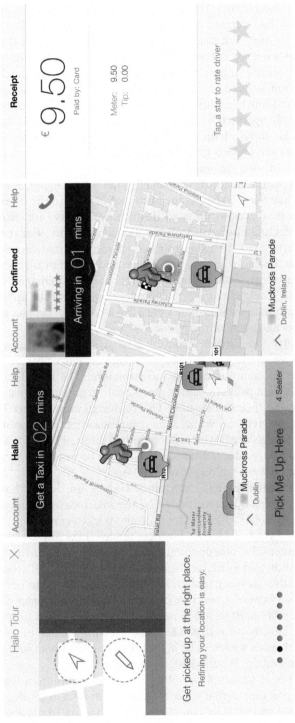

Figure 10.2 From left to right: Hailo tour feature (location refinement), taxis near Muckross Parade, tracking the driver in real time and automatic card payment

Source: Hailo app screenshots. Dates: (a) 11 November 2013; (b), (c) & (d) 7 March 2014

136   *James Merricks White*

is fundamental to its mobility, the arrangement of hardware, code and data transmission protocols recruited by Hailo far exceed the media interface manipulated by its user. When a user orders a taxi using Hailo, the phone transmits data to a nearby cell tower, which then routes this data onto the Internet and on towards Hailo's servers. If the user then phones the driver to confirm the location, instead of routing data on to the Internet, the cell tower passes it to the fixed-line telecommunications infrastructure. In Ireland, these networks are largely operated by Eircom, a formerly state-owned monopoly, which was floated on the Irish and New York stock exchanges in 1999. Individual carriers lease access to this infrastructure at a cost, which is ostensibly passed on to the user through fees and contracts.

Both code and (meta)data are crucial in allowing this exchange of information to occur. While the interface is the most visible layer to the users, many of the communicative actions initiated through normal use are carried out by the code architecture upon which the application operates. For reasons of security, third-party access to a smartphone's underlying hardware is strictly mediated by both the phone's operating system and the firmware running on its baseband processor. A smartphone's functionality is managed through code libraries and frameworks used in the development of an application. The Hailo application reveals itself as a cohesive whole but is in fact interwoven with the code–hardware of the phone.

This permeability goes further. Transmitted data are bundled up with specific information about the data to ensure that they are correctly received and processed by the telecommunications infrastructure. The metadata, found in the header of a data packet, include a protocol version number as well as the data's source and their destination. This information is of crucial importance to data transference – without it, communication could not occur. Transmission protocols are not a form of control directed by any one actor, but rather a commonly adopted standard. Control becomes endogenous to the technological system itself (Galloway 2004).

The layered assemblage that determines Hailo's use is simultaneously recruited by the application and hidden by the interface at the moment of normal use (Chun 2004). This network-in-the-pocket capacity of mobile computing is generative of Hailo's business model. Taxi hire companies in Dublin operate in a market of individualised licensing. In addition to plying for hire (being in motion and available for hire) and standing for hire (being stationary and available for hire), taxi drivers can increase their number of fares by enrolling the services of a taxi hire company. When a customer phones a taxi hire company, its radio-enabled network is then leveraged to source an available driver. This model is dependent upon the installation of a communications unit in driver's vehicle. The hire of this is incorporated into the cost of the service – in Dublin, around €100 a week.

Hailo does not need to install any of its own radio communication equipment, instead relying on external telecommunications infrastructure. In comparison with traditional taxi hire companies, Hailo has low fixed capital costs

Moving applications 137

and low associated installation and maintenance costs. Where code performs the role of the radio operator, there are also presumably fewer attendant labour costs. This leads to a considerably different pricing model. Rather than charge a subscription fee, Hailo extracts a 12% commission – minus VAT and card processing costs – on every fare sourced through the app. This flexibility lowers the threshold on driver uptake and constitutes a significant threat to existing taxi hire companies.

There is, however, an important geographical caveat to be made. In cities such as Dublin – where there is a confluence of high population density, a high number of taxis per head and a high usage of smartphones – the benefits of Hailo to both drivers and passengers outweigh those offered by the radio network of taxi hire companies. In a geographical location where taxi or smartphone use is more sparsely distributed, Hailo has less opportunity to draw upon existing infrastructure. Where I work in Maynooth – a small university town 25 km west of Dublin – it is very difficult to find a taxi using Hailo. In such locations, both spatial scarcity and community loyalty lead to less competition between Hailo and existing taxi hire services. In these instances, the volume of jobs rather than the rate of commission is the dictating competitive factor.

On the whole, it is the geographically dispersed hardware external to Hailo that allows it to compete favourably with existing taxi services. The ability to leverage an already existing general purpose hardware–code stack, rather than design, implement and install a bespoke infrastructural architecture, allows smartphone applications to grow quickly and flexibly. This mechanism underlies many of the disruptive economics of apps, and poses a challenge to the necessarily slow-moving regulatory frameworks at local and national scales.

Moves and the automatic extraction of value

Moves was launched on the Apple App Store in January 2013 by Finnish developer ProtoGeo Oy. The app is a life-logger, which collects personal information for the analysis of physical exercise and daily activities. Rather than depend on a device worn on the user's wrist (as in other commercial solutions, such as Nike's FuelBand or Sony's SmartBand), Moves runs in the background during everyday smartphone use, collecting information available to it from the phone's hardware (the GPS receiver, the GSM and Wi-Fi modules and the accelerometer) to determine how a user moves in and through space. This information is then represented in a visually accessible way. In this section, I draw on the hardware–code–data(base)–interface model to emphasise the importance of the graphical user interface to the familiarity of the application and then the extensibility of its data to its longevity. I argue that its acquisition by Facebook for an undisclosed sum in April 2014 was predicated upon the perceived value and future monetisation of this granular user information.

138   *James Merricks White*

There are essentially two modes to Moves' user interface. The first shows periods of low or no movement as oval nodes and periods of movement between them as coloured lines (see the left-hand panel of Figure 10.3). Nodes are initially represented by the app as a small map; a spatial region. These

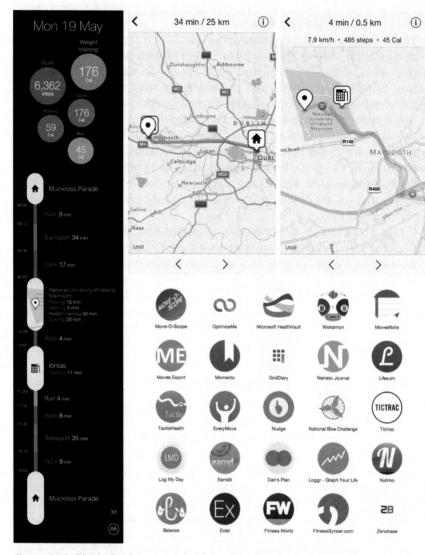

Figure 10.3 Clockwise from top left: Moves interface mode (temporal representation), two views of Moves interface mode (spatial representation) and third-party services built using the Moves API

Source: Move app screenshots (except 7.3(d)). Dates: (a) this is an edited composite of 5 screenshots; 12 August 2014; (b) & (c) 12 August 2014; (d) this an edited composite of 2 screenshots from https://apps.moves-app.com; 17 July 2014

Moving applications 139

can be designated as a place by the user (using Foursquare's open database of user-generated locations) and will subsequently be shown using an icon intended to symbolise that place's associated activity. The colours of connecting lines represent the activity estimated to have been undertaken between locations: green showing walking; pink, running; grey, some other form of transportation. By touching on any node or line, the user enters the second interface mode (see the top right panels of Figure 10.3). Here, temporal representation is sacrificed for a clear representation of spatial information by way of a map. In this mode, moving through time is achieved with the arrow buttons at the bottom of the screen. Moves' modal interface is simple to use and intuitive to a regular smartphone user. There is an important sense, then, in which the cultural capacity of interfaces exceeds specific applications.

Visual and gestural cues accrete into norms of interactive behaviour. These are built-on by daily use with an application. Consider one of the most persistent visual devices drawn upon by Moves: the map. Maps are produced in-the-moment for a specific purpose; brought into being through their reading (Kitchin and Dodge 2007). In the mobile computing map, this manifests through a tension between the general and the specific. On the one hand, the map is a visual representation produced by the Moves code, which in turn – in my use of the application on an iPhone – relies on functions specified in iOS's MapKit Framework. This architecture allows maps to be easily embedded within iOS applications and facilitates the translation of pinching and panning gestures between mobile applications and across Apple devices. On the other hand, the map is specifically produced by the code–data–interface stack for an individual user at a specific moment in time. Prior to its visualisation on the screen, the information collected by Moves must be processed and reformatted. Data gathered about location (from the GPS receiver) and movement (from the accelerometer) are sent to Moves' servers, where the various activities undertaken during a specific time are calculated. This is rearranged in a data format (a JSON array), which can act as input to the app's code–interface, and is then sent back to the phone. Moves' map interface is both general in the conventions of its use and specific in the data that it renders on the screen. The visual device of the map enacts a form of knowledge, which moves through space and time, between users and across devices, but is sufficiently mutable to accommodate their particular needs.

While Moves draws on an aesthetic of visual interface design, it refrains from locking the user into its particular media interface. The data collected by the application have been made potentially accessible and manipulable through an application program interface (API), such that Moves itself offers its own architecture for third-party software development (the bottom left panel of Figure 10.3 shows some of the services using data collected by Moves). For example, MMapper is a Processing sketch, offering simple filters for visualisations of Moves data (see the left-hand panel of Figure 10.4), and Move-O-Scope is a Web application allowing the data to be collated and compared across longer periods of time (the right-hand side of Figure 10.4).

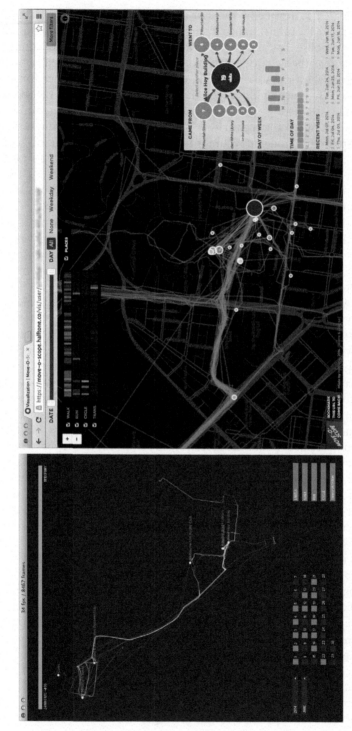

Figure 10.4 Left: MMapper Processing sketch. Right: Move-O-Scope Web application

Source: (a) screenshot of a Processing sketch, MMapper; 17 July 2014
(b) screenshot of https://move-o-scope.halftone.co/vis/user/[id anonymised]; 17 July 2014

Moving applications 141

These applications leverage different hardware–code stacks and represent data to the user through graphical interfaces that have different properties to the Moves app. The potential for its data to be open and fluid reinscribes Moves as a platform for life logging more generally, but begs the question: what is it about data in this instance that is of value beyond the other components of the mobile computing stack?

Life logging might be understood as a mechanism for automatically extracting data from users. I want to suggest that this is a kind of work, closely related to free labour as conceptualised by Terranova (2004), but different in that that inaction and sedentary behaviour are also captured, quantified and rendered as a source of value. There are two important ways in which data might be of value to companies. First, data offer immediate value as a representation of past life: they can be organised, processed and visualised to facilitate benchmarking, decision making and targeted advertising. This can be used as the foundation for products and services, which can be sold back to the user. Second, and more significantly, data act as a form of material fixity for the future realisation of profit. The expectation of as yet performed analysis and calculation upon data, as well as its potential for exposing the body and its movement to financial instrumentation, account for much of the monetary value assigned to data in the present. As such, the acquisition of Moves by Facebook is not only an effort to obtain a platform for the automatic extraction of data, but also serves as a fix for its surplus stores of capital. Understood through their present and anticipated value, data become a deeply political issue, closely entwined with the continual expansion of capitalism (Federici 2004).

Politics beyond software assemblages

Within media and communications studies (Galloway 2004; van Dijck 2013), geographies of software (Thrift and French 2002: Graham 2005: Kitchin and Dodge 2011), and in the emerging area of software studies (Fuller 2008: Manovich 2013), software, what I have been treating here as a combination of code and media interface is often given ontological precedence over hardware and data. This is for two reasons. First, the decentralised execution of algorithms and protocols affords digital computation much of its agentive capacity. Second, code itself does work as a new kind of commodity entangled with, and co-productive of, the forces of globalisation. Increasingly, to understand global capital, labour markets, production and everyday economic practices, it is crucial that researchers have a solid grasp of software. While it is not my intention to deny the need for such engagement, I feel that it is important to acknowledge that the flows of software are predicated upon networked hardware and data infrastructures. To give ontological priority to software de-emphasises this stack of interdependence and the politics by which it is given context.

By considering the significance of hardware, the spatial is reintroduced and with it the local materialities with which software interacts. Hailo shows why

142 *James Merricks White*

this is crucial to an understanding of mobile computing. Hardware is fixed capital where software is fluid. Where network infrastructure permeates the city, external to but spatially colocated with everyday life, potentially disruptive business models can emerge and with them a suite of situated legal and regulatory issues. By considering the significance of data as a dynamic running transverse to software, the politics of computation can be freshly conceptualised. Moves is a good example of how data can exceed the software configurations in which it is represented. Data are more than just a representation of reality, however. Data can also become a kind of life to those who analyse them and value to those seeking to acquire them. Just as software is significant to an understanding of the fluxes and flows of globalisation, so too are data. As a methodological tool, the multilayered hardware–code–data(base)–interface model is able to express these political and economic entanglements in a way that research prioritising software is not always able to. It is only through proper examination of the ways in which these various assemblages are hierarchically arranged that we might properly appreciate how computation and the city are mutually constituted (Chapter 2; see also, Kitchin and Lauriault 2014).

In this examination of mobile computing, I have drawn loosely on theorisations of actor-networks and assemblages without trying to fit the proposed model within a theoretically fleshed-out ontology. Here, I want to briefly touch on what an engagement with this literature might offer the proposed model. The target of Bruno Latour's actor–network theory is no less than the social itself – or, at the very least, the way in which sociality and social bonds are fetishised for their explanatory power within Durkheimian analyses (Latour 2005). Rather than understand phenomena through these top-down forces, Latour urges the social scientist to slowly follow the connections between human and non-human actors, 'redefining sociology not as the "science of the social", but as the tracing of associations' (Latour 2005: 5). By providing a rich, descriptive exploration of the ways in which local phenomena assemble, the social might begin to be rebuilt from the bottom up, taking proper account of the agency of things. In his determination to reboot the project of social enquiry, I worry that Latour leaves too little room for the systemic political and economic forces which I have drawn on in relation to Hailo and Moves.

By contrast, Foucault (1980) uses the idea of the dispositif, or apparatus, to draw attention to the complex arrangement of discourses and institutions that enables the formation and maintenance of knowledge in service to a strategic political function. Here, the social solidifies into expressions of power or knowledge, which are, in the first instance, political. Similarly, Deleuze and Guattari (1987) employ the notion of the assemblage in an effort to open up new forms of political engagement (Tampio 2009). Of importance in their use of the concept is externality – 'relations are external to their terms' (Deleuze and Parnet 1977: 41) – by which they mean that any actor in an assemblage has the potential to exceed that particular arrangement of its relations. This is in keeping with my exploration of Hailo and Moves, where hardware and

Moving applications 143

data do considerable work beyond their configuration within the mobile application assemblage under review.

McFarlane (2011) and Anderson *et al.* (2012) have respectively explored what assemblage theory might mean for urban theory and social-spatial theory more broadly. Through an engagement with the materialist and realist philosophy of Manuel DeLanda (2006), they propose four areas that might be fruitful for geography: an experimental realism; an emphasis on relations within and beyond assemblages; a rethinking of agency and causality in distributed terms; and, an awareness of shifting capacities as assemblages mutate and stabilise. These have informed my approach even in my reluctance to assert the realism of the hardware–code–data(base)–interface stack.

While these approaches have their various strengths and weaknesses, there seems to remain an issue of ontological disconnect between empirical tracings of socio-technical systems, on the one hand, and the political and economic forces at play in the city, on the other. Perhaps, as suggested in Chapter 2, there is an opportunity 'to scale the socio-technical perspective up, and drill the urban studies focus down so that they overlap in view and epistemology'. As a geographer thinking about the relationship between code and the city, my interest is in placing urban research in dialogue with philosophy. While I have presented some literature to this effect, I remain cognisant of the need to further develop the ontological frame of this methodological approach.

Conclusion

In this chapter, I have explored the mobile applications Hailo and Moves through the proposed socio-technical stack: hardware–code–data(base)–interface. This multilayered model is able to account for the way in which networked devices move through space and for non-human as well as human agency, without reifying one concept at the expense of the others. While I have argued for a flattening of the ontological relationship between software and its supporting infrastructures, I have tried to remain aware of two tensions that undermine such an approach. First, that mobile computing is stabilised in hierarchical relationships, such that the capacity for each layer to access the one below it is tightly controlled. And second, that each of these layers is itself transduced in a citational and performative manner by human and non-human actors. These layers are hidden at the moment of their recruitment – obscured by the cohesiveness of a seamless, well-engineered user experience – but they inform the economics and politics of everyday smartphone use in the city, and so deserve proper critical attention.

Acknowledgement

The research for this paper was conducted under *The Programmable City*, a project funded by a European Research Council Advanced Investigator award (ERC-2012-AdG-323636-SOFTCITY).

144 *James Merricks White*

Note

1 By media interfaces, I mean, following Manovich (2013), graphical, audial and haptic feedback mechanisms that convey information through normal use. I do not wish to mean graphical user interfaces exclusively, nor interfaces more broadly. For an exploration of interface theory see de Souza e Silva and Frith (2012), Farman (2012) and Galloway (2012).

References

Anderson, B., Kearnes, M., McFarlane, C. and Swanton, D. (2012) 'On assemblages and geography', *Dialogues in Human Geography*, 2(2): 171–89.
Benkler, Y. (2006) *The Wealth of Networks: How Social Production Transforms Markets and Freedom*, New Haven: Yale University Press.
Chun, W.H.K. (2004) 'On software, or the persistence of visual knowledge', *Grey Room*, 18(Winter), 26–51.
de Souza e Silva, A. and Frith, J. (2012) *Mobile Interfaces in Public Spaces: Locational Privacy, Control and Urban Sociability*, New York: Routledge.
deLanda, M. (2006) *A New Philosophy of Society: Assemblage Theory and Social Complexity*, London: Continuum.
Deleuze, G. and Guattari, F. (1987) *A Thousand Plateaus: Capitalism and Schizophrenia*, trans. B. Massumi, London: Continuum.
Deleuze, G. and Parnet, C. (1977) *Dialogues*, New York: Columbia University Press.
Farman, J. (2012) *Mobile Interface Theory: Embodied Space and Locative Media*, New York: Routledge.
Federici, S. (2004) *Caliban and the Witch: Women, the Body and Primitive Accumulation*, Brooklyn: Autonomedia.
Foucault, M. (1980) 'The confession of the flesh', in C. Gordon (ed.) *Power/Knowledge: Selected Interviews and Other Writings 1972–1977*, New York: Pantheon.
Fuller, M. (ed.) (2008) *Software Studies: A Lexicon*, Cambridge, MA: MIT Press.
Gabrys, J. (2014) 'Programming environments: environmentality and citizen sensing in the smart city', *Environment and Planning D: Society and Space*, 32(1): 30–48.
Galloway, A.R. (2004) *Protocol: How Control Exists After Decentralization*, Cambridge, MA: MIT Press.
Galloway, A.R. (2012) *The Interface Effect*, Cambridge: Polity.
Graham, S. (2005) 'Software-sorted geographies', *Progress in Human Geography*, 29(5): 562–80.
Graham, S. and Marvin, S. (2001) *Splintering Urbanism: Networked Infrastructures, Technological Mobilities and the Urban Condition*, London: Routledge.
Kinsley, S. (2014) 'The matter of "virtual" geographies', *Progress in Human Geography*, 38(3): 364–383.
Kitchin, R. (2014) *The Data Revolution: Big Data, Open Data, Data Infrastructures and Their Consequences*, London: Sage.
Kitchin, R. and Dodge, M. (2007) 'Rethinking maps', *Progress in Human Geography*, 31(3): 331–44.
Kitchin, R. and Dodge, M. (2011) *Code/Space: Software and Everyday Life*, Cambridge, MA: MIT Press.
Kitchin, R. and Lauriault, T. (2014) 'Towards critical data studies: charting and unpacking data assemblages and their work', Programmable City Working Paper 2,

Moving applications 145

Social Science Research Network, available from http://ssrn.com/abstract=2474112 [accessed 24 August 2015].

Latour, B. (2005) *Reassembling the Social: An Introduction to Actor-Network-Theory*. Oxford: Oxford University Press.

Lauriault, T.P. (2012) *Data, Infrastructures and Geographical Imaginations: Mapping Data Access Discourses in Canada*, PhD thesis, Carleton University.

Losey, J. (2014) 'Networked entrepreneurism: how technology can shape alternative democracy', *Citizenship in the Digital Republic Workshop*, IT University of Copenhagen, Copenhagen, Denmark, 13 March.

McFarlane, C. (2011) Assemblage and critical urbanism, *City*, 15(2): 204–24.

Manovich, L. (2013) *Software Takes Command*. New York: Bloomsbury.

Tampio, N. (2009) 'Assemblages and the multitude: Deleuze, Hardt, Negri, and the postmodern Left', *European Journal of Political Theory*, 8(3): 383–400.

Terranova, T. (2004) *Network Culture: Politics for the Information Age*, London: Pluto Press.

Thrift, N. and French, S. (2002) 'The automatic production of space', *Transactions of the Institute of British Geographers*, 27(3): 309–35.

van Dijck, J. (2013) *The Culture of Connectivity: A Critical History of Social Media*, Oxford: Oxford University Press.

Wilson, M.W. (2011) 'Data matter(s): legitimacy, coding, and qualifications-of-life', *Environment and Planning D: Society and Space*, 29(5): 857–72.

Zittrain, J. (2008) *The Future of the Internet: And How to Stop It*, New Haven: Yale University Press.

11 Exploring urban social media

Selfiecity and *On Broadway*

Lev Manovich

Introduction

User-generated visual media, such as images and video shared on Instagram, YouTube, Sina Weibo, VK, Flickr and other popular social media services, open up amazing opportunities for the study of contemporary visual and urban culture. By analysing media shared by millions of users daily, we can understand what people around the world imagine and create; how people represent themselves and others; what topics, styles and visual techniques are most popular and most unique, and how these topics and techniques differ between locations, sexes, ages, and many other demographic characteristics.

In 2005, I coined the term 'cultural analytics' to refer to the 'analysis of massive cultural datasets and flows using computational and visualisation techniques' (Manovich *et al.* 2014a) and in 2007 we established a research lab (Software Studies Initiative, Manovich *et al.* (2014b)) to begin practical work. Having developed and tested our techniques and software tools on a variety of smaller datasets, such as 4,535 covers of *Time* magazine from 1923 to 2009, and 1 million Manga pages, in 2012 we started working on larger social media datasets.

In our first project, *Phototrails* (Hochman *et al.* 2013a), we analysed and visualised 2.3 million Instagram photos shared by hundreds of thousands of people in 13 global cities. Given that all users of Instagram app are presented with the same interface, the same filters and even the same square image size, how much variance between the cities do we find? Are networked apps and their tools, such as Instagram, creating a new global visual language, an equivalent of visual modernism a hundred years earlier? Does the ease of capturing, editing and sharing photos lead to more or less aesthetic diversity? Do software and networks result in more repetition, uniformity and visual social mimicry, as food, cats, selfies, and other popular subjects seem to appear to drown everything else? The use of large samples of social media, and computational and visualisation tools, allows us to investigate such questions quantitatively.

Our analysis in *Phototrails* (Figures 11.1 and 11.2) revealed strong similarity between cities in terms of basic visual characteristics – such as tonality

Exploring urban social media 147

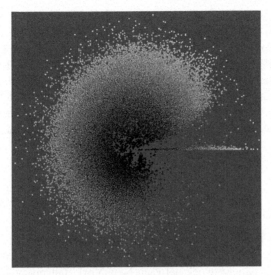

Figure 11.1 50,000 Instagram photos shared in Tokyo in 2012, organised by mean brightness (distance to the centre) and mean hue (angle)
Source: Hochman *et al.* 2013b

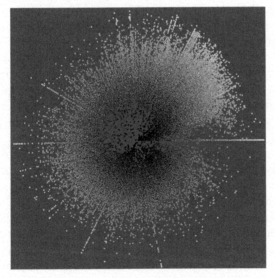

Figure 11.2 50,000 Instagram photos shared in Bangkok in 2012, organised by mean brightness (distance to the centre) and mean hue (angle)
Source: Hochman *et al.* 2013b

and colours of images – and also the use of filters. But these findings were partly an artefact of the method we used. We disregarded the content of photos, the differences in compositions and other aspects of photographic aesthetics, the relative popularity of various photo types and many other

148   *Lev Manovich*

possible dimensions of difference. Instead, we considered the photos only as assemblages of colour pixels. To compensate for some of the limitations of this first project, in 2013 we started a new project *Selfiecity* (Manovich *et al.* 2014c). Rather than using an arbitrary sample of social media images with any content, we focused on only one kind – the popular selfies (self-portraits captured with mobile phone cameras). In the following section, I discuss how we assembled the selfie dataset, our research methods, the presentation of the work via visualisations and a website, and some of our findings.

Selfiecity

Making Selfiecity

To work on *Selfiecity*, we assembled a large multidisciplinary team. The team includes media theorists, an art historian, data scientists, visual designers and programmers, who work between New York, Germany and California. The project was coordinated by Lev Manovich, while Moritz Stefaner was responsible for creative direction and visualisations. Other team members are Dominikus Baur, Mehrdad Yazdani, Alise Tifentale, Jay Chow, Daniel Goddemeyer and Nadav Hochman. The project presentation online combines findings about the demographics of people taking selfies and their poses and expressions; a number of media visualisations (*imageplots*), which assemble thousands of photos; and an interactive application (*Selfiexploratory*), which allows visitors to explore the whole set of 3,200 selfie photos, sorting and filtering it to find new patterns. In addition, the website selfiecity.net also includes three essays about the history of photography and the selfie phenomenon, the functions of images in social media, and the media visualisation method.

The first stage in working on this project was the creation of a selfie dataset. This involved many steps. When you browse Instagram, at first it looks as though it contains a large proportion of selfies. A closer examination reveals that many of them are not selfies, but photos taken by other people. For our project, we wanted to use only single-person 'true selfies'. The team partnered with Gnip, a third-party company, which at that time was the world's largest provider of social data (gnip.com). After developing software that interfaces with the Gnip service in September 2013 we started to collect Instagram photos in different locations. After many tests, we focused on the central areas in five cities located in North America, Europe, Asia and South America. The size of an area used for the Instagram image collection was the same in every city. Since we wanted to collect images and data under the same conditions we selected a particular week (5–11 December 2013) for the project. The numbers of photos shared on Instagram inside the chosen areas of our five cities during this week, according to Instagram data provided by Gnip (sorted by size) were: New York City, 207,000; Bangkok, 162,000;

Moscow, 140,000; Sao Paolo, 123,000; and Berlin, 24,000; with a total sample of 656,000 photos.

The next step consisted of randomly selecting 140,000 photos (20,000 or 30,000 photos per city) from the total set of photos. We then used the Amazon Mechanical Turk service to identify selfie photos from this set. Each of 140,000 photos was tagged by between two and four workers. We experimented with different forms of a question the workers had to answer, and found that the simplest form – 'Does this photo show a single selfie?' – produced best results.

We then selected the top 1,000 photos for each city (i.e., photos which at least two workers tagged as a single-person selfie). We submitted these photos to Mechanical Turk again, asking the three 'master workers' not only to verify that a photo showed a single selfie, but also to tag the sex and guess the age of a person. As the final step, at least one member of the project team examined all these photos manually. Most photos were tagged correctly (apparently every Mechanical Turk worker knew what a selfie was) but we did find some mistakes. We wanted to keep the dataset sizes the same, to make analysis and visualisations comparable; therefore, our final set contains 640 selfie photos for every city (eliminating the mistakes), for a total of 3,200 photos.

This sample set of 3,200 selfie photos was analysed using state-of-the-art facial analysis software from Orbeus Inc. (rekognition.com). The software analysed the faces in the photos, generating over 20 measurements, including face size, orientation, emotion, presence of glasses, presence of smile, whether eyes are closed or open. We used these measurements in two ways. We compared the measured face characteristics between cities, sexes and ages. We also included some of the measurements in the *Selfiexploratory* interactive application to allow website visitors to filter the selfie database by any combination of selected characteristics (see *Selfiexploratory*). The software also guessed the sex and age of a person in each photo. We found that both sex and age estimates were generally consistent with the guesses of Mechanical Turk workers.

Visualising the selfie photos

Typically, a data visualisation shows simple data such as numbers. However, a single number cannot fully represent everything a photo contains. A single photo is not a 'data point' but a whole world, rich in meanings, emotions and visual patterns. This is why showing all photos in the visualisations (along with the graphs or by themselves) is the key strategy of the project. We call this approach 'media visualisation'. In the words of *Selfiecity* artistic director and visualisation designer Moritz Stefaner:

> Showing the high level patterns in the data – the big picture – as well as the individual images has been an important theme in our project. How can we find summarisations of big data collections, which still respect

the individuals, and don't strip away all the interesting details? This has become a quite central question to us, not only with respect to selfies.

(Gorey 2014)

Moritz Stefaner created a few different types of visualisation for the project, including blend video montages, imageplots and *Selfiexploratory*.

Blended Video Montages presents 640 selfies in a video for each city (Stefaner 2013). It runs through all the images, but not in a simple sequence. Instead, a few selfies are superimposed on the screen at a time, with new ones fading on top of the old ones. The faces are aligned with respect to eye position and sorted by the head tilt angle. This visual strategy is designed to create a tension between individual selfie photos and patterns across many images. We do not show each face by itself. But we also do not superimpose all faces together – which would only produce a generic face template, the same for every city. Instead, we show something else: a pattern and individual details at the same time.

Manual inspection of photos one by one can reveal many interesting details, but it is difficult to quantify the patterns observed. We created histogram-type visualisations, *Imageplots* (Figure 11.3), which show distributions

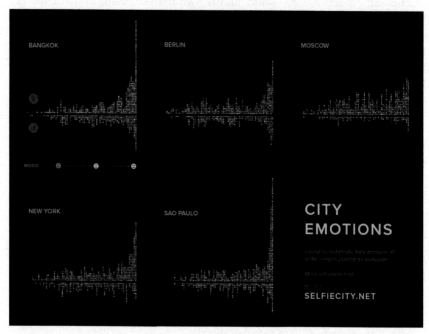

Figure 11.3 Imageplot showing distribution of selfie photos in five cities according to sex (vertical axis) and degree of smile (horizontal axis). The degree of smile was measured by facial analysis software; it can take any value between 0 (no smile) and 100 (strong smile)

Source: Manovich *et al.* 2014c

of sexes, ages and smiles in different cities. Like normal data visualisation, they allow you to immediately see patterns expressed in the shapes of the graphs. But, because these graphs are composed of individual photos, they also provide a different way to explore the interplay between the particular and the general.

A key part of the project is *Selfiexploratory* (Manovich *et al.* 2014d), an interactive visualisation app, which allows website visitors to explore the selfie dataset in many ways. Visitors can filter the photos by city, sex, age and a number of facial measurements extracted by facial analysis software. The application allows visitors to explore the photos using data from both human judgements and computer measurements – two ways of seeing the photos. The sex and age graphs (on the left of the Web page) use human tags and guesses (from Mechanical Turk workers). All other graphs (to the right of the Web page) use software face measurements. Whenever a selection is made, the graphs are updated in real time, and the bottom area displays all photos that match the selection (Figure 11.4). The result is an innovative, fluid method of browsing and spotting patterns in a large media collection.

In addition to presenting the selfie dataset though visualisations, videos and the interactive *Selfiexploratory* application, we also decided to present selected findings in a more conventional format as statistics. Out of a larger set of findings, here we have selected some representative examples:

(1) Depending on the city, only 3–5% of images we analysed were actually selfies.
(2) In every city we analysed, there were significantly more female than male selfies (from 1.3 times as many in Bangkok to 1.9 times more in Berlin). Moscow is a strong outlier – here, we have 4.6 times more female than male selfies. (In the USA the ratio of female to male Instagram users is close to 1.29:1, according to the Pew Research 2015 survey (Anderson 2015)).
(3) Most people in our photos are fairly young (estimated median age 23.7). Bangkok is the youngest city (21.0), whereas New York City is the oldest (25.3). Men's average age is higher than that of women in every city. Surprisingly, more older men (30+) than women post selfies on Instagram.
(4) Computational facial analysis revealed that you can find lots of smiling faces in Bangkok (0.68 average smile score) and Sao Paulo (0.64). People taking selfies in Moscow smile the least (only 0.53 on the smile score scale).
(5) Women's selfies have more expressive poses; for instance, the average amount of head tilt is 50% higher than for men (12.3° vs 8.2°). Sao Paulo is most extreme – there, the average head tilt for women is 16.9°!

These findings present only some of the patterns we found. In general, reviewing all the patterns, we discovered that each of our five cities is an outlier in

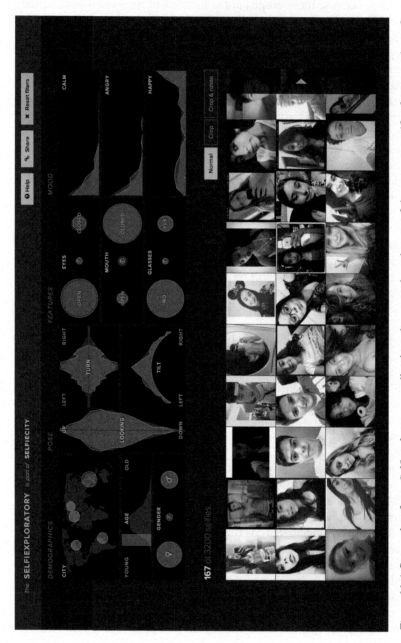

Figure 11.4 Screenshot from *Selfiexploratory* application: the user selected some of the youngest selfies from our data of 3,200 selfies using the age graph (left column, second row)

Source: Manovich *et al.* 2014d

a unique way. However, when we combine many dimensions, Moscow and Bangkok stand out from other cities.

Perhaps our overall most interesting finding is the following. Even though people use the same photo app and service (Instagram), which also allows them to easily see how others photographs themselves around the world, the selfie photos we analysed have significant local specificity. The types of pose change from city to city, and between sexes and ages. So while Instagram may be contributing to the emergence of a uniform 'global visual language', at the same time it still reveals cultural and social differences in how different groups of people represent themselves.

On Broadway

In *Phototrails*, we compared photos from 13 global cities, without filtering them by type or location. In *Selfiecity*, we filtered photos to only compare a single type of photos (selfies), also across multiple cities. For our next project *On Broadway* (Figures 11.5 to 11.7), we decided to zoom closer into the

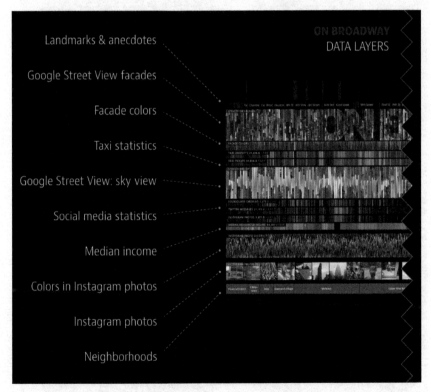

Figure 11.5 Data and image layers used to create the interface to navigating a city street in *On Broadway* project
Source: Goddemeyer *et al.* n.d.

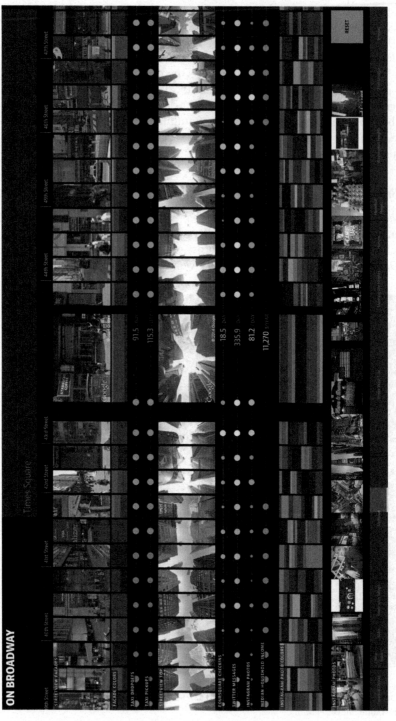

Figure 11.6 Screenshot from *On Broadway* application, showing a zoomed-in view centred on Time Square
Source: Goddemeyer *et al.* n.d.

Exploring urban social media 155

Figure 11.7 Interaction with *On Broadway* installation at New York Public Library (Public Eye exhibition)
Source: Goddemeyer *et al.* n.d.

universe of social media by focusing on the posts along a single city street. At the same time, we expanded our data sources, going beyond Instagram and adding Twitter, Foursquare, Google Street View, taxi pick-ups and drop-offs, and economic indicators from the US Census Bureau.

Representing the city

Modern writers, painters, photographers, filmmakers and digital artists have created many fascinating representations of city life. Paintings of Paris boulevards and cafés by Pissarro and Renoir, photomontages by Berlin's Dada artists, *Broadway Boogie-Woogie* by Piet Mondrian, *Spider-Man* comics (Stan Lee and Steve Ditko), *Playtime* by Jacques Tati and *Locals and Tourists* data maps by Eric Fischer are classic examples of artists encountering the city. The artwork that directly inspired our project is *Every Building on the Sunset Strip* by Edward Ruscha (1996). It is an artist book that unfolds to 25 feet (8.33 metres) to show continuous photographic views of both sides of a 1.5 mile section of Sunset Boulevard.

Today, a city 'talks' to us in data. Many cities make available datasets and sponsor hackathons to encourage the creation of useful apps using their data. (For example, the New York City Mayor's Office's sponsored New York City Open Data website offers over 1,200 datasets, covering everything from the trees in the city to bicycle data). Locals and tourists share massive

156   *Lev Manovich*

amounts of visual geocoded media using Twitter, Instagram and other networks. Services such as Foursquare tell us where people go and what kind of venues they frequent. How can we represent the twenty-first century using such rich data and image sources? Is there a different way to visualise the city besides using graphs, numbers or maps?

Constructing Broadway

The first step in our project was to precisely define the area to analyse, and assemble data from this area. Like a spine in a human body, Broadway runs through the middle of Manhattan Island, curving along its way. We wanted to include a slightly wider area than the street itself, so that we could also capture nearby activities. To define this area, we selected points at 30-metre intervals going through the centre of Broadway, and defined 100-metre wide rectangles centred on every point. The result is a spine-like shape that is 21,390 metres (13.5 miles) long and 100 metres wide. We used the coordinates of this shape to filter Instagram, Twitter, Foursquare, Google Street View, taxi and economic data.

Instagram

Using the services provided by Gnip, we downloaded all geocoded Instagram images shared publicly in the larger New York City area between February 26 and August 3, 2014. The dataset contains 10,624,543 images, out of which 661,809 are from the Broadway area.

Twitter

As a part of a Twitter Data Grant awarded to Software Studies Initiative, we received all publicly shared tweets with images around the world from 2011 to 2014. We filtered this dataset, leaving only tweets shared inside the Broadway area during the same time period that we used for Instagram (158 days in 2014).

Foursquare

We downloaded Foursquare data from March 2009 to March 2014 (1,826 days) through the Foursquare API. Overall, we counted 8,527,198 check-ins along Broadway.

Google Street View images

We experimented with our own video and photo captures moving along Broadway. However, our results did not look as good as Google Street View images, so we decided to include these images as another data source. We wrote a script and used it to download Google Street View images (one image for each of our 713 points along Broadway), looking in three directions: east, west and up. The first two views show buildings on both sides of the streets. The view up is particularly interesting, since it shows the amount of sky visible between buildings to the Google Street View wide angle lens. In the downtown and midtown areas, most of the images in these views are taken near high-rise buildings and only a small part of the sky is visible. However, in the northern part of Broadway, buildings are lower, and this is reflected in larger parts of sky visible in the images.

Taxi

Chris Whong obtained data for 2013 taxi pick-ups and drop-offs from New York City Taxi and Limousine Commission (Whong 2014). In 2013, there were 140 million trips in Manhattan. Filtering this dataset using Broadway coordinates left us with 22 million trips (10,077,789 drop-off and 12,391,809 pickup locations).

Economic indicators

We used the latest data available through the American Community Service. This is a yearly survey of the sample of the US population by the US Census Bureau. The American Community Service reports the data summarised by census tracks. These are areas that are much larger than the 30 × 100 metre rectangles we used to define the Broadway area. Our Broadway consists of 713 rectangles that cross 73 larger US census tracks. Because of these two different scales, any census population statistics available will only approximately apply to the smaller Broadway parts. Given this, we decided to only use a single economic indicator from the American Community Service, estimated average household income. This information was shown as one of the layers in the application.

Navigating the data street without maps

We spent months experimenting with different possible ways to present all these data using a visual interactive interface. The result of our explorations is a visually rich image-centric interface, where numbers play only a secondary role and no maps are used. The project proposes a new visual metaphor for thinking about the city: a vertical stack of image and data layers. There are 13 such layers in the project, all aligned to locations along Broadway. As you move along the street, you see a selection of Instagram photos from each area, left, right and top Google Street View images and extracted top colours from these image sources. We also show the average numbers of taxi pick-ups and drop-offs, Twitter posts with images and average family income for the parts of the city crossed by Broadway. To help with navigation, we added

158 *Lev Manovich*

additional layers showing names of Manhattan neighbourhoods crossed by Broadway, cross-streets and landmarks.

This interactive interface is available online as part of the project website (Goddemeyer *et al.* n.d.). We also displayed it on a 46-inch interactive touch-screen as part of the exhibition *Public Eye* at the New York Public Library (December 2014 to January 2016). Since the exhibition was free and open every day to the public, with dozens of people inside at any given time, we were able to see how ordinary New Yorkers and city tourists interacted with the interface. It became clear that focusing on the visual layers – Instagram photos and Google Street View images – was the key to making the interface meaningful and useful to the public. We saw many times how visitors would immediately navigate and zoom in on a particular block of the city meaningful to them: perhaps a place where they were born, or where they lived for a long time.

This personalisation of the 'big data' was one of our main goals. We wanted to let citizens see how many types of urban data relate to each other, and let them relate massive and sometime abstract datasets to their personal experiences – places where they live or visit.

Conclusion: aesthetics vs politics of big data

Today companies, government agencies and other organisations collect massive data about the cities. These data are used in many ways invisible to us. At the same time, as I already mentioned, many cities make available some of their datasets and sponsor competitions to encourage creation of useful apps using this data. But these two activities – collection of data, and release of the data to the public – are not symmetrical. The data released by cities only covers what city administers and controls – parks and streets, infrastructure repairs, parking tickets, etc. These are data about the city as an entity, not about particular individuals or detailed patterns of their activities. In contrast, the data collected and analysed by social media services, surveillance camera networks, telecom companies, banks and their commercial clients (or government agencies if they are able to get access to parts of this data) are about the individuals: their patterns of movement, communications, expressed opinions, financial transactions.

Some of the data from social media services are easily available via API to anybody with a basic knowledge of computer programming. These data are used in numerous free and commercial apps (for example, when I use Buffer to schedule my posts to Twitter and Facebook, Buffer interacts with them via their APIs to place these posts at particular times on my account pages). The same data have already been used in thousands of computer science papers and conference talks. Many thousands of students in computer science or design classes also routinely download, analyse and visualise social media data as part of their assignments. But ordinary people are not aware that the tweets, comments, images and video they share are easily accessible to

Exploring urban social media 159

anybody via these free API tools. While articles in popular media routinely talk about how individuals' data are collected, aggregated and used for a variety of purposes, including surveillance or customisation of advertising, they typically do not explain that these data are also available to individual researchers, artists or students.

Artists can certainly play their role in 'educating the public' about the access and use of people's data. In our project websites, we have carefully explained where we obtained the data for both *Selfiecity* and *On Broadway*. But our main goal was 'aesthetic education' as opposed to 'political education'. I grew up in a totalitarian society – USSR in the 1970s – where public discussion of art was always geared towards its political use, and art without a clear political message was looked on with suspicion. This experience made me very sensitive to any attempts to reduce art and culture to issues of politics, including currently frequent discussions of big data *only* in terms of surveillance, copyright, access and political and economic issues.

'Big data', including visual social media, is our new artistic medium, and the projects discussed here investigate its possibilities. In fact, we wanted to combine aesthetic questions and research questions: not only what we can learn from social media, but how we use it to create aesthetic representations and experiences. How should we imagine our cities and ourselves in the era of massive data collection and its algorithmic analysis? How can visualisations of such data combine bigger patterns and individual details? What alternative interfaces for exploring and relating to this data are possible, in addition to standard maps, timelines, grids of images and scrollable walls of Facebook, Twitter, YouTube and other large companies? In short: how we can see differently – not only the world around us (this was the key question of modern art) but also our new 'data reality'?

Acknowledgements

Each of the projects described is a collaboration between a team:

Phototrails Nadav Hochman, Lev Manovich, Jay Chow.
Selfiecity Lev Manovich, Moritz Stefaner, Dominicus Baur, Daniel Goddemeyer, Alise Tifentale, Nadav Hochman, Jay Chow.
On Broadway Daniel Goddemeyer, Moritz Stefaner, Dominikus Baur, and Lev Manovich. Contributors: Mehrdad Yazdani, Jay Chow, Nadav Hochman, Brynn Shepherd and Leah Meisterlin; PhD students at The Graduate Center, City University of New York: Agustin Indaco (Economics), Michelle Morales (Computational Linguistics), Emanuel Moss (Anthropology), Alise Tifentale (Art History).

The development of *Phototrails*, *Selfiecity* and *On Broadway* was supported by The Graduate Center, City University of New York, California Institute for Telecommunication and Information (Calit2) and The Andrew W. Mellon

160 *Lev Manovich*

Foundation. We are grateful to Gnip for their help with Instagram data collection. The part of this article about the *Selfiecity* project was adapted from Tifentale and Manovich (2015).

References

Anderson, M. (2015) 'Men catch up with women on overall social media use', *Pew Research Center*, available from http://www.pewresearch.org/fact-tank/2015/08/28/men-catch-up-with-women-on-overall-social-media-use/ [accessed 25 November 2015].

Goddemeyer, D., Stefaner, M., Baur, D. and Manovich, L. (n.d.) *On Broadway*, available from http://on-broadway.nyc/ [accessed 21 November 2015].

Gorey, C. (2014) 'Major study of selfies finds major demographic differences between countries', *siliconrepublic*, available from https://www.siliconrepublic.com/life/2014/02/24/major-study-of-selfies-finds-major-demographic-differences-between-countries [accessed 21 November 2015].

Hochman, N., Manovich, L. and Chow, J. (2013a) *Phototrails*, available from http://phototrails.net/ [accessed 21 November 2015].

Hochman, N., Manovich, L. and Chow, J. (2013b) 'Instagram cities', *Phototrails*, available from http://phototrails.net/instagram-cities/ [accessed 21 November 2015].

Manovich, L., Douglass, J., da Silva, C.I., Yazdani, M., Chow, J., Tifentale, A., Indaco, A., Hochman, N., Crockett, D., Navas, E., Reyes, E. and Huang, C. (2014a) 'Cultural analytics' *Software Studies Initiative*, available from http://lab.softwarestudies.com/p/cultural-analytics.html [accessed 21 November 2015].

Manovich, L., Douglass, J., da Silva, C.I., Yazdani, M., Chow, J., Tifentale, A., Indaco, A., Hochman, N., Crockett, D., Navas, E., Reyes, E. and Huang, C. (2014b) *Software Studies Initiative*, available from http://lab.softwarestudies.com/ [accessed 21 November 2015].

Manovich L., Stefaner M., Yazdani M., Baur, D., Goddemeyer, D., Tifentale, A., Hochman, N. and Chow, J. (2014c) *Selfiecity*, available from http://selfiecity.net/ [accessed 21 November 2015].

Manovich L., Stefaner M., Yazdani M., Baur, D., Goddemeyer, D., Tifentale, A., Hochman, N. and Chow, J. (2014d) 'The selfiexploratory', *Selfiecity*, available from http://selfiecity.net/selfiexploratory/ [accessed 21 November 2015].

Stefaner, M. (2013) *Selfiecity — Five Cities (Short Edit)*, available from http://vimeo.com/moritzstefaner/selfiecity-five-cities [accessed 21 November 2015].

Tifentale and Manovich (2015) 'Selfiecity: exploring photography and self-fashioning in social media', in D.M. Berry and M. Dieter (ed.) *Postdigital Aesthetics: Art, Computation and Design*, London: Palgrave Macmillan.

Whong, C. (2014) 'FOILing NYC's taxi trip data', *Chris Wong*, available from http://chriswhong.com/open-data/foil_nyc_taxi/ [accessed 21 November 2015].

Part III
Governance, politics and knowledge

12 Digital urbanism in crises

Monika Büscher, Xaroula Kerasidou, Michael Liegl and Katrina Petersen

Introduction

As software is becoming 'everyware' (Greenfield 2006; Kitchin and Dodge 2011), it is embedded not only in the rhythms of everyday life, but also in the disruptions of the exceptional. Greater vulnerabilities, created by population growth, urbanisation and austerity, ill-equip societies for an increase in extreme weather and political conflicts in a twenty-first 'century of disasters' (Vidal 2012). However, at this juncture, people also enact a hopeful digital urbanism. With 6.8 billion mobile subscribers worldwide and double-digit growth (Vinck 2013), they have become generators of big data, documenting their lives in intimate detail, which can be highly valuable during crises. Such digital documentations were used, for instance, to connect individuals, communities, emergency agencies, the media and governments locally and globally, to seek and provide information to organise, coordinate and collaborate in the crises in Mumbai, Port au Prince, Tokyo, Oslo, New York, Boston, Tacloban, Gaza and many others.

The most commonly encountered stories of such innovative use of ICT in crises celebrate its potential to increase the efficiency of disaster responses (Katsumi 2013; Morrow *et al.* 2011). But there are also critical voices, drawing on analyses of detrimental effects of surveillance, 'qualculation' or automation in information societies (Graham 2010; Thrift 2004; Suchman and Weber 2014), which are exacerbated under the exceptional circumstances of crises (Büscher *et al.* 2014). This chapter is motivated by the fact that such binary framings fail to adequately open up the ambiguities of socio-technical transformations for adequate analysis. To study the disruptive dynamics of digital urbanism in crises in a way that documents their complexities and opens up alternatives, we have joined design teams who produce ICT architectures for more interoperability and information sharing in disaster responses.[1] This allows us to enter into 'the open', 'where what is to come is not yet ... and might still be otherwise' (Haraway 2010). Examining crises as sites of disruptive innovation (Chesbrough 2003) makes it possible to see how technologies and practices of crisis response and digital urbanism are shaking up taken-for-granted social and organisational conventions, economic and political models, and notions of humanity and justice. These transformations reveal in new ways that 'we have never been human' (Haraway 2008; Hayles 1999) nor singular (Nancy 2000) and open up new approaches to the 'beast' that is situated socio-technical practice.

We investigate how digital urbanisms in crises are experiments with an 'ethics for non-unitary subjects' (Braidotti 2013: 190) that involve reconfigurations of lived experiences of distributed responsibilities as well as practices of noticing and caring about distant others. We argue that by understanding and designing for some of these practices we can define and design 'better' IT for crisis response, which also supports new modes of resistance to more generally problematic aspects of surveillance, qualculation and automation.

Disaster mobilities: from Haiti into the Cloud

On 12 January 2010, a 7.0 Mw earthquake that lasted 35 seconds killed over 160,000 people, and displaced close to 1.5 million Haitians. 60% of hospitals, government and administrative buildings, and 80% of schools were destroyed.[2] For many people, life came to revolve around loss and survival. But how they mobilised socio-technical affordances also marks a turning point in humanitarian disaster response and digital urbanism (Figure 12.1). Digital, mobile and networked technologies made this crisis an exceptional site of emergent informational interoperability.

Figure 12.1 A displaced Haitian fixes mobile phones in a tent city near Port au Prince, Haiti (24 January 2010)

Source: https://www.flickr.com/photos/usairforce/4304491014/in/album-72157623087518481/. (The image is US Gov Work and in public domain).

Digital urbanism in crises 165

Sharon Reader, beneficiary communications delegate for the Red Cross and Red Crescent, who worked in Haiti at the time, explained in a news interview how:

> One of the things that was fairly unique about Haiti was how much of an urban disaster [it] was. You know, it hit Port au Prince and Leogane very heavily ... so you were dealing with a fairly, you know, dense population who do have access to different technologies – Internet, mobile phone ... even [in] countries that like Haiti and right across Africa, this is technology that we can't afford to ignore as humanitarians ...[3]

Her delivery reflects a strong sense of urgency. Many disaster response agencies and policy-makers currently feel pressured to respond to social innovation in ICT use during crises. Despite the widespread use of GIS and other geolocation technologies in formal disaster response, the scale and speed of this exceeds formal response agencies' ability to adapt their processes and regulatory frameworks (Shanley *et al.* 2013). For example, a member of the German Federal Agency for Technical Relief described to us how search and rescue is normally organised by mapping out a grid and carrying out a systematic search. When victims used mobile technologies to call for help after the Haiti earthquake they could precisely locate their needs, which changed the priorities of deployment and disrupted a process designed to ensure the impartiality and rigour of search and rescue.[4]

Mobile ICT practices then disruptively open up new futures. People's ability to put themselves on a global map through social media amplifies the voices of those affected and has the potential to augment formal response efforts by fostering a more relational ethic that allows everyone involved to consider the politics, morality and effects of their actions more broadly (Whatmore 1997). At the same time, it can destructively interfere with formal response practices, undermining distributive justice (as in our example) or challenge the security of command and control communications (Oh *et al.* 2010). In the following, we trace how experiences from Haiti and the subsequent earthquake in Japan inspired attempts to utilise the 'big data' of everyday life for disaster response. In doing so, we also begin to link our discussion of posthuman phenomenologies, socialities and ethics to debates about surveillance, qualculation and automation.

On 11 March 2011, Japan was hit by a 9.0 Mw earthquake and tsunami, killing almost 20,000 people and displacing more than 160,000 (Samuels 2013). The fact that the fourth most powerful earthquake in human history harmed thousands fewer people than the earthquake in Haiti highlights that there is no such thing as a natural disaster (Steinberg 2000). Wealth can hugely affect capacity to prepare and mitigate damage. Amongst other things, it allows technological innovation; the Tohoku earthquake is seen to have proven that 'The Cloud works!' (Katsumi 2013). 'Next-generation ICT services underlying the resilient society' (Kinoshita *et al.* 2012) connected diverse databases, containing citizens' mobility data, life-logging entries, tax and healthcare records. Even though some of the data centres were damaged, such as the IBM centre in Tokyo,[5] they remained operational. This enabled corporations like Amazon and IBM to share their customer management software as a free service to help orchestrate supply and demand matching of relief goods (Katsumi 2013). Inspired by the efficacy of such technological flexibility, a global wave of investment into cloud computing for disaster response is bringing in unprecedented interoperability between diverse agencies and information systems.

The 2013 Geospatial Community Cloud Concept Demonstration orchestrated by the Network Centric Operations Industry Consortium (NCOIC), for example, reflects investment of 1.2 million US dollars to integrate services and information systems globally. NCOIC brought together major transnational industries, including Boeing, defence technology suppliers, IT firms, government and non-government emergency response agencies, culminating in a re-enactment of the international response to the Haiti earthquake to demonstrate the interoperability enabled by their cloud technologies.

In one of the videos that document the event, Kevin Jackson, Vice President of NJVC – an ICT provider for the United States Federal Government and Department of Defense – illustrates how the Cloud allows international response agencies to analyse Twitter and 'what is happening across social media'.[6] In another, Tip Slater, Director of Business Development, NCOIC, calculates the benefits of employing the Cloud.[7] His analysis promises an international federated Cloud system that can be set up 'in hours instead of months'. The cost of IT for emergency agencies is said to be reduced by between 10–80%, much of it because the Cloud enables short-term subscriptions to 'software as a service' rather than requiring permanent investments (NCOIC Rapid Response 2013).

Such ascription of enhanced control and efficiency to technology is common, but questionable, because it hides deeper socio-technical transformations. Ellebrecht and Kaufman (2015), for example, show how the adoption of networked e-triage devices enables efficiencies through delegation of responsibility from physicians to paramedics under conditions of strict control and surveillance, which curtails professional discretion. Technological determinism and *a-priori* assumption of an ethics of efficiency make it harder to see the ambiguous unintended consequences of such change. For instance, in the context of cloud-supported interoperability between international government agencies, emergency services and non-governmental organisations, data security and privacy issues arise (MacAskill *et al.* 2013), and many experts are even more concerned about automated probabilistic prediction (Mayer-Schönberger, in Heaven 2013) and social sorting because they can lead to a 'splintering' of societies and undermine societal virtues of humanity, equality and solidarity (Graham and Marvin 2001). Kafkaesque accumulations of error, indifference, lack of accountability and abuse (Solove 2011; Büscher *et al.* 2014) could undermine the beneficence of interoperable emergency response.

Digital urbanism in crises

In this section, we exhibit practices of an emergent digital urbanism. Digital technologies were used in new ways by Haitians and a global group of 'digital humanitarians' or 'voluntweeters', reconfiguring distributed responsibilities and practices of caring for distant others. We develop some concepts that can provide analytical purchase on these practices and how they perform digitally augmented 'posthuman' experience and agency. We argue that the phenomenologies, socialities and ethics that emerge in these reconfigurations can not only help us understand the ambiguities of disruptive digital innovation more deeply, but also inspire design that can more constructively address some of the problematic aspects of surveillance, qualculation and automation.

After the earthquake, 60–80% of Haitians had access to a mobile phone and network. In parallel, as the first news swept the globe, a group of students working with Patrick Meier in Boston set up the Ushahidi Haiti Project – a digital humanitarian initiative (Figure 12.2). A collaboration developed between Haitians on the ground, the students in Boston, the developers of the Ushahidi mapping platform, the globally distributed Haitian diaspora community, and a group of 'voluntweeters' (Starbird and Palen 2011; Meier 2012; Munro 2013). A freephone number, 4636, which had already been in use to obtain weather reports was appropriated as 'Mission 4636' – an initiative that repurposed the number to receive, process and respond to situation reports from people affected by the earthquake (Table 12.1).

Table 12.1 shows a message sent by people affected by the earthquake. Most of the messages were in Kreyòl and referred to places in slang terms, which were hard to match to places on a map. The international emergency response agencies, who were assisting the almost entirely collapsed local administration, could not use such messages directly to enhance situational

Table 12.1 Example of messages sent by Haitians, which were translated, categorised as 'actionable' or not, and augmented with location name and coordinates and emergency categorisations

Haitian Kreyòl	Nou bezwen aide nan Morija Diquini 63 pa gen dlo ni tente pou nou domi.yo pa pote anyen pou nou lot kote yo jwen,f
English	'We need help in Morija Diquini 63. There is no water nor tents for us to sleep in. They have not brought anything for us. Other places have gotten things. Do what you can to send aid for us.
	God will bless you. – Additional Notes: This area is near the Adventist Hospital of Diquini.'
Intel type	Actionable
Coordinates	−72.3793,18.5355
Location Categories	Morija Diquini 63
Date received	1/25/2010 17:06

(adapted from Munro 2013: 217)

168 *Monika Büscher* et al.

awareness. To add to these challenges, there were no detailed shareable digital maps available, on which to plot such data.

A group of 'Mission 4636' volunteers, non-governmental organisations and Ushahidi Haiti Project participants mobilised help, including 600 volunteers from all over the globe:

* to translate the messages into English;
* to decipher location information and georeference the reports;
* to categorise the information as actionable;
* to map needs.

When they started, the OpenStreetMap of Port Au Prince only detailed main roads and basic infrastructure. A few days later, there were street names, details of land use and the damage caused by the earthquake, and locations of field hospitals and shelters (Meier 2012). Standards like 'Tweak the Tweet' (Starbird and Stamberger 2010) emerged, which provided uniform formats to report needs, locations and contact information and facilitated computational parsing and mapping of tweeted information (Figure 12.2). The ways in which the affordances of this novel assembly of people, mobile phones, the Internet, GIS and social media were grasped supported new ways of self-organising disaster response. But before we discuss these, it is important to briefly explore the significance of this effort.

One marker of the value of crowdsourced information is the fact that the US Department of State analysts and US marines used maps like the one seen on Patrick Meier's laptop screen in Figure 12.2, to identify 'centres of gravity' for the deployment of field teams (Morrow *et al.* 2011). Moreover, the distributed collaborative effort also put people who were not on the relief agencies' radar on the map. For example, a number of messages were sent from Diquini 63 (Table 12.1), which refers to a street address. Several persons reported that this district had received no aid 13 days after the earthquake. Mapping these messages drew attention to this area, one of many places that were difficult to reach. The World Food Program later made an aid delivery and reported that there were about 2,500 people at this location.

The globally connected volunteers self-organised the mobilisation of digital and physical material resources. Starbird and Palen (2011) analysed almost 300,000 Twitter messages that enabled this, and offer several examples. In one case, a local person reported that they were running out of credit on their phone, impeding their ability to send situation reports, and a US-based volunteer, MelyMello (Table 12.2) realised that the Haitians' phones could be credited from afar. The voluntweeters set up a PayPal account that could accept donations. In another case, a collaboration between people in Turkey, the USA and Haiti mobilised a supply truck and confirmed its arrival (Starbird and Palen 2011).

But things did not always go so smoothly. For example, when Ushahidi Haiti Project volunteers looked for translators amongst the global Haitian

Digital urbanism in crises 169

Figure 12.2 Ushahidi Haiti Project situation room in Boston
Source: www.flickr.com/photos/digitaldemocracy/4379912183/in/photolist-7F3chv-7F3cjk-7F74CU-7F3cii-7Aqcrn. Reproduced by permission of Emily Jacobbi on behalf of Digital Democracy.

Table 12.2 Crowdsourcing funding for Haiti 'first responders'

Exchange of tweets
MelyMello (Jan 15 24:26): @ayitiJo we can top up your phone, can't we? add more minutes to it for you? Just need your phone #
...
deJacmel (Jan 16 ~19:00): @MelyMello Please Add min 2 ths cell numbers for me. They R helping Amer families to contact their Haiti relatives.
MelyMello (Jan 17 13:11): @janeSM want to help? Help me add minutes to a WACK of phone numbers I have been sent!

(adapted from Starbird and Palen 2011: 1076)

diaspora on Facebook, automated spam detection mechanisms identified their actions as suspicious. Robert Munro, one of the volunteers at Mission 4636, shows a log of how they discovered this and dealt with it (Table 12.3).

170   *Monika Büscher* et al.

Table 12.3 Excerpt from a chat running alongside the Mission 4636 effort

Facebook message exchange	Message logs
'Facebook just told me I'll be banned for spamming if I keep trying to get the word out to Kreyòl speakers.'	Claire, 21 Jan 2010, 16:14:36 (chat-log:4338)
'@Claire – I am talking to FB right now. Can you please give me the exact details of what happened? The message; the group; your FB id (just copy the URL on your profile page).'	Robert_Munro, 21 Jan 2010, 20:53:09-27 (chat-log:4397-40)
'The message was a pop-up, sorry, not showing up in my history, saying that I was engaging in abusive behaviour; presumably because I was sending the same message to many group admins.'	Claire, 21 Jan 2010, 20:55:47-59 (chat-log:4405-6)
'Nasyon Kreyol'	Claire, 21 Jan 2010, 21:00:37 (chat-log:4420)
'Support the Victims of the Earthquake in Haiti, etc.'	Claire, 21 Jan 2010, 21:01:24 (chat-log:4422)
'Thank you – that is enough for them to go on!'	Robert_Munro, 21 Jan 2010, 21:03:16 (chat-log:4424)

(adapted from Munro 2013: 237)

When the issue was flagged in this chat, Munro contacted Facebook and provided them with the name of one of the Kreyòl language groups that Claire, one of the volunteers, was addressing to elicit help with translation – 'Nasyon Kreyol'. Thus prompted, Facebook engineers were able to track what had happened and whitelist these activities (Munro 2013).

Before we move to our concluding conceptual discussion, we must highlight three important lines of analysis that critically highlight some ambiguities in this 'digital humanitarianism'. First, while these efforts clearly made some difference, some professional responders called it a 'shadow operation that was not part of the emergency response plan' (Morrow *et al.* 2011: 16). Second, studies have shown that these success stories neglect wider implications and effects. Mimi Sheller (2013) highlights the asymmetries of power re-enacted through the activities. She shows that the physical and digital influx of highly mobile international responders, from the World Bank to the voluntweeters, with their birds-eye maps, coincided with a local population who mostly had neither the means nor the right to move outside the danger zone. Third, many Haitians were unaware of the digital humanitarian response or did not have a voice in evaluating its usefulness (Clémenzo 2011).

Bearing these lines of critique in mind, we now trace how 'posthuman' phenomenologies, socialities and ethics come together to understand how the information practices we have described have real-world effects on lived experiences that do not have to stop at placating forms of participation, but can engender true spaces of collaboration. They open up opportunities for

Digital urbanism in crises   171

more 'carefully radical' design (Latour 2008) and act as a potential nucleus for a hopeful, 'better' socio-technical 'beast'.

Discussion: designing IT 'better'

A few years back, Donna Haraway echoed Latour's statement, 'We have never been modern' (1993) by saying, 'We have never been human' (2008). From fire, to shoes, to IT, technologies have always been an integral part of what it means to be human. There simply is no purely human or techno-logical. We are, though, exceptionally good at denying this, intellectually and in practice, with quite problematic effects. Binary analyses of IT-based transformations of urban living, which, on the one hand, focus on efficiency gains (Kinoshita *et al.* 2012) and, on the other, warn that new, digitally enhanced modes of surveillance, qualculation and automation put cities and citizens 'under siege' (Graham 2010), do not challenge the users, designers and developers of technology, social, organisational and policy innovations effectively enough. Even though more critical voices draw out socio-technical entanglements, they rarely offer alternatives to dominant IT use and design philosophies, which enable disembodied surveillance that transcends human scale limits of volume, space and time (Solove 2004). They do not question how novel probabilistic quantitative and qualitative calculation, or 'qualcu-lation', which is alien to – and some argue, incomprehensible for – human reasoning (Thrift 2004, Heaven 2013), could be designed differently, and they do not pursue far enough how automation could be designed to enable a better understanding of how responsibilities are distributed across situated human-machine configurations and contexts.

Making critique more constructive does not have to blunt its teeth. On the contrary, an orientation towards the hopeful can deepen analysis. Crises are an opportune setting for the development of critique that enables 'radically careful' and 'carefully radical' design (Latour 2008), because they bring productive ambiguities to the surface. As people are forced to worry about being physically safe, and where their loved ones are, necessity makes for socio-technical innovation. In the process, people's responses to crises reveal some of the seams that hold the human and the technological together in ways that may allow us to design for a more richly sensory perception of digital seams and extensions. A journalist's photograph of three Haitians searching for a mobile phone signal in the Bel Air neighbourhood in Port au Prince, taken on 16 January 2010[8] mundanely but emblematically captures this. They are holding their phones in the air, looking quizzically at their screens, witnessing others talking on their phones, which documents that, at least for some, networks are available. From such observations, inspiration for more 'seamful' design that makes network availability more explicitly perceivable can be drawn (Chalmers 2003). This would really help people understand what is or is not available to them. With our analysis, we seek to exhibit existing and emergent practices like these to inspire design that

172   *Monika Büscher* et al.

notices where people sense their 'posthuman' phenomenologies, or engage in posthuman socialities and ethics and tries to design for 'better' sensory, cognitive, social and material practices that could support this. Three examples will illustrate this.

First, the social practices of self-organising collaboration between local and global actors, are so deeply enmeshed with technology as to make separation between the human and the technological impossible. The use of the 'Tweak the Tweet' standard, for example, shows how people thought and acted through the capabilities of computational technologies to map 'needs' and invented social and technical mechanisms that allowed new ways of representing how people had been affected (Starbird and Palen 2011). This lived posthuman sociality drew some volunteers into an intense involvement and sense of relational ethical obligation, which suggests a technologically enmeshed 'cyborg' phenomenology that is not experienced as singular, but relational. For some participants, this extended phenomenology, sociality and ethics constituted an overwhelming experience. 'Discovering social media's soul' as one participant puts it (Starbird and Palen 2011:1077), created, on the one hand, an exhilarating 'buzz' of sociability and solidarity, and satisfaction at being able to help rather than just watch, but the sheer number of cries for help also haunted some volunteers and led them to exit the social media sphere, at least for some time. One might wonder, with Susan Sontag, whether such engagement enabled the voluntweeters to:

> set aside the sympathy [...] for a reflection on how our privileges are located on the same map as their suffering and may – in ways we might prefer not to imagine – be linked to their suffering
>
> (Sontag 2003: 91–92)

While there is some indication that experiences of relational ethics through mapping Haiti collectively led to more long-term collaborations, such as the Humanitarian OpenStreetMap Team's Haiti Project,[9] four years after the earthquake, the United Nations found that 817,000 Haitians still needed humanitarian assistance (Oxfam 2014). How could technologies be designed to support more sustained practices of relational ethics?

Second, the collectively organised activity of getting one's needs put on a map makes it possible to record absolute space qualitatively, in a way that is quite different from commercial forms of 'qualculation', which, for example, utilise the big data of everyday life to calculate qualitative profiles and tailor personalised advertising for Web-browsing or mobile customers. The collective mapping for Haiti made it possible to see space and time as relative in specific ways. The process by which the geolocation of specific people and needs had to take place, the lived experience of doing it, the very perception of its possibility, and the way that it was initiated by the locals and their technological experience with the freephone number 4636 reveals opportunities for design that supports such grassroots qualculation. This also offers a productive path forward for supporting sensory perception and

Digital urbanism in crises   173

thinking creatively through commercial and government forms of qualculation and surveillance. As citizens appropriate such techniques for themselves, these are no longer just top-down activities, but a way of learning about self-positioning and self-placing, singularly and collectively.

Third, the way in which the Mission 4636 team noticed and addressed the operation of 'blacklisting' algorithms in Facebook reveals how people perceive the seams of posthumanity by pushing technological limits in crises. The collective found a social channel to address the obstacles this produced, leveraging social networks to make contact with Facebook developers. This circumvented a much longer administrative process that would normally be needed to change 'blacklisted' activities to 'whitelisted' activities. However, it also taught people something about how these algorithms operate, fine-tuning their perceptual apparatus for such operation in other socio-technical contextures.

Together, these observations document an emergent digital urbanism, sharpened and made more creative under the duress of crisis. Our observations resonate with analyses that see people increasingly acting like human pantographs, 'measuring out the world and themselves at once' in what threatens to become 'Lifeworld Inc.' (Thrift 2011: 9), contributing to the digital city as a shared nervous system (Bratton 2008). Our observations show how people develop new senses that understand in new ways their displaced or multiplied embodiment, their addressability or 'awhereness' (Thrift 2011), their connected presence (Licoppe 2004) and comobility (Southern 2012), as well as their subjection to new forms of surveillance, qualculation and automation. In the analysis of digital urbanism in crises, we see emergent practices that appropriate these techniques and thereby strengthen people's rational and sensory capabilities to notice and understand their agency in relation to these digital seams and extensions, and to creatively exploit them for their own purposes. At least in part, this seems to turn them into more 'hopeful monsters' (Richards 1994) in the sense that they also unfold more benign socio-technical evolutionary paths. Addressability, for example, is often seen as a worrisome affordance, because it makes it possible to pinpoint and locate people precisely, for purposes of profiling, personalised advertising, governance, or surveillance (Thrift 2011). However, the examples we have discussed show that addressability also allows dialogue. In many cases, the voluntweeters and Mission 4636 translators contacted the people reporting, to confirm information, receipt of aid or resources, to get more information or engage in conversation. So addressability could be two-way. How to design for this is one of the key questions that arises from our analysis.

Acknowledgements

The research is part of research funded by the European Union 7th Framework Programme in the BRIDGE project (Grant no 261817) and the SecInCoRe project (Grant no 261817).

174 *Monika Büscher* et al.

Notes

1 EU projects: BRIDGE (BRIDGE Project 2015) and SecInCoRe (SecInCoRe n.d.)
2 (Disasters Emergency Committee 2015; Turine *et al.* 2015)
3 Transcribed from CBC Radio Canada (2012)
4 Personal communication
5 See IWGCR (2011)
6 NCOIC (2013a; minute 12:16)
7 NCOIC (2013b; minute 3:42)
8 (Thew, S. 2010)
9 (Chavent n.d.)

References

Braidotti, R. (2013) *The Posthuman*, Cambridge: Polity.
Bratton, B.H. (2008) *iPhone City*, available from http://www.bratton.info/projects/texts/iphone-city/pf/ [accessed 1 April 2015].
BRIDGE Project (2015) *Bridge*, available from http://www.bridgeproject.eu/en [accessed 21 November 2015].
Büscher, M., Perng, S-Y. and Liegl, M. (2014) 'Privacy, security, liberty: ICT in crises' *International Journal of Information Systems for Crisis Response and Management*, 6(4): 76–92.
CBC Radio Canada (2012) *Jan 26 & 29: from Port au Prince, Haiti – Kingston, Jamaica – Butare, Rwanda – Nicaragua – Bas Me Limbe, Haiti*, available from http://www.cbc.ca/dispatches/episode/2012/01/26/jan-26-29-from-haiti---kingston-jamaica---butare-rwanda---nicaragua/ [accessed 25 August 2015].
Chalmers, M. (2003) 'Seamful design and UbiComp infrastructure', *Proceedings of UbiComp Workshop, 'At the Crossroads: The Interaction of HCI and Systems Issues in UbiComp'*, available from http://citeseerx.ist.psu.edu/viewdoc/download?doi=10.1.1.61.6779&rep=rep1&type=pdf [1 April 2015]
Chavent, N. (n.d.) 'Haiti', *Humanitarian Open Street Map Team*, available from https://hotosm.org/projects/haiti-2 [accessed 25 August 2015].
Chesbrough, H.W. (2003) *Open Innovation: The New Imperative for Creating and Profiting from Technology*, Boston: Harvard Business Press.
Clémenzo, J-Y. (2011) *Ushahidi Project and Mission 4636 in Haiti: Participation, Representation and Political Economy*, MA thesis, London School of Economics, available from http://jeanyvesclemenzo.ch/Nouveausite/Recherches/DFA24093-B92E-4A34-9746-564DE2E4BC0A_files/ResearchUshahidi.pdf [accessed 1 April 2015].
Disasters Emergency Committee (2015) *Haiti Earthquake Facts and Figures*, available from http://www.dec.org.uk/articles/haiti-earthquake-facts-and-figures [accessed 21 November 2015].
Ellebrecht, N. and Kaufmann, S. (2015) 'Boosting efficiency through the use of IT? Reconfiguring the management of mass casualty incidents in Germany', *International Journal of Information Systems for Crisis Response and Management*, 6(4): 1–18.
Graham, S. (2010) *Cities under Siege: The New Military Urbanism*, London: Verso.
Graham, S. and Marvin, S. (2001) *Splintering Urbanism*, London: Routledge.

Digital urbanism in crises 175

Greenfield, A. (2006) *Everyware: The Dawning Age of Ubiquitous Computing*, San Francisco: Peachpit Press.

Haraway, D.J. (2008) *When Species Meet*, Minneapolis: University of Minnesota Press.

Haraway, D.J. (2010) 'Staying with the trouble: xenoecologies of home for companions in the contested zones', *Cultural Anthropology Online*, July 27, available from http://www.culanth.org/fieldsights/289-staying-with-the-trouble-xenoecologies-of-home-for-companions-in-the-contested-zones [accessed 1 April 2015].

Hayles, N.K. (1999) *How We Became Posthuman: Virtual Bodies in Cybernetics, Literature, and Informatics*, Chicago: University of Chicago Press.

Heaven, D. (2013) 'Not like us: artificial minds we can't understand', *New Scientist*, 2929(8 August 2013): 33–5.

IWGCR (2011) 'Japan earthquake puts data centers and Cloud services at risk', *International Working Group on Cloud Computing Resiliency*, available from http://iwgcr.org/japan-earthquake-puts-data-centers-and-cloud-services-at-risk [accessed 25 August 2015].

Katsumi, B.T. (2013) 'The resiliency, dependability and "survivability" of Cloud computing', *CloudScape V*, available from http://www.cloudscapeseries.eu/Content/Agenda.aspx?id=264 [accessed 1 April 2015].

Kinoshita, K., Yukio I., Hideaki K. and Maeda, Y. (2012) 'Technologies and emergency management for disaster recovery – with focus on the great east Japan earthquake', *IEICE Transactions on Communications*, E95.B(6): 1911–4.

Kitchin, R. and Dodge, M. (2011) *Code/Space: Software and Everyday Life*. Cambridge, MA: MIT Press.

Latour, B. (1993) *We Have Never Been Modern*, Boston: Harvard University Press.

Latour, B. (2008) 'A cautious Prometheus? A few steps toward a philosophy of design (with special attention to Peter Sloterdijk)', in F. Hackney, J. Glynne, and V. Minton (eds) *Networks of Design, Proceedings of the 2008 Annual International Conference of the Design History Society*: 2–10.

Licoppe, C. (2004) '"Connected" presence: the emergence of a new repertoire for managing social relationships in a changing communication technoscape', *Environment and Planning D: Society and Space*, 22(1): 135–56.

MacAskill, E. Borger, J. Hopkins, N. Davies, N. and Ball, J. (2013) 'GCHQ taps fibre-optic cables for secret access to world's communications', *The Guardian*, June 21, available from http://www.guardian.co.uk/uk/2013/jun/21/gchq-cables-secret-world-communications-nsa [accessed 1 April 2015].

Meier, P. (2012) 'How crisis mapping saved lives in Haiti – News Watch', *National Geographic Explorers Journal*, 2 July 2012, available from http://newswatch.nationalgeographic.com/2012/07/02/crisis-mapping-haiti/ [accessed 1 April 2015].

Morrow, N., Mock, N., Papendieck, A. and Kocmich, N. (2011) 'Independent evaluation of the Ushahidi Haiti Project', *Development Information Systems International Ushahidi Haiti Project*, available from www.alnap.org/pool/files/1282.pdf [accessed 1 April 2015].

Munro, R. (2013) 'Crowdsourcing and the crisis-affected community: lessons learned and looking forward from Mission 4636', *Information Retrieval*, 16(2): 210–66.

Nancy, J-L. (2000) *Being Singular Plural*, Redwood City: Stanford University Press.

NCOIC (2013a) *NCOIC Cloud Computing Demo – Video 2*, available from https://www.youtube.com/watch?v=lydf9xGOfHQ [accessed 25 August 2015].

176 *Monika Büscher et al.*

NCOIC (2013b) *NCOIC Cloud Computing Demo – Video 1*, available from https://www.youtube.com/watch?v=Wkeha_GKkAU [accessed 25 August 2015].

NCOIC Rapid Response (2013) NCOIC Rapid Response Capability Process – NCOIC, available from http://www.ncoic.org/10-technology/41-tech-prod-process-nrrc [accessed 1 April 2015].

Oh, O., Agrawal, M. and Rao, H.R. (2010) 'Information control and terrorism: tracking the Mumbai terrorist attack through Twitter', *Information Systems Frontiers*, 13(1): 33–43.

Oxfam (2014) 'Haiti earthquake: 4 years later', *Oxfam International*, available from http://www.oxfam.org/en/haitiquake [accessed 1 March 2014].

Richards, E. (1994) 'A political anatomy of monsters, hopeful and otherwise: teratogeny, transcendentalism, and evolutionary theorizing', *Isis*, 85(3): 377–411.

Samuels, R.J. (2013) *3.11: Disaster and Change in Japan*, Ithaca: Cornell University Press.

SecInCoRe (n.d.) *The SecInCoRe Project*, available from http://www.secincore.eu/ [accessed 21 November 2015].

Shanley, L., Burns, R., Bastian, Z. and Robson, E.S. (2013) *Tweeting up a Storm: The Promise and Perils of Crisis Mapping*, Washington, DC: Wilson Centre, available from https://www.wilsoncenter.org/sites/default/files/October_Highlight_865-879.pdf [accessed 1 April 2015].

Sheller, M. (2013) 'The islanding effect: post-disaster mobility systems and humanitarian logistics in Haiti', *Cultural Geographies*, 20(2): 185–204.

Solove, D.J. (2011) *Nothing to Hide: The False Tradeoff between Privacy and Security*, New Haven: Yale University Press.

Sontag, S. (2003) *Regarding the Pain of Others*, London: Penguin Books.

Southern, J. (2012) 'Comobility: how proximity and distance travel together in locative media', *Canadian Journal for Communications*, 37(1): 75–91.

Starbird, K. and Palen, L. (2011) '"Voluntweeters": self-organizing by digital volunteers in times of crisis', *Proceedings of the SIGCHI Conference on Human Factors in Computing Systems*, 1071–80.

Starbird, K. and Stamberger, J. (2010) 'Tweak the Tweet: leveraging microblogging proliferation with a prescriptive syntax to support citizen reporting', *Proceedings of the 7th International ISCRAM Conference*, 1–5.

Steinberg, T. (2000) *Acts of God: The Unnatural History of Natural Disaster in America*, New York: Oxford University Press.

Suchman, L. and Weber, J. (2014) 'Human-machine autonomies', *Symposium: Autonomous Weapons Systems – Law, Ethics, Policy, Florence, European University Institute*, 24–25 April.

Thew, S. (2010) 'Hatian [sic] earthquake photo preview 01991418', *European Press Photo Agency*, available from http://www.epa.eu/disasters-photos/earthquake-photos/hatian-earthquake-photos-01991418 [accessed 25 August 2015].

Thrift, N. (2004) 'Movement-space: the changing domain of thinking resulting from the development of new kinds of spatial awareness', *Economy and Society*, 33(4): 582–604.

Thrift, N. (2011) 'Lifeworld Inc – and what to do about it', *Environment and Planning D: Society and Space*, 29(1): 5–26.

Turine, G., Gabriner, A., Bicker, P. and Laurent, O. (2015) 'Haiti earthquake: five years after', *TIME*, 12 January 2015, available from http://time.com/3662225/haiti-earthquake-five-year-after/ [accessed 21 November 2015].

Vidal, J. (2012) 'Earth faces a century of disasters, report warns', available from http://www.rawstory.com/2012/04/earth-faces-a-century-of-disasters-report-warns/ [accessed 1 April 2015].

Vinck, P. (2013) *World Disasters Report: Focus on Technology and the Future of Humanitarian Action*, Geneva: International Federation of Red Cross and Red Crescent Societies, available from http://www.ifrc.org/PageFiles/134658/WDR 2013 complete.pdf [accessed 1 April 2015].

Whatmore, S. (1997) 'Dissecting the autonomous self: hybrid cartographies for a relational ethics', *Environment and Planning D: Society and Space*, 15(1): 37–53.

13 Coding alternative modes of governance

Learning from experimental 'peer-to-peer cities'

Alison Powell

Introduction

Coded infrastructure impacts city life, in ways that can largely be unconscious. Codes do not necessarily have to be imposed on the city from outside of it. They may emerge from within the city, and by doing so demonstrate different ways of constructing urban experience. Coding can be sense making, and building coded infrastructures can in turn require sense making – including decisions about how the code work should fit into a particular urban space, and how it ought to be managed and sustained. This chapter develops a perspective on peer-to-peer engagements on the coded city by analysing how coding practice is related to the development of other social and cultural 'codes' that propose alternative ways of integrating technology into space. It argues that peer-to-peer coded cities are most significant because they suggest alternative ways of governing the interface between technology, the social and the spatial.

Dominant visions of 'smart' or 'coded' cities reinforce top-down governance via centralised control. Bottom-up visions stress participatory engagement in urban space and politics through the use of information, sensors and data processing as part of citizen engagement. This chapter identifies how ICT projects of the past were imagined as providing opportunities for collaborative development and governance of particular urban spaces, in opposition to top-down efforts at urban communication governance taking place at the same time. We will see how these past projects, which often focused on providing access to communication enact a 'politics of the minor' (Feenberg 2011; Osborne and Rose 1999) and introduce new possibilities for governance of augmented urban spaces that are relevant for today's 'smart city' proposals.

This understanding of governance includes 'all processes of governing, whether undertaken by a government, market or network, whether over a family, tribe, formal or informal organisation or territory and whether through laws, norms, power or language' (Bevir 2013: 1). In this case, the object of such governance is the city – or more precisely the code-mediated city – and the governance itself consists of a set of norms, frameworks or decisions that configure how ICTs ought to be integrated into city space and life. While a narrow view of civic governance might focus on the role of a formal organisation (the *government*), our broader view of governance here is concerned with the role of informal organisations, including loose organisations who use peer-to-peer methods to develop coded infrastructures that they establish in city space.

Previous attempts at creating peer-to-peer urbanism suggest that ICT-enabled cities need meaningful governance of the integration of technologies into cities – which encompasses how projects are conceived and discussed (discourse), how they are established in space (practice) and how they are built (architecture). These three elements are simultaneously co-produced, and all of them have an impact on the ability of people who live in cities to speak and be heard. I examine how peer-to-peer urbanism, as represented by community wireless networks, establishes alternative governance modes through discourse, practice and architecture. The analysis, I contend, is a step towards constructing a framework for good governance that can then be applied to future coded or 'smart' cities.

The top-down 'smart city'

'Smart' systems are intended to augment urban spaces: as Aurigi and De Cindio (2008: 1) write: 'The gradual development of an enriched media environment, ubiquitous computing, mobile and wireless communication technologies, as well as the Internet as a non-extraordinary part of our everyday lives, are changing the ways people use cities and live in them.' These augmentations include blending mediated data with built spaces, presenting media on large screens or on personal devices, and providing ways to visualise movements, decisions and contextual information. Dodge and Kitchin (2005) describe the ways that these projects layer software-controlled spaces over physical and geographical spaces, providing interfaces and data processing layers that become embedded into the experience of particular kinds of space. These software elements sort and control the people and things that move through spaces, altering their relationships. The software-controlled layer is often perceived as being able to provide information and calculations that are of broad social benefit, such as community sensing (Salim 2012) and data visualisation (Moere and Hill 2012).

These technological layers create data that are available for use by various actors in various ways. Smart cities are seen, on the one hand, as being able to enact more efficient control of the complex systems of cities by creating more data for cybernetic control systems (Townsend, 2013) and, on the other hand, to improve the day-to-day decision making of individuals through 'street computing' that allows everyday users to take advantage of otherwise-hidden computational interfaces within the city. This is achieved by building or gaining access to sensor networks, tapping into publicly collected open data, or employing APIs to capture, use and remix data collected by mobile

180 *Alison Powell*

phone companies. This apparent opposition between smart cities facilitating better cybernetic management and smart cities providing more opportunities for citizens to improve their own experiences seems straightforward, but both the dominant paradigm of centrally governed cities *and* the alternative paradigm of emergent citizen use of data-collecting ICTs depend on strong interlinkages with commercial infrastructure and processing power. The ethic of 'street computing' is, on one level, participatory and empowering, as it seeks a way for individuals to make sense out of data flows. On another level though, it is deterministic and celebratory – for example, Moere and Hill (2012: 28) write, 'Recent advances in sensing devices, wireless network connectivity, and display hardware have made the ultimate vision of ubiquitous computing finally possible, in which the "computer" as we know it becomes embedded in physical objects and surfaces of everyday life.' Not only does this framing imply a technologically driven vision for the city, it also implies some linear, forward motion towards that vision, which is evoked as being not just desirable but inevitable.

Dominant perspectives: technology and cities as neutral

Dominant smart city rhetoric and smart city projects imply a neutral, if not straightforwardly positive role for technology within the city. The city augmented by technology is an improved city, with efficiency of service provision created as a result of data collection architectures and without too much of the messiness and dynamism otherwise associated with city life. This means that smart cities are often commercial cities or cities of privatised technology, when vendors deploy particular systems into urban spaces. In his critique of the dominant imaginary of smart cities, urban scholar Adam Greenfield suggests that one problem with smart city narratives is that they seem to refer to cities as if they were not real, actual, varying places. He writes, 'The canonical smart city almost *has* to be staged in any-space-whatever; only by proposing to install generic technologies on generic landscapes in a generic future can advocates avoid running afoul of the knotty complexities that crop up immediately any time actual technologies are deployed in actual places' (Greenfield 2013). Greenfield notes how the discourses used to describe smart city projects encode a hypothesis that the contemporary urban environment is too difficult for ordinary, unaided human beings to understand and manage, and that some higher power (in this case, information processing and computer-aided decision making) is required.

One of the consequences of this is that the dominant vision for smart cities imagines them as 'clean' and 'legal' places where data calculation systems pre-empt disruptive or illegal activity. Data collection thus functions like centralised surveillance systems: as a system of discipline in which the fear of being observed drives exemplary behaviour. Idealising cities as entities that can be abstracted and rationalised has a long history that encompasses but extends past modernity. Expectations of both abstraction and rationality

Coding alternative modes of governance   181

characterised imaginings of the nineteenth century city – the industrial, well-ruled and orderly city – as the model for government, even while representations of the time returned over and over to the actual city's problematic immanence; its ungovernability, crime, destitution, vice, gambling and drunkenness (Foucault 1984; Osborne and Rose 1999). But because there is more than one way of imagining the data city, and more than one way of structuring the systems that are part of it, there are alternative visions for smart cities too – much as there were alternative visions for previous visions of exemplary city life.

Alternative perspectives: a coded city of 'minor politics'

These alternative visions focus on the capacity of citizens to leverage features of new technologies to experience urban life differently. Urbanist Anthony Townsend suggests that sensor networks and mobile technologies (especially smartphones) have made it possible for 'a motley assortment of activists, entrepreneurs, and civic hackers' to tinker with technology as a means to 'amplify and accelerate the natural sociability of city life' (2013: 9). Townsend focuses on how these people imagine a different kind of data city – one that builds mechanisms to share data and creates interfaces that allow different perceptions and navigations of city spaces. This creates a 'lattice' interconnecting local space and technology. This architectural layer forms one element of peer-to-peer urbanism. Beyond these technological capacities, however, peer-to-peer alternatives establish alternative organisational practices, and promote different kinds of spatial engagement, essential components of an expanded concept of peer-to-peer urban governance.

Peer-produced or grassroots ICT projects suggest that instead of a centralised ICT-enabled city with established top-down governance, it might be possible to develop a peer-to-peer smart city featuring heterarchical organisational practices and distributed modes of architecture. These notions leverage a 'minor politics' of urbanism (Osborne and Rose 1999) that stresses the local and contingent nature of urban experience (Thrift 2014). The real variation of experiences at the point where technology, organisation, culture and place combine suggests that the small, messy or unsustainable interventions enacted through peer-to-peer urban projects like community wireless networks have significant value in rethinking ideas of governance in the era of the smart city.

Peer-to-peer: from coding practice to governance norm?

'Peer-to-peer' refers to a relational dynamic based on equipotency between members. Originally referring to a modification of client-server information processing architecture that partitions processing work between a number of interlinked nodes, the concept has been extended into social and economic fields, reflecting the influence of ideas about society's networked organisation

182 *Alison Powell*

(Castells 2001). 'Peer-to-peer' came to describe the relational dynamics at work in distributed networks within organisations or communities of practice. Yochai Benkler (2006) develops the concept of commons-based peer production to refer to the economic and social impacts of collaborative and contributory projects, including free and open source software production and the development of Wikipedia. He claims that the network form and peer production practices create a networked information economy where freely given peer-to-peer contributions also contribute to markets. Such a networked information economy supports individual autonomy and other liberal values. In the wake of Benkler's work, theoretical and empirical critiques have focused on the relationship between peer-to-peer processes, economic and organisational shifts, and the value systems of liberal and neoliberal capitalist systems. Peer-to-peer contribution systems have been perceived as more democratic than other systems of production for software code or knowledge in general, as oppositional to contemporary neoliberal information orders, or as disruptive to existing intellectual property regimes. They have also been imagined as intrinsically linked with a minor or 'micropolitics', which are 'distinguished from such large-scale interventions as elections and revolutions that aim at state power' (Feenberg 2011). How might peer-to-peer urbanism unfold, and would it create a different locus of control for the coded informational layers of the city – perhaps even an opposition to centralised data collection and control?

The legacy of community wireless networks illustrates how F/OSS (free and open source software) modes of peer production expand from coding to other practices and how coded architecture illustrates alternative ways of conceiving space.

History and legacy of community wireless networks – peer-to-peer coded urbanism

Community wireless networks (CWNs), based on local experimentation with wireless radio technology, emerged around the world in the years following the drop in price of radio communication equipment that used unlicensed or license-exempt radio, which could be reconfigured using F/OSS. These projects exemplify the interplay of culture, organisation and technical production that characterise the potential importance of peer-to-peer coded cities and their minor politics of governance.

In 2002, the first 'free information advocates' met in Berlin to talk about free information infrastructures. In 2003, Freifunk ('free radio') was founded with the goal of providing Internet connectivity across underserved areas of East Berlin. In the following decade, hundreds or perhaps thousands of these community based networks were set up, bringing together people interested in experimenting with open wireless technologies and those interested in improving civic life. In general, projects embraced one of two architectural forms: either using wireless as a means of broadcasting a single point of

Internet access, or as a means of establishing meshed networks that interlinked individual wireless routing devices. Like other alternative imaginations of technology-enhanced cities, they influenced dominant imaginations, in some cases inspiring the development of municipal scale wireless connectivity projects.

These projects espoused a range of aims and goals that included providing Internet access to underserved areas or using wireless networks as a mechanism for social engagement, but also focused on F/OSS development, open hardware, reuse and repurposing of computer technology, and public engagement with communication policy issues. Community wireless networks depended on some form of community contribution of expertise, time, money, hardware or software (Abdelaal and Ali 2008). They experimented with peer-to-peer urbanism through cultures of peer production derived from F/OSS development strategies (Gaved and Mulholland 2008; Forlano *et al.* 2011) by positioning alternative coded architectures as alternative spatial engagements (Powell 2008; Antoniadis *et al.* 2008), and promising alternative modes of social engagement (Shaffer 2013). The links between the codes of F/OSS development and the reimagining of space reveal how alternative conceptions of the coded city establish new ways of engaging and governing local space. This valorises unstable, temporary and contingent encodings of urban space, which permit us to think about governance of the smart city as a form of politics of the minor.

Peer-to-peer production and modes of participation

Community wireless network projects depended on the existence of F/OSS software that permitted modification of wireless equipment in order to effectively run their projects. This software was collaboratively developed by an international community of practice who shared the code online, and by local activists who subsequently modified it and (not always legally) installed it onto wireless networking hardware. The different options for F/OSS wireless networking software also linked with the different ways that activists imagined that CWNs could fit into their city neighbourhoods – from the expansion of convivial 'third places' imagined by participants at Montreal's Ile Sans Fil network to the alternative media and file-sharing network constructed using high-powered wireless technology by the members of the Athens Metropolitan Wireless Network. The Athens Metropolitan Wireless Network was built by friends who lived around the hills in the centre of Athens, and used antennae mounted on the tops of apartment buildings to link together these private spaces in a network that never connected to the public Internet. In contrast with the provision of Internet in existing public spaces imagined by Ile Sans Fil, this presents a highly private view of the city. Other networks imagined wireless connectivity as a form of media (in Lawrence, Kansas, the CWN launched a local online newspaper) or security infrastructure (in Lompoc, California, the network managers installed virtual

184　*Alison Powell*

networks so that police and fire services could use it for their work, and also provided temporary service to contractors at the local air base and prison) (see Forlano *et al.* 2011).

Social organisation and legitimacy

The social dynamics within peer-to-peer processes are also variable. Peer-to-peer processes are often described as being inherently more democratic than other modes of engagement, especially because they aim to create shared commons of assets (Bauwens 2005). In the expansion of coded work into city space, some parallels with the dynamics of peer-to-peer production online emerge. Although some CWNs developed their technical projects using hierarchies where one person was ultimately responsible for the quality of the code, other strategies were required in order to maintain interest and participation in projects over the long term, as well as to secure the roll-out and maintenance of Wi-Fi infrastructure. These included distributed, heterarchical models of organisation, characterised around strong participation in developing the physical wireless access network and the social, organisational and cultural capital also required to make projects 'go live'.

These varying strategies align with the two forms of peer production: 'heavy' and 'lightweight' (Haythornthwaite 2009). 'Heavyweight peer production' is characterised by 'strong-tie affiliation with community members and community purpose, enacted through internally negotiated, peer-reviewed contribution' (here and below, Haythornthwaite 2009: 1). Strongly organised CWNs with institutional ties to other organisations followed this form. In contrast, 'lightweight peer production' functions 'by weak-tie attachment to a common purpose, enacted through authority-determined, rule-based contribution', including the CWN projects that invited people to list their open Wi-Fi hotspots but also in projects that required only technical interconnection to become 'part of the project'. For example, at Berlin's Freifunk network, participation in the network was both limited to and required the construction of a mesh network node – although in the end this was such a difficult task that for many it transformed into a form of 'heavyweight peer production'. Regardless, the instigators of the Freifunk network were clear that anyone who was willing to build a network node was welcome to participate in the construction of the network: 'Freifunk is just a concept, it is not an entity', reported one of the network's founders (Forlano *et al.* 2011: 36). Each node host owns an equal portion of the network, making the network the property of its participants.

In contrast, other CWNs employed more structured and hierarchical relationships. This happened both through the choices made about project architecture and through organisational structures. In rural Denmark, the Djursland project used secured anchors. Finally, some CWNs moved from grassroots organisational forms to hybrid organisational forms including

Coding alternative modes of governance 185

community–university partnerships (Vienna, Austria), municipally owned networks (Fredericton, NB; Wireless Philadelphia), and municipal–community partnerships (Montreal, QC) (Tapia *et al.* 2009). These structural relationships encoded methods of collaboration between very different kinds of entity, with the shared project of extending the communicational benefits of coded infrastructure to all.

Architectural choices

In addition to showing the variable ways that F/OSS might augment urban space, and the intersecting modes through which legitimacy is constructed for CWN proponents, CWNs also demonstrate the extension of code into space by politicising architectural choices. These political positionings emerge with the architectural possibilities available for setting up wireless networks. Two architectural forms – broadcast and distributed networks, combined with the social structures that developed around CWNs – establish frameworks for an alternative diagramming of the city. Broadcast networks require Internet connectivity at a central point that is of high enough quality to transmit a signal to receivers in the area, bearing in mind that the radio spectrum used by CWNs is of low quality. By contrast, a distributed network architecture in which wireless routers are linked together, each sharing a portion of their connectivity, suggests a reciprocal, peer-to-peer diagram of civic relationships. These different modes imply different relationships between people within the city, and even different conceptual frames for civic relations. Osborne and Rose (1999) use the concept of 'diagramming' to suggest the relationship between space and government of cities. They write, 'The vicious immanence of the city is a never-ending incitement to projects of government. Such projects seek to capture the forces immanent in the city, to identify them, order them, intensify some and weaken others, to retain the viability of the socialising forces immanent to urban agglomeration while civilising their antagonisms' (Osborne and Rose 1999: 738).

We could take community networks as literal 'diagrams' of cities, which propose alternative spatial tendencies by establishing nodes and links that connect different kinds of space, some physical and some virtual. We could also take them as invitations to employ the different 'diagramming' modes as proxies for understanding the social and relational aspects of local city governance. A 'broadcast lilypad city' might valorise centres of exchange, such as local community centres (used by many CWNs as installation points for wireless broadcast antennae), and more aggregate modes of social relation in keeping with the traditions of social mapping derived from the Chicago School of Sociology in the 1930s. These modes focus on a knowable city that can be mapped. In contrast a 'distributed, peer-to-peer city' might valorise more informal social links not based around cultural institutions, or the creation of hybrid, commercial–community 'third spaces' (Oldenburg 1989).

186 *Alison Powell*

Spatial engagements: a coded city's alternative diagrams

Community wireless networks reiterate how such diagramming of the city can be a socio-technical project linking new infrastructures to existing social and spatial practice. In other words, CWNs and their interventions create a way for advocates to talk about and explore what their cities mean to them. For example, in his report on the Consume network active in London in the early 2000s, Julian Priest (2004) argued that attempts to map the location of Consume network nodes was actually more successful as a proxy for measuring the location of geeks living in London, since geeky participants in the Consume project were likely to have wireless network nodes on their personal property. Unfortunately, for the 'success' of Consume, the distribution of geeks was concentrated in particular areas of the city, and outside of these areas their density was simply not high enough to create a functioning wireless network. In analysing Adelaide Wireless in southern Australia, Jungnickel (2014) focused on the messiness of aims to create a meshed network linking individual residences, which by necessity included *ad-hoc* and informal meetings of wireless network creators in backyards and on rooftops. These meetings were social; in addition to helping create wireless networks, they also spawned relationships to other civic technologies (like bicycles).

Outcomes and implications

The proliferation of CWNs as code-based civic interventions in particular urban spaces was short-lived. By some measures, the vast majority of these projects failed: in 2005, individuals added thousands of wireless nodes to collaborative online maps, such as nodeDB or the Wikipedia page for CWNs. At present, only a fraction of these networks are still in operation. This lack of sustainability also suggests some lessons for governance within 'minor politics'. Some of the CWN legacies rest in social, rather than technical transformations that appeared at the time to be temporary or contingent. The network of people who initially set up Serbia's BGWireless network found that their monthly picnic hackathons were more valuable than a functioning network and have continued to hold the parties without supporting the code. Other legacies are technical: CWNs actively contributed to the development of F/OSS software and hardware, including gateway software, such as WiFiDog, and mesh networking software, such as the Mesh Potato, a version of which was used to relay activist communications during the Arab Spring. These collective efforts go quite some distance to establish an information commons: 'the "open and free" availability of the raw material; participatory "processing"; and commons-oriented output' (Bauwens 2009: 122). Since these products of peer-produced efforts remain in common ownership, they maintain the possibility of peer-produced F/OSS code production and the expansion of peer-to-peer cities (Corsin-Jimanez, 2014). Finally, some projects achieved sustainability through encoding new social relationships

Coding alternative modes of governance   187

amongst techno-enthusiasts, small businesses, city governments and non-governmental organisations. These efforts created locally specific modes of integrating technology into the minor politics of the urban. They succeeded in producing technology in space, as engagement with space, in ways that were appropriate to the spaces they were in, for as long as it made sense to be there. Some remain as parts of infrastructure and others leave traces in the cultural and social spaces of cities, and in the codes that can still be used to augment them.

Conclusion

This chapter has contrasted two modes of combining citizenship, technology and space, the 'hierarchical city' espoused in many 'smart city' technology projects, and the 'peer-to-peer' city suggested by some CWN projects. Such projects establish a range of alternative means of organising access to communications. The 'coding' includes the integration of F/OSS social and cultural codes into the city, and the way that wireless architecture is imagined as being integrated into the city.

The extent to which projects oriented around the smart city can produce forms of 'technological citizenship' depends on how citizenship, space and technology are combined. Although it is tempting to automatically oppose dominant and alternative visions of cities, history does not work that way. The alternatives of the peer-to-peer city have also influenced the dominant imaginaries, at least in the way they have organised infrastructures and positioned discourses that facilitate the development – temporary, contingent – of coded city projects that can generate alternative modes of imagining a smart city. However, CWNs offered only an alternative to technological citizenship based around the consumption of ICT connectivity. Another way of looking at the partnerships created as these networks became more sustainable would be as an appropriation of the alternative into the dominant (Cammaerts 2011). Indeed the very notion of citizenship has now been challenged by the dominant neoliberal political order. Can peer-to-peer forms effectively challenge this political form?

This challenge poses a problem for the emerging forms of encoding that are bound in to the contemporary city. The augmentation of the city through technology is now based less on the opportunity to be 'connected' (as it was for CWN projects) and more on the production and processing of data via information networks. As the technological city shifts from being a place where new innovations are discussed as creating new ways to listen and speak, and towards a place where subjects produce and clients consume data, the alternative modes of techno-social governance sketched here will need to be better developed. In the coming reiteration of the smart city, who writes the codes? How will data be able to speak for people's interest? As these develop and mature, we need to examine how they, too, might be governed – and what techno-social alternatives remain.

188 *Alison Powell*

References

Abdelaal, A.M. and Ali, H.H. (2008) 'A graph theoretic approach for analysis and design of community wireless networks', *AMCIS 2008 Proceedings*, available from http://aisel.aisnet.org/amcis2008/310 [accessed 25 November 2015].

Antoniadis, P., Le Grand, B., Satsiou, A., Tassiulas, L., Aguiar, R., Barraca, J. and Sargento, S. (2008) 'Community building over neighborhood wireless mesh networks', *IEEE Technology and Society Magazine*, 27(1): 48–56.

Aurigi, A. and de Cindio, F. (2008) (eds) *Augmented Urban Spaces: Articulating the Physical and Electronic City, Design and the Built Environment*. Farnham, UK: Ashgate.

Bauwens, M. (2005) 'The political economy of peer production', *1000 Days of Theory*, available from http://www.ctheory.net/articles.aspx?id=499 [accessed 25 August 2015].

Bauwens, M. (2009) 'Class and capital in peer production', *Capital & Class*, 33(1): 121–41.

Benkler, Y. (2006) *The Wealth of Networks: How Social Production Transforms Markets and Freedom*, New Haven: Yale University Press.

Bevir, M. (2013) *A Theory of Governance*, Berkeley: University of California Press.

Cammaerts, B. (2011) 'Disruptive sharing in a digital age: rejecting neoliberalism?', *Continuum: Journal of Media and Cultural Studies*, 25(1): 47–62.

Castells, M. (2001) *The Internet Galaxy*, Oxford: Oxford University Press.

Corsin-Jimanez, A. (2014) 'The right to infrastructure: a prototype for open source urbanism', *Environment and Planning D Society and Space*, 32(2): 342–62.

Dodge, M., and Kitchin, R. (2005) 'Code and the transduction of space', *Annals of the Association of American Geographers*, 95(1): 162–80.

Feenberg, A. (2011) 'Agency and citizenship in a technological society', *Course on Digital Citizenship*, IT University of Copenhagen.

Forlano, L., Powell, A., Shaffer, G. and Lennett, B. (2011) *From the Digital Divide to Digital Excellence: Global Best Practices for Municipal and Community Wireless Networks*, Washington, DC: New America Foundation.

Foucault, M., and P. Rabinow (ed.) (1984) *The Foucault Reader*, New York: Pantheon.

Gaved, M. and Mulholland, P. (2008) 'Pioneers, subcultures and cooperatives: the grassroots augmentation of urban places', in A. Aurigi and F. de Cindio (eds) *Augmented Urban Spaces: Articulating the Physical and Electronic City. Design and the Built Environment*, Farnham, UK: Ashgate.

Greenfield, A. (2013) *The City is Here for You to Use: Part I Against the Smart City*, New York: DO projects.

Haythornthwaite, C. (2009) 'Crowds and communities: heavy and lightweight models of peer production', *Proceedings of the Hawaii International Conference on System Sciences*, available from https://ideals.illinois.edu/bitstream/handle/2142/9457/HICSS%2042%20PPVCC%20Jan%202009.pdf?sequence=2 [accessed 25 August 2015].

Jungnickel, K. (2014) *DiY WiFi: Re-imagining Connectivity*, London: Palgrave MacMillan 'Pivot'.

Moere, A.V. and Hill, D. (2012) 'Designing for the situated and public visualisation of urban data', *Journal of Urban Technology*, 19(2): 25–46.

Coding alternative modes of governance   189

Oldenburg, R. (1989) *The Great Good Place: Cafés, Coffee Shops, Community Centers, Beauty Parlors, General Stores, Bars, Hangouts and How They Get You through the Day*. New York: Paragon House.

Osborne, T. and Rose, N. (1999) 'Governing cities: notes on the spatialisation of virtue', *Environment and Planning D: Society and Space*, 17(6): 737–60.

Powell, A. (2008) 'Wi-Fi publics: producing community and technology', *Information, Communication and Society*, 11(8): 1034–56.

Priest, J. (2004) *The State of Wireless London*, available from http://informal.org.uk/people/julian/publications/the_state_of_wireless_london/ [accessed 25 August 2015].

Salim, F.D. (2012) 'Probing streets and the built environment with ambient and community sensing', *Journal of Urban Technology*, 19(2): 47–67.

Shaffer, G. (2013) 'Lessons learned from grassroots wireless networks in Europe', in A. Abdelaal (ed.) *Social and Economic Effects of Community Wireless Networks and Infrastructures*, Hershey, PA: Idea Group Inc.

Tapia, A.H., Ortiz, J.A. and Powell, A. (2009) 'Reforming policy to promote local broadband networks', *Journal of Communication Inquiry*, 33(4): 354–75.

Thrift, N. (2014) 'The "sentient" city and what it may portend', *Big Data and Society*, 1(1): 1–21.

Townsend, A. (2013) *Smart Cities: Big Data, Civic Hackers, and the Quest for a New Utopia*, New York: W.W. Norton and Co.

14 Encountering the city at hacking events

Sophia Maalsen and Sung-Yueh Perng

Introduction

Software developers have long held community events in which they build code and discuss issues or bugs they encounter. The open source community first coined the term 'hackathon' for an event held on 4 June 1999 when developers converged on Calgary, Canada, to work on Internet identity and security protocols (OpenBSD n.d.). In its early stage, and within the OpenBSD community, attending hackathons had both technological and symbolic significance. Although participation was not on a paid-for basis, attendance at the events was by invitation only, targeting those with demonstrated abilities; these were not 'developer training events'. Hackathons have since diversified and spread beyond elite tech communities. Meyer and Ermoshina (2013: 3) categorise hackathons into three types: 'issue oriented', centred around solving specific real-world problems; 'tech oriented', focused on developing prototype systems; and 'data oriented', wherein datasets are supplied by the organisers. The value of the events is more than technological and includes building 'new alliances and partnerships, discovering and developing new ideas and approaches to problems, and providing the muscle needed to make the new ideas and approaches a reality' (Popyack 2014: 40). From a personal perspective, attending a hackathon can provide a route into a new community, lead to potential new employment or a start-up enterprise, enhance skills and build friendships.

Since 2009, the social and ethical benefits derived from the use of open government data have led to an increase in 'civic hackathons'. Following the American 'coding for democracy' movement, civic hackers are described as 'technologists, civil servants, designers, entrepreneurs, engineers – anybody – who uses a minimum of resources and a maximum of brainpower and ingenuity to create, enhance or fix something' (Meyer and Ermoshina 2013: 3). Thus, for Meyer and Ermoshina (2013), hackathons contain an experimental element of bricolage as well as being collaborative, heterogeneous and constituted by hybrid expertise. This creates an innovation and problem-solving space and a set of tools in which social challenges can be addressed through technology and which produces a community of experts, professionals, activists and citizens, who can mutually support each other and contribute their individual skills.

Despite their benefits and ethics of openness, hackathons nonetheless pose questions and difficulties with respect to the politics of membership, which has implications for which issues are addressed, how they are tackled, and to whom the end product is designed. Usually taking place at weekends to attract working developers, and often consisting of intensive ten-hour-plus working days, hackathons tend to exclude those who have weekend and family commitments. Moreover, the decision making process during the event can prioritise the views of technology and coding experts and marginalise the roles played by domain experts, social scientists, urban planners, activists, public sector employees, local volunteers and interest groups. More crucially, the timing and format can ignore the opinions and experiences of local residents, whose everyday lives are to be analysed, programmed and reconfigured and potentially altered and disrupted. This is most acutely reflected in the production of apps intended to shape the 'smart city', leading to questions as to whom the smart city is being designed by and for. As Porway (2013) reflects, rather than addressing broader social problems faced by cities, there is a danger that hackathons only 'solve the participant's problems because as a young affluent hacker, my problem isn't improving the city's recycling programs, it's finding kale on Saturdays'.

In this chapter, we examine how the energy, data, creativity and imagination play out when code is mobilised to address urban problems and the implications and challenges that emerge in that process. To do so, we draw on our ethnographic participant observation conducted in Dublin, Ireland, in 2014. We focus on Code for Ireland events, but are also informed by the participation in a number of other coding or hacking events. Although we both have relatively weak coding skills, much of which were learnt through the hackathons, these events became increasingly inclusive over time, with an emerging appreciation of a diversity of skills beyond coding, and thus we could contribute to the hackathons in other ways (such as providing feedback, domain knowledge, facilitating team negotiation). Moreover, we engaged in dialogue with event organisers concerning our observations, opening up two-way communication that enabled a more reflexive research practice. In particular, we use our fieldwork at Code for Ireland to examine the productive tension in the aims and ambitions between two forces often found at work at Code for Ireland 'meet-ups' which do not always seamlessly interact: what the developers want to do and what the government or companies running the hackathon desire. The following sections comment on the making of hacking space, the fluidity and messiness of the hackathon process, and questions whether the end-products live up to the promotional rhetoric of hackathons.

192   Sophia Maalsen and Sung-Yueh Perng

Placing civic hacking

The mundane question of where participants hack and develop apps is often overlooked when highlighting the value, ethics and culture within the hacking community. However, the place of hacking is important because the social relationships and practices of assembling code have to be brought together to be materialised in chips, parts and infrastructure to take effect (MacKenzie 2001), and venues and their configuration produce particular kinds of sociality and spatiality that influence interactions and dynamics within teams and projects, and also influence attendance. To decode how Code for Ireland provides a 'place' for hacking and how their goals and achievements are contextualised, in this section we attend to practical issues, such as choice of venue, the internal spatial arrangement and its temporality, to highlight how ethical values and organisational challenges meet and materialise.

Code for Ireland was launched in January 2014 and since then has had regular, monthly gatherings in Dublin where participants can meet face-to-face, catch up with the progress of each other's projects, work on their projects, and network with developers, community members and other interested individuals. The meet-ups are scheduled for the last Thursday evening of each month, and the evening often starts with socialising until the organiser gathers participants to start the event. The organiser introduces the motivation and goal of the meet-up, highlighting that Code for Ireland is a voluntary organisation that promotes the idea of openness, transparency and connecting communities and technologies. The opportunity that Code for Ireland want to harness is to leverage the participants' diverse skills sets, including developing and designing software, marketing and data analysis, to produce apps that serve community needs. Alongside the meet-up participants, there are usually guests present from government agencies or companies who may have access to required datasets, the knowledge to source data if not readily available, or required domain expertise.

Realising the goals of the organisation is not a trivial task and the organisers have gradually developed strategies to pursue these. Rather than a weekend event creating a quick fix, they recognise that they are taking a longer-term approach. This requires regular meet-ups and various ways to maintain momentum: using social media, maintaining a website populated with details about ongoing projects, creating a database of diverse skill sets using online forms, and developing problem-evaluating methods to help their projects get started. Their efforts created a regular flow of new participants with backgrounds ranging from local authorities and tech companies to non-governmental organisations and local businesses. The momentum created by Code for Ireland is demonstrated in the turnout for the July 2014 meet-up. Held in the Dublin offices of LinkedIn, in a warm, breezy and bright summer evening, the meet-up had around 70 people registering their interests and about 40 people attending, working on six different projects.

Encountering the city at hacking events   193

With a longer-term approach comes sustained logistical issues, for example, the venue and the means to accommodate participants. Part of Code for Ireland's remit is to establish an inclusive group of participants to pursue projects for addressing community issues. To provide the participants with a place to discuss and work on projects during 2013 and 2014, the meet-ups took place in the headquarters of Facebook, Google and LinkedIn in Dublin's 'Silicon Docks'. The only exception was for the launch event, which took place in Dublin Castle, a popular historical venue for high-profile conferences and cultural events, providing social and symbolic significance to the organisation. Within the company venues, meet-ups took place in or near the canteen area, where at the end of each event the sponsored pizza and beer became a catalyst for networking and catching up before the night concluded. The venues are all open-plan, providing enough space for individual groups to occupy their own corners for discussion, as well as allowing event participants to move in between projects. This gives a sense of openness to members, encouraging them to contribute wherever they can, at any stage in a project's development, with their ultimate goal of being open for reappropriation and reproduction of ideas and code elsewhere by other groups of people and for different purposes.

This focus on inclusion and community, however, is simultaneously in tension with the corporate host venues, as some participants commented. Several times, participants had to sign confidentiality agreements to enter the building while participating in an event advocating openness and transparency. Almost always, participants were shepherded by company staff into the canteen. We were left wondering if this is simply because we might be lost in the often vast and complex buildings, or in fear that we might take the opportunity to wander off and enter restricted areas 'by accident'. In other words, the hack events often seemed to be hosted in a liminal space, with participants always an insider to the event but an outsider to the venue. Despite this, these same major tech companies set aside budget, encourage their employees to take 'social responsibility' and, in effect, contribute to the stability and sustainability of Code for Ireland with sufficient space and generous supplies to keep the initiative going.

Further, Code for Ireland encourage their members to work towards the vision that any solution they create in Dublin can be taken up by other cities in Ireland and beyond for wider reuse and redeployment. There have been increasingly frequent reminders for participants to build products from open source software and deposit code in GitHub, an online service providing repository, version tracking functionalities and other code services, especially as projects come close to completion. In early hacking history, the right to access was a critically important motivation, driving the writing of free and open source software (F/OSS), with associated licensing to ensure that the software would not be privatised (Coleman 2013).

Behind such a material arrangement for code is an emphasis on building modular and scalable apps that cut across geographical boundaries and social needs. Indeed, Code for Ireland is inspired by Code for America to build apps that work well in a local context and can then be reappropriated for another community. An often cited example in the meet-up is an American app in which citizens are encouraged to 'adopt' a hydrant being quickly tweaked to replace the hydrant with a park so that Dublin communities can take more responsibility for their neighbourhoods. Code here becomes an 'immutable mobile' (Latour 1987), where the core architecture remains the same even though the purpose and context of use change. However, what is less stable is the interest and the motivation that enables code writing in the first place. Finding existing solutions is a good software development practice to save time and resources, which are both scarce in voluntary activities. But the translation of the motivation for adopting hydrants, which is to prevent the hydrants from being covered by the snow after winter storms in Boston, into the context of encouraging community participation and responsibility in Dublin, while truly inspiring, has to undergo series of brainstorming, outreach and reorientation before specific goals for the project can be set and software specifications decided. In other words, code becomes mutable (Law and Mol, 2001) when brought into the city, organised under a different framework, extended with new functionality, tweaked and refined, and responds to specific dynamics and requirements from local communities. At the meet-ups we attended, considerable time was spent discussing ideas and subsequent variations of the original idea, what it could be used for and how it could be made, so much so that the actual coding and app development was delayed perhaps longer than it should have been.

Exploring the 'placing' of civic hacking also led us to rethink the often singular, fixed, streamlined and goal-specific backdrops that contextualise hackathons. Frequently, what the aim is and what would be a good approach to achieve it are developed and negotiated through conversational interaction during the events; this process is never fixed but is in a constant state of renegotiation throughout the project. Interestingly, the dynamic of the Ireland chapter of the Code for All events was also seen to be different from that in other countries. For example, one of the organisers had recently attended the Open Knowledge Festival in Berlin with representatives from international chapters of the Code for All movement. He observed that the discourse in Berlin was strongly centred around transparency, measuring the outcome of projects, and whether they could influence government policy and action. Code for Ireland, in contrast, was less focused on influencing government and more on enabling change at a community level and in people's lives by situating them in a more community- and ethics-driven environment. As such, the approach to project management was less controlling and there was a strong focus on making the event relevant to participants' lives and enjoyable, with coding seen as something of a social and leisure activity. The organiser thus referred to Code for Ireland 'hacking the system with apps', wherein the apps become a means to the mission, but are not the mission itself.

The individual

The hackathon could not exist without those who participate. Although there is rhetorical discussion as to what hackathons can do for the city and communities, less emphasis is placed on what hackathons can do for those who are involved in the event. As Coleman notes, much of the research on hacking and F/OSS development focuses on the more intangible spaces of bits and bytes but often neglects the existence of 'face-to-face interactions amongst these geeks, hackers and developers'. The reason Coleman (2013: 45) offers for this lack of interest is the fact that much of the communication and interaction between participants is 'unremarkable – the ordinary stuff of work and friendships'. And yet, the social element of hackathons is a strong influence on participation, as we have clearly observed at the coding events we have attended.

So what attracts people to hacking and coding events? Some participants mentioned that it was a way to meet people; indeed with PyLadies and Coding Grace, the programs were designed to encourage women to participate and engage with technology in a supportive environment. As for Code for Ireland, while there may be some spectacle lent to Code for Ireland by virtue of the venues – the googleness of Google – and the emphasis on the project's PR, the majority of the interpersonal communications reflect those of normal interactions and decision making processes: discussing ideas, suggesting ways to approach the topics, somebody always typing, and ideas boards being added to.

Moreover, there is often fluidity between the groups, encouraged by the organisers and enacted by participants. The organisers promote mobility between groups as a way of sharing experiences and ideas. Allowing participants to move freely between groups can be an effective way of sustaining their interests in the event. For the participants, even if they are not 'affiliated' to a particular group, they can still show up and provide their thoughts and experiences to various groups in one evening. Even when some people attach themselves to one project at a meeting, at the next meeting they may join another 'more-interesting-at-that-moment' project, or a project that they feel has more potential to be followed through or to produce a useful product. However, group members may also not show up at all, with an e-mail sent to the online project management site about work commitments preventing attendance being the most common form of apology. Indeed, at one event we attended, there was only one representative in each of the two groups we had participated in at the previous meeting. This stalled the process of development and made decision making difficult. In one case, a project idea was changed quite substantially when only one key member of the group was present who was left to make decisions on behalf of the larger group in consultation with a government representative who was persuading him to reframe the project along new lines. Absences, then, can have considerable impact on whether a project will be followed through to completion and in what form.

196 *Sophia Maalsen and Sung-Yueh Perng*

Furthermore, while there was a general acknowledgement that the projects were not operating in isolation and that the ideas were intended to benefit the wider community, often the main driver for people to attend was some type of self-gain. In our case, we were obviously motivated by research and the need to study the field, but talking to other participants brought up other reasons. As a result, practices of sharing and individual gains cannot be easily separated from each other. By virtue of Dublin promoting itself as a tech hub and attracting international companies, such as Google and Facebook, we observed that there were people involved from such organisations. Importantly, such companies often import part of the workforce with them to Ireland. One participant revealed that he had moved to Dublin for work from San Francisco and that he was not just attending the event to donate his skills but to meet new people. For others, it is a way to develop skills and to engage with a broader community of programmers and developers, with a social occasion, including free pizza and beer as an added bonus. The way that hackathons can serve individuals is described in a post on the Kansas City IT Professionals' website that highlights 'seven reasons why you need to attend hackathons' (Gelphman 2014):

(1) connect with passionate developers;
(2) demonstrate your skills;
(3) push yourself;
(4) get feedback;
(5) learn and grow;
(6) become part of the community;
(7) change your life.

Certainly, these reasons were motivators at the events we attended. However, there is an individual element that is often overlooked in the hackathon and the smart city discourse. Gelphman goes on to indicate that hackathons can be framed instead as a way to become part of a community in which the emphasis can switch from what the individual can do for the community, to what the community can do for the individual. It is not simply what people can do for the hackathon but also what the hackathon can do for the people involved. Mattern (2014) alludes to this sense of individualism when she discusses what she terms the 'widgetisation' of urban resources, which conveniently translates 'our messy city into my efficient city', producing an individualised civics.

Mattern's critical appraisal of what kind of city is produced through the hackathon and who it is envisioned by is shared by Porway. He critiques the usefulness of 'throwing data' at hackers and expecting something good and useful to emerge: 'Most companies think that if you can just get hackers, pizza and data together in a room, magic will happen' (Porway 2013). He does not dismiss hackathons *per se*, but he does emphasise the need to start with a clear question and definition of the problem to be solved, and make use of

Encountering the city at hacking events 197

subject matter experts to articulate the problems to which the data are related to the hackers and to assess the results so that the process not only addresses the 'what' of the data but also the 'why'. The lack of a clear question and focus certainly delayed many of the projects we observed, and Porway's suggestions could be one way of negotiating such stalling. Like Mattern, Porway sees the individuality of many of the apps as problematic. Using the example of the New York City Reinvent Green Hackathon, he demonstrates how the winning apps, including a 'bikepool' app and a farmer's market inventory app, reflect the participant's 'problems' and do not solve the wider sustainability problems of the city.

However, this is not to say that there is no reflection from the participants on the process of pursuing individual interests under the name of citizen collaboration. One of the Code for Ireland participants raised concerns over the ambiguous relationship and the lack of reciprocity with government agencies, which release data to facilitate projects pursued by the initiative. Here, the participant is reflecting on the ethics of taking the data without necessarily providing something in return. His concerns are appeased by the event organiser and his framing of the activity as a broader opportunity to effect change at a community level. Nonetheless, the mechanism and scope for benefitting the government or the general public seems to be missing. However, such a 'reciprocal relationship' between the government and participants is presently being trialled as the initiative develops its own project and alliances with relevant government agencies. An example referred to by one of the Code for Ireland organisers was a queuing time estimation service for a highly congested public office. The organiser described the difficulty of obtaining data from the government for improving estimation accuracy, the alternative approaches the project undertakes to acquire data, and to prove to relevant agencies that such service is needed and that there is a viable solution under development.

These tensions and opportunities between hacking for individual or communal gain are underlined by the broader ethics of the F/OSS community, and we cannot understand the motivators behind the hacking and coding events described here without paying some attention to the ethical practice that informs them. There are parallels between the openness of data and the openness of source code that converge in the place of the hacking events and inform the practice of the individual. Both share a 'vibrant ethic of information freedom', and projects can also be understood 'as a site for the production of ethics' (Coleman and Hill 2005: 277). Coleman and Hill (2005) note that F/OSS ethics and politics are oppositional to market-based software production and associated intellectual property regimes. Instead, F/OSS developers take advantage of copyleft licenses, in which the code source remains accessible. Importantly, they describe this as a material and symbolic reterritorialisation of knowledge, which means that developers can access and use source code legally. Thus, F/OSS is characterised by an aesthetic of openness and collaboration for the greater good. This parallels with the

198 *Sophia Maalsen and Sung-Yueh Perng*

politics of civic hacking, e.g., the corporate hosting, the contextualisation of success or the individualised interests, as discussed here, and the associated openness of the data providers, in this case, most often Dublin City Council.

The hacking events, the F/OSS and the individual participants encounter the city in a way that is mediated by their own ethical and political code. The tensions between individual and broader community gain are negotiated by a practice of openness and it is this that helps maintain the energy of the projects. Although unifying, an ethics of openness does not negate the plurality of approaches, or the multiplicity of the issues that participants want to address. Nor does the mutability of code necessarily allow an easy transfer of ideas from one country or region to another to produce a successful outcome, as advocated by Code for Ireland organisers. The hackathons themselves become sites of encountering the city, often in messy ways, as various agendas and politics compete, despite an overriding motivation to make the city better for all. It is this tension that may be responsible for the relative lack of apps that successfully address urban issues and governance. Such events do, however, produce opportunities that benefit participants in more social and localised ways; thus, the value of hacking events cannot be discounted.

Conclusion

This chapter is an opening scene for our research on hacking events. We have asked whether such events deliver on the promises they make to find workable solutions to civic issues and city governance. We addressed these questions through observations made during our fieldwork and found hacking and coding events to be dynamic spaces, with the mutability of code, the social relationships facilitated through the events, and the city and communities they address, interacting in mutually informing ways.

Such events were seen by some as creative and legitimate ways to approach city problems, as evidenced by the presence of local government representatives at some events suggesting issues they would like addressed and offering access to data, the enthusiasm of the organisers to encourage participation and openness across projects, and the commitment of individuals. However, the success of the events and their products in solving these issues was rarely validated. For the individual, hacking and code events provided them with a chance to acquire and develop skills, network, make friends, socialise and channel their energies into issues that mattered to them. In this sense, we must remember that hacking and coding events are not necessarily all work, but can be spaces of leisure.

The hacking events we observed were spaces of interaction, discussion, creation and leisure and, as such, can be seen to mediate positive encounters with the city regardless of output. Further, there is a need for making the plurality of code and coders more explicit, so as to understand who and what kinds of activity are still missing in this approach. In so doing, we also expand the discourse on the smart city by focusing on the people and the

Encountering the city at hacking events 199

relationships they establish in proactively creating 'smart city' spaces and tools. Indeed, a focus on civic hacking places people back into the smart city, addressing the critique that much of the smart city discourse forgets about community by focusing predominantly on technology.

Acknowledgement

The research for this paper was conducted under *The Programmable City*, a project funded by a European Research Council Advanced Investigator award (ERC-2012-AdG-323636-SOFTCITY).

References

Coleman, G. (2013) *Coding Freedom: The Ethics and Aesthetics of Hacking*, Princeton: Princeton University Press.

Coleman, G. and Hill, B. (2005) 'The social production of ethics in Debian and free software communities: anthropological lessons for vocational ethics', in S. Koch (ed.) *Free/Open Source Software Development*, Hershey, PA: Idea Group Inc.

Gelphman, M. (2014) '7 reasons why you need to attend hackathons', Kansas City IT Professionals, available from http://www.kcitp.com/2014/07/01/hack-midwest-kansas-city-hackathon/ [accessed 15 July 2014].

Latour, B. (1987) *Science in Action: How to Follow Scientists and Engineers through Society*, Cambridge, MA: Harvard University Press.

Law, J. and Mol, A. (2001) 'Situating technoscience: an inquiry into spatialities', *Environment and Planning D: Society and Space*, 19(5): 609–21.

MacKenzie, A. (2001) 'Open source software: when is a tool? What is a commodity?', *Science as Culture*, 10(4): 541–52.

Mattern, S. (2014) 'Interfacing urban intelligence', *Places*, April 2014, available at https://placesjournal.org/article/interfacing-urban-intelligence/ [accessed 17 June 2014].

Meyer, M. and Ermoshina, K. (2013) 'Bricolage as collaborative exploration: transforming matter, citizens and politics', *i3 Conference Cooperating for Innovation: Devices for Collective Exploration, TELECOM ParisTech*, Paris, 2 December 2013, available from http://www.i-3.fr/wp-content/uploads/2013/04/Meyer_conferenceI32013.pdf [accessed 15 July 2014].

OpenBSD (n.d.) 'Hackathons', *OpenBSD*, available from http://www.openbsd.org/hackathons.html, [accessed 19 March 2015].

Popyack, J.L. (2014) 'Prohacktivity, *or* one giant hack for mankind', *ACM Inroads*, 5(2): 40–52.

Porway, J. (2013) 'You can't just hack your way to social change', *Harvard Business Review Blog*, 7 March 2013, available from http://blogs.hbr.org/2013/03/you-cant-just-hack-your-way-to/ [accessed 15 July 2014].

15 Semantic cities

Coded geopolitics and the rise of the Semantic Web

Heather Ford and Mark Graham

Introduction

Cities are much more than just bricks and mortar. They are also digital. A core aspect of places and the ways that we enact them and bring them into being is computation and digital data (Kitchin and Dodge 2011; Graham *et al.* 2013). Platforms such as Google Maps, Baidu, OpenStreetMap, Wikipedia, Twitter, Facebook and Yelp! all encourage users to embed and deploy digital content in their everyday spatial practices. Graham *et al.* (2013: 465), for example, argue that 'representations of place, in conjunction with myriad other layerings and discourses' can be seen as augmentations of the city. Because these augmentations are such an integral element to contemporary urban environments, it is crucial to understand how they are produced and reproduced, and made visible and invisible by both large organisations and the cumulative efforts of millions of contributors (Leszczynski and Wilson 2013; Leszczynski 2015; Wilson 2014).

A major contributor to the rise of digital layers of the city has emerged from the phenomenon called 'volunteered geographical information'. This is a practice and phenomenon whereby individuals voluntarily provide geographical information on sites and platforms, enabling the capture of user-generated content (Elwood *et al.* 2011: 573). The idea that there are now many different ways for citizens to contribute to the representation of their cities has led some to argue that the representation of place has become democratised. Lawrence Lessig, for instance, has noted that, 'For the first time in a millennium, we have a technology to equalize the opportunity that people have to access and participate in the construction of knowledge and culture, regardless of their geographic placing' (Lessig 2003).

But not only is digital content impacting on how cities are experienced, the infrastructure of the Web itself is undergoing a significant phase of transformation – one related to the way in which information is structured and represented. In 2001, Berners-Lee *et al.* (2001) outlined a new vision for the creation of a Semantic Web as a 'web of data' to replace the 'web of documents' that had been the result of the Web's original design. The goal of the Semantic Web was to enable the development of principles and standards for the structuring and sharing of data between different websites.

Over a decade after this vision for the Semantic Web was published, Google launched a service called the Knowledge Graph, which adopts many of the same principles of the Semantic Web. The goal of the Knowledge Graph was to answer basic search queries without the user having to navigate to other websites. A search for 'Paris', for example, would result in a prominent table on the right-hand side of the Google search page listing facts about Paris (in addition to regular search results on the left-hand side of the page). These facts include the status of Paris as the capital city of France, a paragraph of text about the city (taken from Wikipedia), followed by a series of statistics including its size, weather and population (attributed to figures from UNdata) and a series of labelled images under the heading, 'Points of interest', as can be seen in Figure 15.1.

In 2012, the Wikimedia Foundation (the organisation that administers Wikipedia) announced a new project called Wikidata that would boost Wikimedia's efforts to support Semantic Web principles. Funded in part by Google, Wikidata would develop a semantically organised knowledge base[1] sourced with information from Wikipedia and other Wikimedia Foundation projects, as well as other sources of open data. Wikidata's goals are twofold: to support Wikipedia and other Wikimedia projects by enhancing consistency across different projects and language versions, and to support the many different (third-party) services and applications that reuse Wikipedia data in a structured way (Vrandecic and Krotzsch 2014). In other words, Wikidata stores structured information in formats that allow websites and machines (instead of human beings) to easily reuse it.

With two of the world's most popular websites (Google and Wikipedia) now applying Semantic Web principles to the organisation of information, we ask what effects these data integration practices have on the representation of places. Using the example of the city of Jerusalem, we explore data sharing practices at the intersection of Wikipedia and Google by tracing the representation of the city as data moves from Wikipedia to Google and Wikipedia to Wikidata through the process of automated data extraction and database linking. By analysing the practices by which data is extracted and then linked according to the logic of the Semantic Web, we argue that, far from enabling shared meaning across different sites, as promised by the original designers of the Semantic Web, meaning is significantly different across these sites.

When data moves from Wikipedia to Wikidata and to Google, it becomes less nuanced, its provenance is obscured, the agency of users to contest information is diminished and the use of personalised filters means that users cannot see what information is being presented to them. Because the dominant discourses surrounding the move towards a more semantic web frame these changes as inherently technical rather than political, we conclude that there needs to be a renewed debate about the politics encoded in and performed through geographically linked databases.

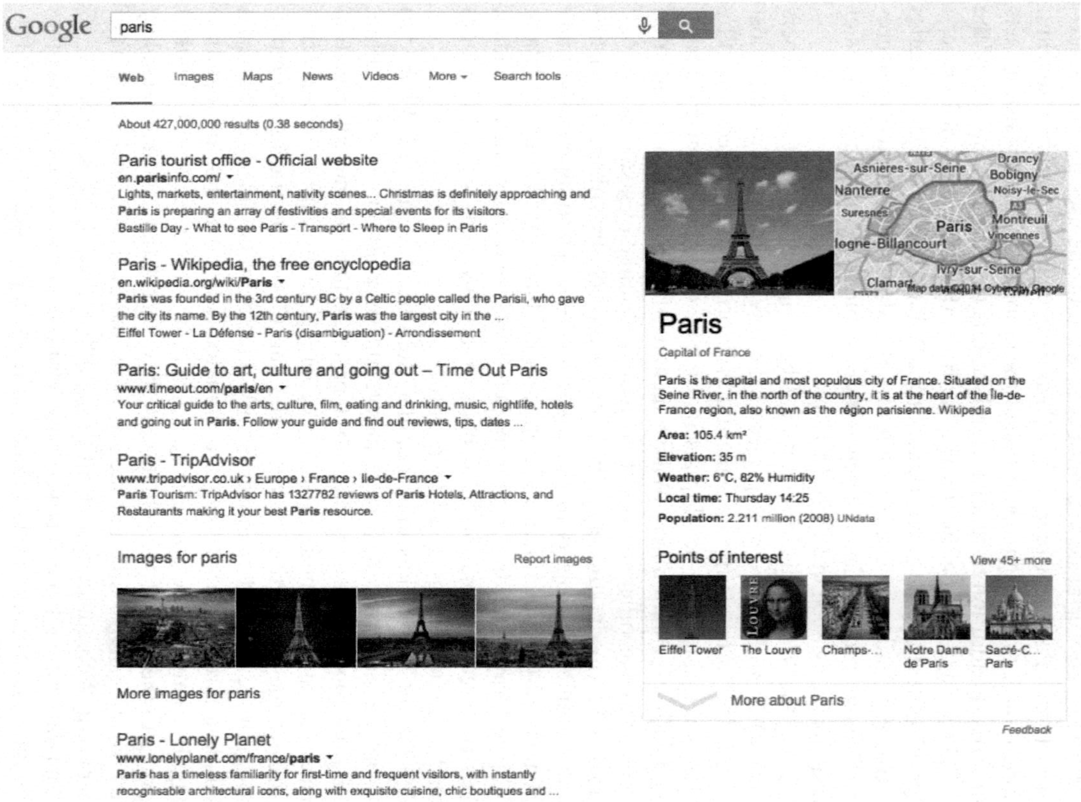

Figure 15.1 Results of a search for 'Paris' on Google (4 December 2014)

Semantic cities 203

Jerusalem is a city in the Middle East with a capital claimed by both the State of Israel and the State of Palestine and whose status as a capital city is one of the longest running disputes on Wikipedia (Wikipedia contributors 2014). The city's borders and governance have changed significantly over the years, most recently after the 1967 (Six-Day) war between Israel and the neighbouring states of Egypt, Jordan and Syria, when Israel annexed East Jerusalem from Jordan. Many Palestinians foresee Jerusalem as their future capital, but there is no widespread international recognition for Jerusalem (as composed of both East and West parts) as the capital of either Israel or a Palestinian State. Such disagreement is reflected in the very different perspectives on what are the basic facts about Jerusalem in the Arabic and Hebrew versions of Wikipedia and in the heated and long-running disagreements on the text of the English version – for instance, see Graham *et al.* (2013) and Graham and Zook (2013) for examples of the divergent representations and contestations of Jerusalem on Google and Wikipedia.

To understand how the city's contested political contexts are embedded into its digital layers, we traced how the city is digitally represented and the debates about such representations. We did this by analysing representations of Jerusalem across the Arabic, Hebrew and English versions of Wikipedia (working with a translator on the Arabic and Hebrew versions), as well as on the platforms of Wikidata, Freebase and Google. Other search engines, such as Microsoft's Bing, also display data from Wikipedia, but we decided to focus on Google because of its widespread usage in much of the world as the default search engine.

The impact on representational power of mediating technologies

Research into the political implications of technologies has a rich history in such fields as science and technology studies, but the analysis of search engines is still nascent in contemporary technology research, albeit for a few notable examples. Introna and Nissenbaum (2000), for example, have shown how search engines 'systematically exclude (in some cases by design and in some accidentally) certain sites, and certain types of sites, in favour of others' (Introna and Nissenbaum 2000: 169), and that this is a sign of increasing centralisation and commercialisation of the guiding forces of the Internet. Similarly, in the *Society of the Query Reader*, König (2014) reiterates the importance of search engines for the public health of the Internet, and calls for an opening up of the 'black boxes' of search algorithms, and for a recognition of the increasingly concentrated, monopoly-like nature of the search engine market. But it is also important to look beyond the effects of algorithms on representations, and focus attention on the practices through which large databases are constructed. In the process of extracting data from these systems, Groth (2013: 1) notes that 'we remove nuance, context and provenance'.

In this chapter, we situate these arguments in the context of the urban

204 *Heather Ford and Mark Graham*

environment, a context in which digital representations can quickly translate into material practices. By analysing the features of this intersection between people, practices, tools, laws and economics in a spatial account, we are able to recognise the features of practice that produce digital results. Furthermore, despite the resurgence in research about search engines, the majority of previous research has considered *individual* platforms, focusing on Google, Facebook and other major corporations, rather than addressing the increasing interdependence of different organisations in the development of Web logics. By tracing practices between interconnected sites such as Wikipedia and Google, we note the underlying logics that are guiding the development of the Web in general, rather than focusing on the idiosyncrasies of one particular site.

The digital dimensions of Jerusalem

We first trace how Jerusalem is represented on the Arabic, English and Hebrew versions of Wikipedia, and then on Wikidata, Freebase and Google. We then go on to describe the affordances of each of these platforms for users interacting with the platforms.

A search for 'Jerusalem' on Google reveals the multitude of sources from which Knowledge Graph results are produced. Google extracts data from information repositories such as Wikipedia, the CIA World Factbook and Freebase for its factual statements, and draws on data about what people search for in the presentation of results for the section 'Points of interest'.[2] In the Jerusalem example, the paragraph about Jerusalem is extracted from the English version of Wikipedia,[3] but the foundation date and area size are mirrors of the Freebase item on Jerusalem. The population figures presented in search results are attributed to UNdata. Perhaps most interestingly, the results represent Jerusalem as the 'Capital of Israel', a claim disputed by most of the world's national governments.

When we trace the material effects of the cleaning, tweaking and joining of databases according to Semantic Web logics in the case of Google's Knowledge Graph and Wikimedia's Wikidata project, we observe four key trends. As information is extracted from a variety of data sources, there is a resulting loss of nuance, and a loss of important contextual information. As data are extracted from a number of different sources, the provenance of the data becomes obscured. Furthermore, as statements are extracted from user-generated content systems (such as Wikipedia), which are populated by volunteer labour and then housed in Google's system, the agency of the users diminishes, with concurrent limitations on their ability to edit or functionally contest information originally provided by them. Finally, the logic of the personalised agent present in Semantic Web logic means that the perspectives of other users on the same topic are obscured. We discuss each of these results next.

Loss of nuance

Although Google employs data from Wikipedia, its representation of the status of Jerusalem as the 'capital of Israel'[4] is significantly less nuanced than the representation of the status of the city in English Wikipedia. The Jerusalem article in English Wikipedia contains an infobox[5] listing both Israel and Palestine as 'claimants' to the city, followed by the statement that Jerusalem is 'administered by Israel' and a listing of both the 'Israeli District' and 'Palestinian Governorate', as can be seen in Figure 15.2. Google, on the other hand, represents Jerusalem unequivocally as the 'capital of Israel', even in searches conducted in Arabic and searches conducted from the Palestinian Territories.

Figure 15.2 Section of the Jerusalem infobox on English Wikipedia as at 13 July 2014

The Wikidata entry for Jerusalem has suffered from a similar loss of nuance. Struggles to define the description tag for the Jerusalem item on Wikidata have been ongoing since the page was created at the end of October 2012, with editors reverting between different versions of Jerusalem's status in relation to Israel and Palestine. After a statement was added that associated Jerusalem with Israel, Israeli editors added statements asserting Jerusalem's status as the capital city of Israel. It was only almost two years later, in July 2014, that a user created the statement that Jerusalem was also associated with the State of Palestine with reference to East Jerusalem. Israeli editors continue to revert edits referring to Palestine and to add further statements supporting the Israeli claim (such as the most recent edit, at the time of writing, which stipulated that East Jerusalem also belonged to Israel with a reference to Jerusalem Law). During this time, Wikidata is being used by other sites to represent facts about the world, including the 30–40 apps that have been written to extract data from Wikidata and present them in other contexts.

When information moves from the highly contested and editable space of Wikipedia to structured databases, such as Wikidata and Google, it loses a direct connection to its contested and unstable origins. The ideal of the Semantic Web is based on the ideal that computers need to be able to process the semantics (meaning) that human beings attach to their words. Using Semantic Web logic, the computer would 'know whether we meant Paris, the perfume, Paris, the place, or Paris, the celebrity' by structuring information in a way that computers could understand, and then interconnecting those structured databases so that computers could understand what was meant by users' queries (Berners-Lee *et al.*, 2001).

The problem with this logic is that Google may be able to disambiguate the difference between Jerusalem, the play, and Jerusalem, the city, but it is unable to distinguish between different lived understandings of the city. The Israeli government sees Jerusalem as its capital city but most other states do not; Jerusalem is seen by the Palestinians as their future capital but Ramallah is the *de-facto* capital of the Palestinian administration. Such complex perspectives are difficult to represent in a structured database also intended to represent every other city in the world because they are largely unique and context-dependent. Although Wikidata enables competing claims to be represented within the same item, the initial extraction of data from Wikipedia did not reflect this nuance, and, after almost three years, there seems to be no evidence that the qualifying claims (that the city's status is contested) are being represented when the data travels to other sites.

The way in which facts are constructed is in the process of separating the social context of their production from the statements themselves (Latour and Woolgar, 1986). This means that there are political implications to the loss of complexity and nuance. The more that statements are represented as fact-like, the more they will be recognised and accepted as facts. For this reason, Google's representation of Jerusalem as the unequivocal capital of Israel has potential material effects on the conditions of people in the region.

The provenance of data is obscured

Neither the reasoning behind Google's decision to show particular facts nor the sources of those facts are always visible. In addition, facts or statements that *are* attributed are not always accurately sourced. Following the link from Google's population number for Jerusalem, for example, a user is taken to a Google 'Public Data' page that indicates that the source of population statistics for Jerusalem is 'UNdata' (see Figure 15.3). This is done instead of providing users with either specific datasets or metadata about how the data were selected.

UNdata (data.un.org) collects census figures from national governments and is therefore not the direct publisher of data in this instance. For this to be revealed, a user would have to click on the UNdata hyperlink in Google, search for 'Israel'[6] on the UNdata website and read the notes that indicate that the data is provided by Israel and that these figures include East Jerusalem. Google has limited affordances for accurate sourcing, since it divorces the content that it provides from the source (and consequently the methodological details) of that information.

Population statistics are inherently political. By definition, they serve as a signifier for who is actually counted and contained within the borders of a city. That is, they tell us something about both the boundaries of the city and who is counted as being within those boundaries. In a city like Jerusalem, where fundamental disagreements exist about what the city itself is and who it contains, population statistics can be particularly revealing about who counts and who is counted. In Jerusalem, population statistics furthermore often depend on government institutions such as the Israeli Central Bureau of Statistics, even though such institutions are not recognised by Palestinians and are dependent on which of the contested borders are being recognised by the counting body. As the data moves from national statistics offices to UN statistics offices to the UNdata platform and to Google and Freebase, the numbers are iteratively stripped of the national and institutional context that gave rise to their very particular result. This stripping of contextual information is not a de-politicisation of the data, but rather, the presentation of data that advances one political position (in this case, the Israeli position) at the expense of others.

Wikidata outlines how users should add citations to particular statements and asks for editors to replace current references (indicating the Wikimedia site from which the data was imported) with a 'reliable, secondary' source. In the case of the Jerusalem item in Wikidata, only a single secondary source is identified (with the qualifying statement that East Jerusalem (also) belongs to Israel with reference to 'Jerusalem Law') (Wikidata contributors 2014).

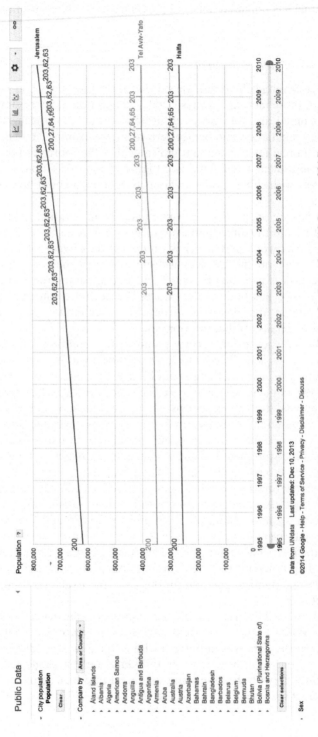

Figure 15.3 Screenshot of Google results after clicking on the population figure for Jerusalem (19 January 2015)

Semantic cities   209

The diminishing agency of users

When information is housed on Google's platform, the affordances for that information to be edited or challenged by ordinary users are significantly reduced. Google does not allow editing by users and interaction is limited to restricted forums where users can provide feedback. Clicking on the 'feedback' button in small grey lettering at the base of the Knowledge Graph results box makes a series of buttons labelled 'wrong?' appear next to each statement (see Figure 15.4). Users have the option of adding a description of what is 'wrong' with the information reflected, as well as to provide a URL with supporting evidence. No information is available about what happens to a user's feedback once they have provided it and any feedback is not displayed publicly. The result is that feedback and potential revisions submitted by the public are left disassociated from the data.

In another example, when users click on the population figure for Jerusalem in Google, they are taken to the Google Public Data platform

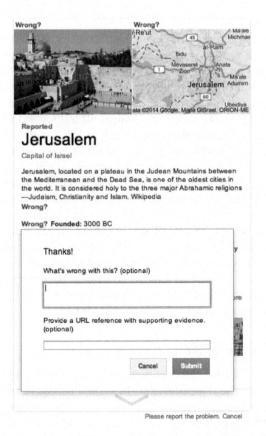

Figure 15.4 Screenshots after clicking on 'feedback' and the 'Wrong?' hyperlink above the Jerusalem headline on google.com

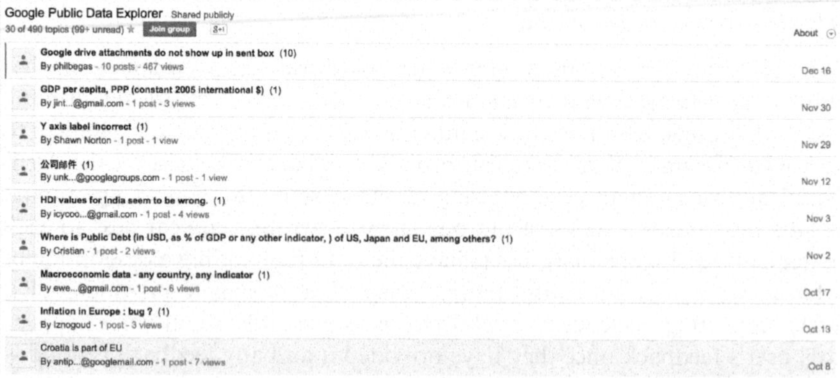

210　*Heather Ford and Mark Graham*

Figure 15.5 Screenshot of Google Public Data Explorer Forum as at 21 December 2014

Source: https://groups.google.com/forum/#!forum/public-data-labs, accessed 21 December 2014

(see Figure 15.5), where they might click on a button entitled 'discuss', which links to a Google group. Users have, however, been posting questions and comments about incorrect information to the forum that have remained unanswered for months (see Figure 15.5). Although users are able to discuss problems amongst themselves, such discussion is not helpful if users do not have permissions to make necessary changes after discussion.

Even though a piece of information, such as the population of Jerusalem, can exist in the 286 possible language versions of Wikipedia, if it were to be entered on Wikidata (as a first step to populate Wikipedia infoboxes that use this data), it could only be discussed in English on Wikidata. This is because, on Wikidata, there is only a single talk page for discussing an item. This consequently restricts the ability of non-English speakers to participate fully in debates. Wikipedia's talk pages, in contrast, are almost always open for any user in any language version of Wikipedia to contribute to. As data moves from Wikipedia to Wikidata, there is a decrease in the ability of people speaking languages other than English to fully participate in debates about how information is reflected. Here, centralisation affords greater efficiency but this has an impact on who is able to participate.

Personalised results make others' filters less recognisable

On Google, users receive personalised results and cannot view what results other users obtain. The algorithms that drive personalised results are opaque to users and there are no informational cues about whether other users are seeing information differently (Gillespie 2010; 2014). The unintended consequence of personalisation is that, while individual users are able to potentially obtain more accurate results filtered according to their own needs, the corollary of

Semantic cities 211

this is that users are not able to see how others view the same subject. This has a potentially negative effect on public discourse when users become isolated from information that disagrees with their viewpoints (Pariser, 2012).

As data are extracted and combined within Google's Knowledge Graph and Wikipedia's Wikidata project, nuance is lost as important contextual information is left behind during the extraction process. Extracted data also suffer from the obscuring of the data's sources and a concurrent disconnection of information from its source. This disconnection also involves a loss of agency of the user to engage actively with public information systems, where debate and contestation is obscured and isolated from the display of that information. As information is increasingly personalised, the perspectives of other users are obscured by the system, preventing shared perspectives on important public topics. On their own, these effects are effective in closing off the opportunity for debate and contestation, but they are reinforced by the discourses that prescribe how the Semantic Web and linked data are imagined.

Technical discourses

Underlying the Semantic Web and linked data are powerful narratives about the apolitical and purely technical processes of structuring and linking data. In the Wikidata talk page for Jerusalem, for example, many editors accuse one another of 'pushing a political agenda'. 'Ymblanter', the administrator who started the page, was accused by an editor, 'Hanay', of 'pushing a political agenda' when he changed the description in the Jerusalem article from 'city in Israel' to 'city in Israel which Israel claims to be its capital' after 'Hanay' tried changing it to 'capital city of Israel' and another editor tried changing it to 'a city in Israel and Palestine'. Both 'Hanay' and 'Ymblanter' accused one another of pushing a political agenda, asserting their own versions of what is the 'clearly neutral' description.

> Wikidata, on the other hand, does not have any political aims in making statements acknowledging the existence of certain facts.
> ('Yair rand', Wikidata talk page for Jerusalem, 5 February 2013)

As information moves from Wikipedia to Wikidata, from Wikipedia to Google, not only does information itself change, the process of editing becomes increasingly complex, its discourses focus on the sites as apolitical and highly technical spaces, and the corresponding rules for, and expertise in dealing with controversy are increasingly obscured. This impacts on the ways in which local people are able to participate, challenge and speak back to representations of place.

Conclusion: code, content and cities

As our cities become increasingly digital, and as the digital becomes increasingly governed by the logics of the Semantic Web, there are important questions to ask about how these new alignments of code and content shape how cities are presented, experienced and brought into being. What we found is a paradoxical situation whereby, through connecting datasets, Semantic Web initiatives detach localised information from the contexts of its creation. By divorcing content from its contexts, this process establishes new contexts in which necessarily political decisions are being made, with far-reaching consequences.

Linked data organised through the Semantic Web can be easily integrated, repurposed, collected, classified, published and indexed. It is, however, important to recognise that such efficiencies come with a price. By automatically extracting content from different sites and presenting it in new frames, knowledge bases are increasingly distancing (and in some cases cutting off) debate about contested knowledges of places. This effect is achieved by transferring data about cities from Wikipedia's participatory framework to sites like Wikidata and Google, where the affordances are less participatory, where the rules are increasingly opaque to the average user and where the framing discourses are that these platforms are apolitical and highly technical. When user-generated knowledge reaches the veiled confines of Google search, users lose the ability to effectively contest and change information that forms a key component in the representation of places.

The move to the Semantic Web also means that many decisions about how places are represented are increasingly being made by people and processes far from, and invisible to, people living under the digital shadows of those very representations. Contestations are centralised and turned into single data points that make it difficult for local citizens to have a significant voice in the co-construction of the digital augmentations of their own cities.

Despite this pessimism, we believe that much can be done to remedy this situation. Mediators like Google could do more to lay bare the origins of the information that they host, and to provide opportunities for ordinary users to participate in the improvement and contestation of those data. The Wikidata community, similarly, could recognise that it, too, is a site for political contestation and that they need to build the functionality and experience within their administrator community to deal with such disputes when they arise. Despite Wikidata employees claiming that 'Wikidata will not be about the Truth' (Vrandencic in Graham 2012), Wikidata is employed as a repository for all manner of truths, and will therefore exert significant impacts on our informational environments.

Because platforms like Wikipedia and mediators like Google are becoming not just central gatekeepers of information, but also integrated parts of our cities, it is important that different communities are able to create, reproduce and represent different truths and worldviews on, and through, those platforms. And while certain truths are universal (Paris is generally considered to be the uncontested capital city of France), others are more messy and unclear (for example, whether the population of Israel should include occupied and contested territories).

The reason that the rise of the Semantic Web and linked data matters is because they not only eliminate some of the scope for culturally contingent representations of places, processes, people and events, but also depoliticise and obfuscate some of those processes of representation. Potentially, even more concerning is the fact that centralised and linked data organised under the logics of the Semantic Web are unlikely to reflect the opinions and beliefs of traditionally marginalised groups. Disagreements over places and the ways in which they are represented are no longer simply confined to specific informational silos: they are, instead, extracted and linked in increasingly complex formations that are difficult to trace and engage with. Said simply, structured data is not conducive to the representation of minority opinions.

In following contested urban information through the Semantic Web, we have shown how the governance of linked data and logics of the Semantic Web is ultimately making the messy political informational layers of cities more transparent to machines and more opaque to human beings. Linked data and the Semantic Web have important implications for representation, voice and ultimately power in cities, and we need to ensure that we are not seduced into codifying, categorising and structuring in cases when we should be describing the inherent heterogeneity of meaning in certain situations. If we ever hope to move towards a goal of more inclusive informational cities, we first need to better understand how the Semantic Web changes urban life.

Notes

1 Knowledge bases are systems used to store structured data, consisting of facts and rules, which are structured according to specific formats.
2 Because Google does not cite the source of factual data, we assume that it is being sourced from Freebase, based on public comments about the sources of its data.
3 Searches in other languages draw data from the relevant language version of Wikipedia.
4 The same results were available using Arabic and Hebrew settings and by users located in Tel Aviv (Israel) and East Jerusalem (Palestine).
5 An infobox is a summary or list of facts added to the top right-hand corner of Wikipedia articles.
6 The UNdata site houses a population figure for Jerusalem that is significantly larger than the Google figure – probably because the UNdata site houses the more recent figures.

References

Berners-Lee, T., Hendler, J. and Lassila, O. (2001) 'The Semantic Web', *Scientific American*, May 2001, available from http://www.scientificamerican.com/article. cfm?id=the-semantic-web [accessed 25 August 2015].
Elwood, S. Goodchild, M.F. and Sui, D.Z. (2011) 'Researching volunteered geographic information: spatial data, geographic research, and new social practice', *Annals of the Association of American Geographers*, 102(3): 571–90.

214   *Heather Ford and Mark Graham*

Gillespie, T. (2010) 'The politics of "platforms"', *New Media and Society*, 12(3): 347–64.

Gillespie, T. (2014) 'The relevance of algorithms', in T. Gillespie, P.J. Boczkowski and K.A. Foot (eds) *Media Technologies: Essays on Communication, Materiality, and Society*, Cambridge, MA: MIT Press.

Graham, M. (2012) 'The problem with Wikidata', *The Atlantic*, (6 April 2012).

Graham, M. and Zook, M. (2013) 'Augmented realities and uneven geographies: exploring the geolinguistic contours of the Web', *Environment and Planning A*, 45(1): 77–99.

Graham, M., Zook, M. and Boulton, A. (2013) 'Augmented reality in urban places: contested content and the duplicity of code', *Transactions of the Institute of British Geographers*, 38(3): 464–79.

Groth, P. (2013) 'The knowledge-remixing bottleneck', *IEEE Intelligent Systems*, 28(5): 44–8.

Introna, L.D. and Nissenbaum, H. (2000) 'Shaping the Web: why the politics of search engines matters', *The Information Society*, 16(3): 169–85.

Kitchin, R. and Dodge, M. (2011) *Code/Space: Software and Everyday Life*, Cambridge, MA: MIT Press.

König, R. (ed.) (2014) *Society of the Query Reader: Reflections on Web Search*, Amsterdam: Institute of Network Cultures.

Latour, B. and Woolgar, S. (1986) *Laboratory Life: The Construction of Scientific Facts*, Princeton, NJ: Princeton University Press.

Lessig, L. (2003) 'An information society: free or feudal', *World Summit on the Information Society*, Geneva, Switzerland, available from http://www.itu.int/wsis/docs/pc2/visionaries/lessig.pdf [accessed 25 August 2015].

Leszczynski, A. (2015) 'Spatial media/tion', *Progress in Human Geography*, 39(6): 729–51.

Leszczynski, A. and Wilson, M.W. (2013) 'Guest editorial: theorizing the geoweb', *GeoJournal*, 78(6): 915–19.

Pariser, E. (2012) *The Filter Bubble: What the Internet is Hiding from You*, London: Penguin.

Vrandecic, D. and Krotzsch, M. (2014) 'Wikidata: a free collaborative knowledge base', *Communications of the ACM*, 57(10): 78–85.

Wikidata contributors (2014) *Wikidata Jerusalem Entry*, available from https://www.wikidata.org/wiki/Q1218 [accessed 23 July 2014].

Wikipedia contributors (2014) *Wikipedia: Requests for Arbitration/Palestine-Israel Articles*, available from https://en.wikipedia.org/w/index.php?title=Wikipedia:Requests_for_arbitration/Palestine-Israel_articlesandoldid=617668489 [accessed 23 July 2014].

Wilson, M.W. (2014) 'Continuous connectivity, handheld computers, and mobile spatial knowledge', *Environment and Planning D: Society and Space*, 32(3): 535–55.

16 Cities and context
The codification of small areas through geodemographic classification

Alex Singleton

Geodemographic place coding

Geodemographic analysis continues an extensive history of empirically driven models of urban socio-spatial structure, extending back to the work of human ecologists in the 1920s and 30s and, more recently, the large body of empirically driven work producing social area analysis models (Shevky and Williams 1949; Shevky and Bell 1955) for various urban locations (see Timms 1971: 56). Representations created through such models attempted to reduce the complexities of population and built structure into meaningful and simplified typologies, giving order to multiple attributes about small areas (Abler *et al.* 1971). Some of the earliest published work on geodemographics was also described as social area analysis (Webber 1975) and focused on single cities (in Webber's case, Liverpool, UK). It was only later that geodemographic techniques were expanded to create classifications with national coverage (Webber 1977; Webber and Craig 1978). Such geodemographic systems were presented by Webber (1978: 275) as a methodological solution for handling the highly dimensional 1971 UK census:

> What is needed is a strategy which will pick out a pattern from the detail, without losing too much of the original information, and which will admit more detailed examination of parts of the pattern which become relevant to a particular issue or local area as and when required.
>
> (Webber 1978: 275)

Webber (1978) also makes two further points. First, that geodemographics provide utility as a method of performing analysis on sparsely populated census variables that otherwise might suffer statistical unreliability at the local level. This has contemporary relevance in the context of the USA, where the national census now only represents a limited number of questions, and is supplemented by more uncertain small-area estimates from the American Community Survey (Spielman and Singleton 2015). Second, geodemographics are a useful framework within which non-census indicators could be evaluated over time and, again, would be familiar to contemporary users of

216 Alex Singleton

geodemographics with respect to spatial policy evaluation (Batey *et al.* 2008) and small-area population profiling (Singleton 2010a).

Although this early history concerned analysis in the public sector, during the 1980s geodemographics were adopted widely by the private sector as a tool for customer segmentation (Sleight 1997), as it was found that the grouping of areas into clusters showed strong correspondence with the consumption of certain product categories. This led to the creation of numerous commercial classifications. However, more recently, there has been a resurgence of interest in geodemographic applications within the public sector (Longley 2005). Although many geodemographic classifications are commercial, and, as such, have cost implications, within the UK a series of academic classifications have been built that correspond to the decennial release of the 1981 (Charlton *et al.* 1985), 1991 (Blake and Openshaw 1995), 2001 (Vickers and Rees 2007) and 2011 (Office for National Statistics, 2015) censuses.

Although of demonstrated utility (Harris *et al.* 2005, Singleton and Spielman 2014), geodemographics have been criticised as geographically oversimplified (Twigg *et al.* 2000), or of masking diversity within small areas (Voas and Williamson 2001). However, there is evidence to suggest that geodemographic classifications perform well in comparison with more complex statistical models (Brunsdon *et al.* 2011). In the mid-1990s, as part of a wider critique of GISs, there was also extended critique of the negative images that place-based marketing initiatives may elicit (Goss 1995, 2003). Uprichard *et al.* (2009) more recently raised concerns about the 'automatic production of space' (Thrift and French 2002), through recursive, reiterative and transformative practices that are embedded within software.

Sociologists (along with numerous other social science disciplines) have widely utilised classifications based on occupation (e.g., in the UK, the National Statistics Socio-Economic Classification) to code individuals into occupational class based groupings or hierarchies. However, since the mid-2000s, interest has grown over the use of contemporary geodemographic classifications as part of research into the spatialisation of class (Parker *et al.* 2007). Geodemographics have been argued as 'emblematic of a significantly changing relationship between class and status' (Burrows and Gane 2006: 805), and, within this context, geodemographics are seen as usefully encapsulating a wide range of social transactional data that are otherwise of restrictive access to academia. Additionally, geodemographics are seen to be engaging with a 'rhetoric of sociological discourse' (Savage and Burrows 2007: 887), albeit arguably only at the level of cluster description. Other theoretical work has also sought to identify how geodemographics fit within Bourdieu's field-capital theory (Tapp and Warren 2010). Most commercial geodemographic classifications are optimised on the basis of discriminating patterns of consumption (Webber 2007), which have been shown to have similar stratification to patterns of occupational groups (Sivadas 1997); and, as such, it is perhaps not unsurprising that parallels between

Cities and context 217

these two classification approaches are drawn, despite their very different methodologies.

Subjectivity and classification builder preferences

A geodemographic is created using algorithms that aim to optimise the assignment of small areas into groups that offer the greatest similarity over a typically large set of attributes. However, such representations are explicitly linked to those methodological decisions taken in their construction. Such choices can be informed empirically, theoretically and more pragmatically, based on the practitioner or collective of industry experience. As such, the process of geodemographic classification building is regularly described as both art and science (Harris *et al.* 2005).

The research presented in this chapter does not attempt to provide an evaluation of geodemographics relative to other techniques, nor does it aim to provide an exposition about the 'best' method of building a geodemographic, or how this might be assessed. The empirical focus here is to explore how output geodemographic patterns can be sensitive to changes in methodological approach. Some potential options that a classification builder might take when building a geodemographic classification are outlined in the remainder of this section.

Geographical extent

The choice of geographical extent affects how similarity between areas are considered by clustering algorithms. Geographical extent selection has three impacts. First, by altering the statistical distributions of attributes, for example, the minimum, maximum and average values, each variable will change relative to the selected geographical extent. This alters the shape of the 'attribute space' that is searched when a clustering algorithm is seeking an optimal partitioning of areas into groups. As such, it could be argued that classifications built for and from data about more localised extents are likely to demonstrate greater sensitivity (Openshaw *et al.* 1980), and some have argued that national classifications are not necessarily more complete relative to local models (Reibel and Regelson 2011). However, to some extent, this also reflects a difference of view that geodemographics are seen as either a method (e.g., application of clustering to uncover patterns) or a tool (use of a classification system to illustrate patterns or contexts) (Singleton and Spielman 2014).

The second impact of switching from a national to constrained geographical extent is that the benefits of appending national surveys onto a classification are lost unless an adequate sample within the restricted extent can be extracted. Descriptive detail that could be obtained by appending such additional data potentially impacts the range of possible end-user applications. These issues may, however, be minimised in the future, as greater volumes

218   *Alex Singleton*

of open data, which can be partitioned into different geographical extents, become available.

Finally, changes from the national extent impact the ability to use geodemographics as a measure for comparing places. Furthermore, they can be expensive to maintain and update, an issue acute for the public sector (Webber 1980).

Scale, zones and input variables

The arrangement of areas into geodemographic clusters is impacted by the choice of zonal geography, as this affects the calculation of summary values for input attributes. This is a prescient issue in statistical analysis involving aggregate geographical data, and is referred to as the modifiable areal unit problem (Openshaw 1984). Although of concern, Richard Webber has contended: 'I have yet to come across any real-world example of a conclusion being invalidly reached as a result of this hypothetical possibility' (cited in de Smith *et al.* 2009:133). Nonetheless, sensitivity to this issue is required in selecting an 'appropriate' geography and interpreting results derived at this selected scale. An 'appropriate' zonal geography can be guided by a number of factors, such as the availability of data inputs, the intended applications, stability of patterns over different scales or other motivations to provide more detailed classifications, such as leveraging competitive advantage.

Variable choices can be driven by multiple perspectives ranging from theories about what influences socio-spatial structure, empirical investigation of attribute influence on cluster formation, and pragmatic choices based on the experiences of the classification builder or the overarching purpose of the classification (e.g., general purpose versus bespoke; see Singleton and Longley 2009a). Precursors to geodemographics, such as social area analysis (Shevky and Bell 1955), were constructed from a theory about the key drivers of small-area differentiation and change, although some have argued that these were *ex-post-facto* rationalisation of earlier works featuring more *ad-hoc* choices (Timms 1971). Geodemographics were, however, established with a more applied focus. In one of the earliest national classifications, Webber and Craig (1978: 6) note, '[A] general purpose classification should by definition represent as wide as possible a variety of characteristics without over representing any particular aspect.' Correlated attributes have a 'weighting' effect that gives greater emphasis to such combined dimensions, potentially influencing cluster assignment. Inputs into this classification were organised around 'dimensions' not dissimilar to those presented in social area analysis models, and such typology of input attributes has also remained a feature of many present-day classifications.

Knowledge about the input variables used to build geodemographics ranges in degrees of transparency. For many commercial classifications, the exact specification of inputs will be commercially sensitive, and, as such, will typically not be fully disclosed (Singleton and Longley 2009b). Conversely,

Cities and context   219

in 'open geodemographics' (Vickers and Rees 2007), a full specification of variables would normally be made, including links to where these data may be obtained in the public domain. For open geodemographic classifications, transparency requires that all data be publicly available, and, as such, this could also restrict inputs to certain variable types where licences permit redistribution.

Finally, the choice of variables is also related to the selection of scale or extent, given that each affects whether or not certain attributes would be available to the classification builder, and how they might be amalgamated (e.g., individual versus concatenated age ranges). For example, open data within one context may not be available in another, or attributes available more universally might be restricted in scale for a target area.

Measurement, weights and transformations

A classification can be built with attributes of numerous measurement types, such as proportions (e.g., percentages), averages, ratios, continuous measures (e.g., distance) or relative scores (e.g., index scores). The choice depends to an extent on the attributes of interest. For example, density would typically be presented as a ratio of population divided by area, whereas an example of a continuous measure might be the distance of an area from the coast or another feature of interest. However, the measurement of attributes using either rates or relative scores is more nuanced. The former relates to the expression of an attribute within an area on a standard scale, whereas the latter takes a rate for a given attribute, and then compares areas by the extent these deviate from the national average. Measurement types impact the range of values that an attribute can hold, for example, percentage scores range between 0 and 100, whereas other measures can hold a wider range of values; such differences may alter the shape of output classification.

Historically, managing a large number of attributes when building geodemographic classifications was more difficult with restricted computing power. Principal component analysis (PCA) was introduced as a method of reducing attribute dimensions (see Webber 1975), and also reducing the impact of correlated attributes (since PCAs, by definition, comprise linearly uncorrelated variables). As computing power has increased, the necessity for PCA has been reduced, and given that PCA can remove non-linear association between variables emergent within specific geographical contexts, some have argued against its use (Harris *et al.* 2005).

Weights can be added to attributes to increase their importance in a clustering solution; however, the choice of weights can be considered subjective, and as such, has been avoided in a number of open geodemographics (Vickers and Rees 2007). Weighting does, however, see extensive use in commercial geodemographics, and has also been noted as a method to control unhelpful effects caused by highly skewed or otherwise problematic attributes (Harris *et al.* 2005).

220 *Alex Singleton*

Finally, prior to clustering, data standardisation is required, to ensure that all attributes are measured on the same scale and, as such, have the same influence on the final cluster solution. However, the exact methods chosen can either constrain or enhance the impact of outliers. For example, standardisation with a z score measures how distant an attribute score is relative to the mean in standard deviation units; however, this can accentuate the effect of outliers. Other techniques, such as the commonly used range standardisation, redistribute attribute scores onto a fixed scale, typically 0–1, compressing outliers into this range, and suppressing their impact. Decisions on which techniques are appropriate are framed within classification builder views on whether outliers are an issue to correct or an interesting local pattern that is desirable to influence final cluster assignment. Such decisions will also be guided by practicality, given that outlier clusters will, by definition, be small in nature, and this may not be viewed as a useful feature to appear in a final typology.

Clustering methods

Clustering algorithms attempt to seek an optimal grouping of areas into clusters by maximising some measure of within-cluster homogeneity or between-cluster heterogeneity. Methods of optimisation vary between clustering approaches; however, the choice of algorithm can influence the assignment of areas to clusters. A further key decision must be made about how many clusters are desirable in a final solution. Such decisions are commonly guided by experience (Harris *et al.* 2005); however, they can also be assessed empirically through analysis of divisions that 'fit' the data most effectively. Common techniques include the use of 'elbow criterion' measures (Vickers and Rees 2007) or such methods as silhouette plots (Adnan *et al.* 2010). A final consideration is whether the classification is to be hierarchical, and if so, whether it is to be built from the top down (most aggregate groups first) or from the bottom up (most disaggregate groups first).

Case study – national versus local geodemographics

In this final section, two geodemographic classifications are compared, illustrating how, from the same input data and methods, two different assignments of areas into clusters can be created by adjusting the geographical extent of the classification boundaries. The 2011 Office for National Statistics Output Area Classification (OAC) will be used as the national classification, and the methodology repeated for the localised extent of Liverpool.

The full methodology for the 2011 OAC is presented elsewhere (Office for National Statistics, 2015). However, in brief: the input data for the OAC are sourced entirely from the 2011 census, and are detailed in Table 16.1. Variables are organised around three domains; demographic, housing and socio-economic. These are then divided into a series of subdomains,

Cities and context   221

Table 16.1 2011 Output Area Classification input variables

Domain	Subdomain	Variables
Demographic	Age structure	Age bands
	Family structure	Marriage; children; dependent children
	Ethnicity	Ethnic groups; spoken English; Europe versus new Europe
Housing	Composition	Density; communal establishment; student household; occupancy rating
	Type	Detached, semi-detached, terrace, flats
	Tenure	Socially rented; privately rented; owned or shared ownership
Socio-economic	Health	Day-to-day activities limited, a lot or a little; standardised illness ratio
	Employment	Full time; part time; unemployment
	Occupation	Occupation groups
	Education	Level 1; Level 2; Level 3; Level 4+
	Mobility	Car ownership; private transport; public transport; active transport

Source: 2011 UK census

comprising a total of 60 variables. The input variables to the OAC are all calculated as percentages against an appropriate denominator, with the exception of a standardised illness ratio and population density. Input data were selected on the basis of maintaining similarity to the 2001 OAC (Vickers and Rees 2007), while also exploiting some new variables added in the 2011 census. These requirements were formulated after the outcome of a national consultation exercise delivered by the Office for National Statistics[1] and extensive evaluation.

After the 2011 census, data were assembled and the attribute measures calculated. These were first standardised using an inverse hyperbolic sine function, which transforms the attributes more closely to a normal distribution. It can be argued that more normally distributed input attributes assist clustering algorithms such as k-means, given their optimisation for finding spherical clusters, although there is no statistical requirement for the data to be normally distributed, as might be the case with such techniques as regression analysis. Second, prior to clustering, all of the attributes were standardised onto a 0–1 scale using a range standardisation method, thus ensuring that each variable had an equal influence on the clustering result. The k-means algorithm was then implemented to cluster the UK Output Areas and Small Areas (in Northern Ireland) into eight initial clusters, referred to as 'supergroups'. The data were then split by these clusters, and further divided into between two and four clusters, forming a second level, 'groups', and comprising 26 clusters in total. A final set of splits created a 'subgroup level', comprising a total of 76 clusters. The nested hierarchy of OAC 2011 is shown in Table 16.2 and mapped for the UK and Liverpool in Figures 16.1 and 16.2. Although the eight supergroup clusters are visible in the UK map, within

222   *Alex Singleton*

Table 16.2 2011 Output Area Classification hierarchy

Supergroup	Group	Subgroup
1 – Rural residents	1a – Farming communities	1a1 – Rural workers and families
		1a2 – Established farming communities
		1a3 – Agricultural communities
		1a4 – Older farming communities
	1b – Rural tenants	1b1 – Rural life
		1b2 – Rural white-collar workers
		1b3 – Aging rural flat tenants
	1c – Aging rural dwellers	1c1 – Rural employment and retirees
		1c2 – Renting rural retirement
		1c3 – Detached rural retirement
2 – Cosmopolitans	2a – Students around campus	2a1 – Student communal living
		2a2 – Student digs
		2a3 – Students and professionals
	2b – Inner-city students	2b1 – Students and commuters
		2b2 – Multicultural student neighbourhoods
	2c – Comfortable cosmopolitans	2c1 – Migrant families
		2c2 – Migrant commuters
		2c3 – Professional service cosmopolitans
	2d – Aspiring and affluent	2d1 – Urban cultural mix
		2d2 – EU white-collar workers
		2d3 – Highly qualified quaternary workers
3 – Ethnicity central	3a – Ethnic family life	3a1 – Established renting families
		3a2 – Young families and students
	3b – Endeavouring ethnic mix	3b1 – Striving service workers
		3b2 – Bangladeshi mixed employment
		3b3 – Multiethnic professional service workers
	3c – Ethnic dynamics	3c1 – Constrained neighbourhoods
		3c2 – Constrained commuters
	3d – Aspirational techies	3d1 – Established tech workers
		3d2 – Old-EU tech workers
		3d3 – New-EU tech workers
4 – Multicultural metropolitans	4a – Rented family living	4a1 – Privately renting young families
		4a2 – Socially renting new arrivals
		4a3 – Commuters with young families
	4b – Challenged Asian terraces	4b1 – Asian terraces and flats
		4b2 – Pakistani communities
	4c – Asian traits	4c1 – Achieving minorities
		4c2 – Multicultural new arrivals
		4c3 – Inner-city ethnic mix

Supergroup	Group	Subgroup
5 – Urbanites	5a – Urban professionals and families	5a1 – White professionals
		5a2 – Multiethnic professionals with families
		5a3 – Families in terraces and flats
	5b – Aging urban living	5b1 – Delayed retirement
		5b2 – Communal retirement
		5b3 – Self-sufficient retirement
6 – Suburbanites	6a – Suburban achievers	6a1 – Indian tech achievers
		6a2 – Comfortable suburbia
		6a3 – Detached retirement living
		6a4 – Aging in suburbia
	6b – Semi-detached suburbia	6b1 – Multiethnic suburbia
		6b2 – White suburban communities
		6b3 – Semi-detached aging
		6b4 – Older workers and retirement
7 – Constrained city dwellers	7a – Challenged diversity	7a1 – Transitional eastern European neighbourhoods
		7a2 – Hampered aspiration
		7a3 – Multiethnic hardship
	7b – Constrained flat dwellers	7b1 – Eastern European communities
		7b2 – Deprived neighbourhoods
		7b3 – Endeavouring flat dwellers
	7c – White communities	7c1 – Challenged transitionaries
		7c2 – Constrained young families
		7c3 – Outer-city hardship
	7d – Aging city dwellers	7d1 – Aging communities and families
		7d2 – Retired independent city dwellers
		7d3 – Retired communal city dwellers
		7d4 – Retired city hardship
8 – Hard-pressed living	8a – Industrious communities	8a1 – Industrious transitions
		8a2 – Industrious hardship
	8b – Challenged terraced workers	8b1 – Deprived blue-collar terraces
		8b2 – Hard-pressed rented terraces
	8c – Hard-pressed aging workers	8c1 – Aging industry workers
		8c2 – Aging rural industry workers
		8c3 – Renting hard-pressed workers
	8d – Migration and churn	8d1 – Young hard-pressed families
		8d2 – Hard-pressed ethnic mix
		8d3 – Hard-pressed European settlers

Source: 2011 UK census

Figure 16.1 Supergroup level Output Area Classification – UK
Source: 2011 UK census

Cities and context 225

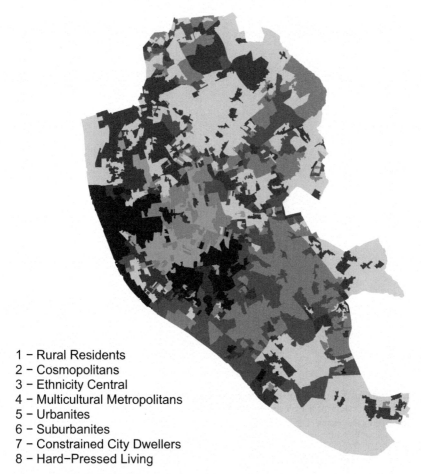

1 – Rural Residents
2 – Cosmopolitans
3 – Ethnicity Central
4 – Multicultural Metropolitans
5 – Urbanites
6 – Suburbanites
7 – Constrained City Dwellers
8 – Hard-Pressed Living

Figure 16.2 Supergroup level Output Area Classification – Liverpool
Source: 2011 UK census

Liverpool, only seven clusters are present, excluding the predominantly rural supergroup '1 – rural residents'.

A subset of 1584 Output Areas were extracted for the extent of Liverpool, and inputs were created that mirrored the attributes, measures, transformation and standardisation methods used for the OAC 2011 classification. Prior to clustering the Liverpool classification, a range of k values were considered for the initial supergroup level by plotting a total 'within sum of squares' statistic for 2–12 cluster solutions. The purpose of this plot was to identify an 'elbow criterion', which is a visual indication of where an appropriate cluster frequency might be set for Liverpool. As can be seen in Figure 16.3, there are no large decreases in the 'within sum of squares', and a minor moderation of the decrease around 7 or 8 clusters; which also mirrors similar patterns

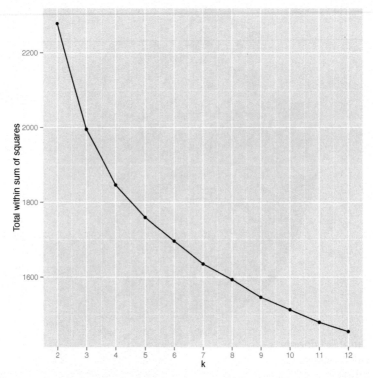

Figure 16.3 An 'elbow criterion' plot used to consider an appropriate number of supergroup clusters in a Liverpool Output Area Classification
Source: 2011 UK census

observed within the UK OAC (Office for National Statistics 2015). As such, and to maintain comparability with the way in which the national OAC is represented within Liverpool, a seven-cluster solution was chosen.

The next stage was to create the seven-cluster solution, and the k-means algorithm was run 10,000 times on the input data. This repetition is necessary as the initial starting conditions for k-means are randomly allocated, and, as such, a pool of outcomes must be generated in order to assess which result represents a best fit of the data. For full details of how the k-means algorithm assigns areas into clusters, see Harris *et al.* (2005); for processes of optimisation, see Singleton and Longley (2009a). The final set of seven clusters for Liverpool is shown in Figure 16.4. To contextualise these assignments, rates for input attributes within each cluster were compared with the Liverpool averages. From these scores, the labels and descriptions shown in Table 16.3 were formulated. Furthermore, the output areas that were closest in attributes to their assigned cluster mean were identified, and a random postcode within these zones selected, where an illustrative photograph was taken (see Figure 16.5).

Cities and context 227

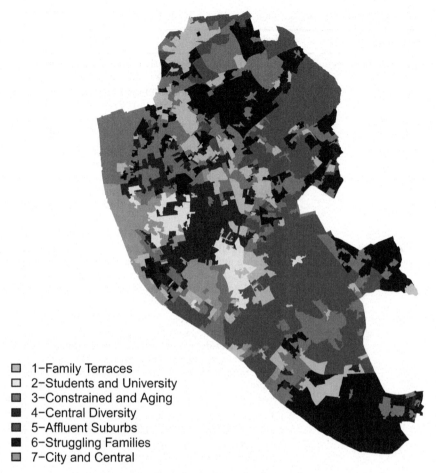

- ☐ 1-Family Terraces
- ☐ 2-Students and University
- ■ 3-Constrained and Aging
- ■ 4-Central Diversity
- ■ 5-Affluent Suburbs
- ■ 6-Struggling Families
- ☐ 7-City and Central

Figure 16.4 Supergroup level Liverpool Output Area Classification
Source: 2011 UK census

The purpose of such descriptive material is to give a very brief overview of the 'typical' characteristics of the clusters. Although this was not the case here, such processes of labelling are often completed by a wider review group rather than an individual. For the 2011 OAC, this involved consultation and approval of names and descriptions by the Office for National Statistics. An alternative method of validation of both the cluster assignment and the descriptive interpretation is illustrated by Longley and Singleton (2009), who used an online public consultation portal to gather feedback on the classification. Such systems give the general public a method of responding to assignments; this feedback could be incorporated into revised classifications.

Although the colours are not comparable, if the arrangement of areas into clusters in the Liverpool OAC in Figure 16.4 and in the subset of the 2011 UK OAC for Liverpool (see Figure 16.2) are compared, the overall patterns

228 *Alex Singleton*

Table 16.3 Liverpool Output Area Classification labels and brief descriptions

Supergroup	Brief description
1 – Family terraces	Within these predominantly terraced areas, there are many families with young children; however, there are fewer ethnic minorities than the Liverpool average. Most property is owner-occupied or rented from the private sector.
2 – Students and university	The majority of students studying in higher education live within these areas in shared accommodation, typically rented from the private sector.
3 – Constrained and aging	These areas have a high concentration of elderly residents and others living in constrained circumstances. There are higher than Liverpool average rates of divorce and unemployment. Many of the properties are flats rented from the social sector.
4 – Central diversity	These centrally located areas have high ethnic diversity. There are many families with young children, although the rate of divorce is higher than the Liverpool average. Unemployment within these areas is high, and those in work tend to work in low-level service occupations.
5 – Affluent suburbs	These affluent suburban areas feature larger detached and semi-detached houses, many of which are owner-occupied. Residents are typically well qualified and in the latter stages of successful careers in the public sector, finance or education. In families who have had children, the children are old enough to be no longer dependent.
6 – Struggling families	Families within these areas typically have young children and live in terraced housing rented from the social sector. There are high levels of unemployment in these areas; those in work typically have blue-collar occupations.
7 – City and central	These central areas are typically occupied by young professionals, with high ethnic diversity, and particularly large proportions of wider-EU residents. Many residents within these areas are single and living in flats rented from the private sector; they are well qualified and work in white-collar occupations.

Source: 2011 UK census

are broadly similar, although there is a greater degree of spatial autocorrelation (less 'noise') in the Liverpool OAC. Such effects would probably occur because the optimisation process in building the local classification forms clusters in relation to local attribute means rather than those of the UK. The effect is that the resulting clusters fit the data better for their locality.

This comparison can be extended by cross-tabulating the assignment of output areas in the two classifications. These are presented as percentage scores in Table 16.4. A number of interesting trends are highlighted. The first

Figure 16.5 Liverpool Output Area Classification supergroups
Source: photos by Alex Singleton

Table 16.4 Percentage of output areas assigned to Output Area Classification supergroups (rows) and Liverpool Output Area Classification supergroups (columns)

	1 – Family terraces	2 – Students and university	3 – Constrained and aging	4 – Central diversity	5 – Affluent suburbs	6 – Struggling families	7 – City and central
2 – Cosmopolitans	7.2	34.3	1.8	1.8	0.0	0.0	54.8
3 – Ethnicity central	0.9	3.7	0.0	80.4	0.0	0.0	15.0
4 – Multicultural metropolitans	15.0	8.8	0.0	69.9	1.8	4.4	0.0
5 – Urbanites	41.7	0.5	5.9	0.0	51.5	0.0	0.5
6 – Suburbanites	0.0	0.5	0.0	0.0	99.5	0.0	0.0
7 – Constrained city dwellers	15.8	0.0	67.7	7.6	0.3	8.2	0.3
8 – Hard-pressed living	23.5	0.0	9.3	0.0	6.6	60.6	0.0

Source: 2011 UK census

is that the OAC supergroup '2 – Cosmopolitans', which represents the gentrified core of most large cities in the UK, is split within Liverpool OAC into a cluster with similar characteristics '7 – City and central', and a further cluster that represents many of the student areas ('2– Students and university'). Such areas are not necessarily as concentrated or extensive in other urban areas of the UK. Other OAC supergroups maintaining similarity to those in the Liverpool classification are '3 – Ethnicity central' and '6 – Suburbanites', with 80.4% and 99.5% similarity, respectively. The UK OAC supergroup '4 – Multicultural metropolitans' maintains broad similarity to the Liverpool OAC supergroup '4 – Central diversity', although some output areas are reassigned into '1 – Family terraces', which has lower ethnic diversity and '2 – Students and university' which, although ethnically diverse, has different age profiles and many more residents in full-time education. Similarly, the UK OAC supergroup '5 – Urbanites' is split into two between the less affluent '1 – Family terraces' and '5 – Affluent suburbs'. The supergroup '7 – Constrained city dwellers' maintains most similarity to the Liverpool OAC supergroup '3 – Constrained and aging' (67.7%); however, output areas are also reassigned into '1 – Family terraces' (15.8%) and '6 – Struggling families' (8.2%). The supergroup '8 – Hard-pressed living' has the majority of output areas assigned to '6 – Struggling families' (60.6%); however, other output areas are assigned into areas that, although less affluent, have either more elderly residents ('3 – Constrained and aging'; 9.3%) or younger families ('1 – Family terraces'; 23.5%). There are also some assignments into the most affluent supergroup in Liverpool ('5 – Affluent suburbs'). This latter difference is interesting, as '8 – Hard-pressed living' might be a cluster where use could be envisioned in public sector targeting of resources – for example –widening university participation or healthcare initiatives. However, in the context of Liverpool, 6.6% of these areas are reclassified as '5 – Affluent suburbs' when examined with the city-focused classification.

Discussion and conclusions

This chapter has provided an overview of how geodemographic classification emerged as a method of describing the characteristics of areas from rich multidimensional census data. The use of contemporary geodemographics is widespread in the public and private sectors, to effectively code people and the places in which they live into aggregate groupings based on shared attribute similarities. As a representational method, details of reality are balanced in favour of generalisation, with the aim of providing a model that has utility in aiding understanding about how places are structured or that can be used as a component of area-based targeting strategies. Such codification is informed first by those choices made when compiling the classification, and second, by the choice of labels and descriptive materials associated with the output typology to provide context. As such, there are no 'correct' or 'true' geodemographic representations and, between classifications, these organise

232 *Alex Singleton*

a variety of different granular geographies into aggregate typologies of varying characteristics.

Methodological decisions that a classification builder might take when building a geodemographic vary, and some typical choices were reviewed, alongside discussion of their probable impacts. A comparison of all possible methods and their combinations would run the length of many doctoral theses; thus, an illustrative case study was selected to focus on the impact of one specific methodological decision, the geographical extent of the classification. In this comparison, the national OAC 2011 was mapped for the geographical extent of Liverpool. The methodology used to create this classification was then repeated to derive a new classification with cluster optimisation restricted to the extent of Liverpool. The impact of this single decision resulted in a classification that arguably represents the geography of Liverpool more appropriately, given that the clusters were optimised based on a constrained geographical area, and as such, do not have to account for the wider variance of a UK dataset. Reassignments from 2011 OAC into the Liverpool classification were considered, and highlighted local sociospatial structures that either deviate from or are similar to national patterns.

It is important to differentiate between a geodemographic method, which is the process by which a classification can be built, and a geodemographic system, in which those classifications are pre-compiled and often integrated into software coding solutions that can be applied to a range of applications. In this chapter, a classification system is compared with an implementation of a method, and the results indicate that, perhaps unsurprisingly, a bespoke classification (in this case optimised for local context) offers a potentially more effective representation than a generic geodemographic system. The purpose here is not to make the case for general purpose versus bespoke classifications, as such arguments have been rehearsed since the inception of geodemographics (see Openshaw *et al.* 1980), and are discussed and evaluated elsewhere (Singleton 2010b). In a geodemographic system, the aim is to provide the 'best' representation for a wide range of purposes. For example, a commercial classification may find utility in the retail, automotive or insurance sectors; however, it is not specifically designed for any of these applications.[2] Whereas geodemographic methods aim to provide contextual structure for a given application or locality, given the divergent aims and objectives of geodemographic systems and methods, the exact choices about how a classification will be created become application-specific. For example, the UK OAC 2011 required input attributes that would be available in all counties of the UK, and as such, ignores those attributes that might only be available within specific countries. Examples could include the input of Welsh language variables in Wales, or within England, attributes about second home ownership.

As illustrated by the case study presented in this chapter, the choice of methods can impact the output representation, and as such, it is critical when building a geodemographic to be open and transparent about methodological specification, and present a clear rationale about why these decisions were taken. This is of particular importance for applications in the public sector where life chances might be apportioned through those decisions informed by geodemographics (Singleton and Longley 2009b). Such methodological clarity engenders greater scientific rigour, as methods are more open to scrutiny, testing and reproduction. Arguably, the best practice in this regard is to place within the public domain – for example, utilising public code sharing repositories such as GitHub – the code, data and written interpretations.[3] Furthermore, and as argued elsewhere (Longley and Singleton 2009), mechanisms that enable end users to be empowered to give feedback about classification reliability should also be encouraged.

Building geodemographics employs scientific methods of data reduction to provide summary measures of the characteristics of typically small-area geography. The art of building geodemographics relates to methodological choices and their justifications, which are typically guided by classification builder expertise. Given this subjectivity, there are no 'best' solutions, although some classifications may perform better for certain applications, either serendipitously, or by design, such as with a bespoke classification. Given their prevalence of use, it is argued here, that for geodemographics to attain greater social responsibility all aspects of the build process should be placed within the public domain, and additionally, mechanisms should be enabled to provide end users (either those who are coded or those who are coding) with the ability to give feedback on the quality of assignments.

Notes

1 Details of the consultation exercise can be found at Office for National Statistics (n.d.).
2 In addition to general purpose classifications, many commercial geodemographic companies also offer systems that have been tailored to markets. For example, CACI produce 'Acorn' (http://acorn.caci.co.uk/).
3 https://github.com/

References

Abler, R., Adams, J.S. and Gould, P. (1971) *Spatial Organisation: The Geographer's View of the World*, Englewood Cliffs, NJ: Prentice-Hall.
Adnan, M., Longley, P.A., Singleton, A.D. and Brunsdon, C. (2010) 'Towards real-time geodemographics: clustering algorithm performance for large multidimensional spatial databases', *Transactions in GIS*, 14(3): 283–97.
Batey, P., Brown, P. and Pemberton, S. (2008) 'Methods for the spatial targeting of urban policy in the UK: a comparative analysis', *Applied Spatial Analysis and Policy*, 1(2): 117–32.
Blake, M. and Openshaw, S. (1995) *Selecting Variables for Small Area Classifications Of 1991 UK Census Data*, Working Paper 95/5, Leeds: School of Geography, University of Leeds.
Brunsdon, C., Longley, P., Singleton, A. and Ashby, D.I. (2011) 'Predicting

234 Alex Singleton

participation in higher education: a comparative evaluation of the performance of geodemographic classifications', *Journal of the Royal Statistical Society, Series A*, 174(1): 17–30.

Burrows, R. and Gane, N. (2006) 'Geodemographics, software and class', *Sociology*, 40(5): 793–812.

Charlton, M.E., Openshaw, S. and Wymer, C. (1985) 'Some new classifications of census enumeration districts in Britain: a poor man's ACORN', *Journal of Economic and Social Measurement*, 13(1): 69–96.

de Smith, M., Goodchild, M.F. and Longley, P. (2009) *Geospatial Analysis: A Comprehensive Guide to Principles, Techniques and Software Tools*, 3rd edn, Leicester: Matador.

Goss, J. (1995) 'Marketing the new marketing: the strategic discourse of geodemographic information systems', in J. Pickles (ed.) *Ground Truth*, New York: Guildford Press.

Goss, J. (2003) 'The instrumental rationality of geodemographic systems', in D. Clarke (ed.) *The Consumption Reader*, New York: Routledge.

Harris, R.J., Sleight, P. and Webber, R.J. (2005) *Geodemographics, GIS and Neighbourhood Targeting*, London: Wiley.

Longley, P. (2005) 'Geographical information systems: a renaissance of geodemographics for public service delivery', *Progress in Human Geography*, 29(1): 57–63.

Longley, P. and Singleton, A. (2009) 'Classification through consultation: public views of the geography of the e-society', *International Journal of Geographical Information Science*, 23(6): 737–63.

Office for National Statistics (n.d.) *User Engagement on a New 2011 United Kingdom Output Area Classification*, available at http://www.ons.gov.uk/ons/guide-method/geography/products/area-classifications/ns-area-classifications/new-uk-output-area-classification/index.html [accessed 25 November 2015].

Office for National Statistics (2015) *2011 Area Classifications*. London: Office for National Statistics, available from http://www.ons.gov.uk/ons/guide-method/geography/products/area-classifications/ns-area-classifications/ns-2011-area-classifications/index.html [accessed 21 August 2015].

Openshaw, S. (1984) *The Modifiable Areal Unit Problem*, CATMOG 38, Norwich: Geoabstracts.

Openshaw, S., Cullingford, D. and Gillard, A. (1980) 'A critique of the national classifications of OPCS/PRAG', *Town Planning Review*, 51(4): 421–39.

Parker, S., Uprichard, E. and Burrows, R. (2007) 'Class places and place classes geodemographics and the spatialization of class', *Information, Communication and Society*, 10(6): 902–21.

Reibel, M. and Regelson, M. (2011) 'Neighborhood racial and ethnic change: the time dimension in segregation', *Urban Geography*, 32(3): 360–82.

Savage, M. and Burrows, R. (2007) 'The coming crisis of empirical sociology', *Sociology*, 41(5): 885–99.

Shevky, E. and Bell, W. (1955) *Social Area Analysis*, Stanford: Stanford University Press.

Shevky, E. and Williams, M. (1949) *The Social Areas of Los Angeles*, Berkeley: University of California Press.

Singleton, A. (2010a) 'The geodemographics of educational progression and their implications for widening participation in higher education', *Environment and Planning A*, 42(11): 2560–80.

Cities and context 235

Singleton, A. (2010b) *Educational Opportunity: The Geography of Access to Higher Education*, Farnham: Ashgate.

Singleton, A. and Longley, P. (2009a) 'Creating open source geodemographics – refining a national classification of census output areas for applications in higher education', *Papers in Regional Science*, 88(3): 643–66.

Singleton, A. and Longley, P. (2009b) 'Geodemographics, visualisation, and social networks in applied geography', *Applied Geography*, 29(3): 289–98.

Singleton, A. and Spielman, S. (2014) 'The past, present and future of geodemographic research in the United States and United Kingdom', *Professional Geographer*, 66(4): 558–67.

Sivadas, E. (1997) 'A preliminary examination of the continuing significance of social class to marketing: a geodemographic replication', *Journal of Consumer Marketing*, 14(6): 463–79.

Sleight, P. (1997) *Targeting Customers: How to Use Geodemographic and Lifestyle Data in Your Business*, Henley-on-Thames: NTC Publications.

Spielman, S.E. and Singleton, A.D. (2015) 'Studying neighborhoods using uncertain data from the American Community Survey: a contextual approach', *Annals of the Association of American Geographers*, 105(5): 1003–25.

Tapp, A. and Warren, S. (2010) 'Field-capital theory and its implications for marketing', *European Journal of Marketing*, 44(1–2): 200–22.

Thrift, N. and French, S. (2002) 'The automatic production of space', *Transactions of the Institute of British Geographers*, 27(3): 309–35.

Timms, D.W. (1971) *The Urban Mosaic: Towards a Theory of Residential Differentiation*, Cambridge: Cambridge University Press.

Twigg, L., Moon, G. and Jones, K. (2000) 'Predicting small-area health-related behaviour: a comparison of smoking and drinking indicators', *Social Science and Medicine*, 50(7–8): 1109–20.

Uprichard, E., Burrows, R. and Parker, S. (2009) 'Geodemographic code and the production of space', *Environment and Planning A*, 41(12): 2823–35.

Vickers, D. and Rees, P. (2007) 'Creating the UK national statistics 2001 output area classification', *Journal of the Royal Statistical Society. Series A. Statistics in Society*, 170(2): 379–403.

Voas, D. and Williamson, P. (2001) 'The diversity of diversity: a critique of geodemographic classification', *Area*, 33(1): 63–76.

Webber, R.J. (1975) *Liverpool Social Area Study, 1971 Data*, PRAG Technical Paper 14, London: Centre for Environmental Studies.

Webber, R.J. (1977) *An Introduction to the National Classification of Wards and Parishes*, Technical Paper 23, London: Centre for Environmental Studies.

Webber, R.J. (1978) 'Making the most of the census for strategic analysis', *The Town Planning Review*, 49(3): 274–84.

Webber, R.J. (1980) 'A response to the critique of the national classifications of OPCS/PRAG', *The Town Planning Review*, 51(4): 440–50.

Webber, R.J. (2007) 'The metropolitan habitus: its manifestations, locations, and consumption profiles', 39(1): 182–207.

Webber, R. and Craig, J. (1978) *Socio-Economic Classifications of Local Authority Areas*, Studies on Medical and Population Subjects 35, London: OPCS.

Index

abstraction 4, 5, 10, 51, 56, 61, 62, 63–6, 67, 69, 72, 125, 180
accelerometer 137, 139
activism 41, 97, 181, 183, 186, 191
actor network theory 67, 133, 142
actuators 1, 3, 28
aesthetics 55, 139, 146, 147, 158–9
agency 6, 7, 9, 45, 50, 51, 52, 53, 57, 91, 118, 120, 124, 126, 127, 131, 142, 143, 167, 173, 201, 204, 209–11; secondary 15, 132
agent-based modelling 5, 61, 62, 64, 65, 68, 69, 70
aggregation 55, 65, 75, 159, 185, 218, 220, 231, 232
algorithms 9, 10, 17, 18, 19, 20, 22, 27, 36, 52, 56, 67, 75, 95, 105, 117, 118, 131, 133, 134, 141, 159, 173, 203, 210, 217, 220, 221, 226
Amazon 149, 166
analogue 2, 32, 92
Android 32, 84, 86
apparatus 18, 19, 23, 82, 122, 132, 142
Apple 32, 130, 137, 139
Application Programming Interface (API) 52, 80, 88, 100, 138, 139, 158, 159, 179
apps 1, 3, 6, 7, 9, 45, 50, 51, 52, 91, 93, 130, 132, 137, 145, 155, 158, 191, 192, 193, 194, 197, 206
ARPANet 33, 39
art installations 3, 6, 116, 118, 123, 124
Arup 49, 52, 55
assemblage 1, 3, 4, 5, 7, 8, 10, 11, 16, 18, 19, 20, 21, 22, 24, 74, 81, 82, 87, 122, 123, 132, 133, 134, 136, 141–3
automation 8, 15, 16, 18, 81, 131, 163, 164, 165, 167, 171, 173, 201

Benkler, Yochai 132, 133, 182
black-boxing 22, 49, 50, 118, 130, 134, 203
buildings 4, 30, 96, 157, 164, 183

capital 19, 141
capitalism 11, 87, 134–7, 141, 182
cellular automata 64
census 8, 155, 157, 207, 215, 216, 220, 221, 231
citizenship 2, 9, 41–2, 187
civic: engagement 36, 40, 42, 56, 97, 118, 119, 122, 179; hacking 8, 9, 181, 190, 192–4, 198, 199
classification 10, 215–33
code: libraries 3, 75–86, 136; traffic 5, 72–86
Code for America 194
Code for Ireland 9, 191, 192, 193, 194, 195, 197, 198
code/space 16, 17, 18, 22, 24, 118, 131, 132
collaboration 76, 159, 167, 168, 170, 172, 185, 197
communications 1, 7, 27, 28, 35, 38, 52, 93, 108, 109, 136, 165, 179, 182, 187, 195
computation 4, 5, 6, 7, 8, 10, 27, 28, 36, 38, 45, 61, 65, 66, 69, 75, 86, 105, 106, 109, 112, 113, 130, 131, 132, 133, 134, 141, 142, 146, 172, 200
computing: cloud 8, 27, 28, 34, 35, 36, 45, 73, 75, 86, 91, 92, 97, 102, 103, 164–6; human-centred 91, 92, 96, 102; mobile 3, 5–8, 130–43; sensor-based 28; street 179, 180; tangible 106; ubiquitous 2, 18, 28, 29, 119, 179; urban 3, 27, 36, 40, 44, 45
context 1, 6, 9, 11, 17, 18, 40, 51, 100,

117, 120, 121, 125, 126, 131, 179, 194, 198, 203, 204, 206, 217
contingency 10, 11, 17, 18, 131, 132, 181, 183, 186, 213
control 1, 4, 5, 8, 32, 34, 37, 45, 46, 49, 51, 54, 63, 66, 68, 72, 75, 76, 81, 82, 120, 131, 136, 165, 166, 178, 179, 182, 194; centre 49; creep 15
crisis 8, 163–73
crowdsourcing 1, 3, 6, 76, 102, 168, 169
cultural: analytics 7, 8, 146–59; capital 184
curation 7, 116, 120, 121, 123, 126, 127

data: analytics 30, 36, 38, 67; assemblage 18, 19, 20; big 2, 8, 18, 27, 149, 158, 159, 163, 165; infrastructure 1, 18, 132; linked 201, 211, 212, 213; model 53; open 18, 50, 51, 52, 155, 218, 219; structures 9, 67, 69
database 6, 7, 20, 54, 80, 81, 95, 110, 111, 116, 118, 124, 132, 137, 139, 141, 142, 192, 202, 203, 204, 206
datafication 6, 116
deconstruction 17, 122, 133
Deleuze, Gilles 74, 108, 142
diagram city 64–6
discursive regime 2, 21–3, 121
dispositif 7, 118, 119–27
disruptive innovation 8, 56, 137, 142, 163, 167, 182
distributed mapping 8, 168
Dodge, Martin 1, 2, 15, 16, 17, 18, 22, 24, 105, 106, 117, 118, 131, 132, 139, 141, 163, 179, 200
Dourish, Paul 4, 17, 27–46, 51, 106

Earthquake 8, 164–8, 170, 172
Embodiment 7, 11, 51, 55, 56, 106, 117, 120, 123, 126, 127, 133, 173
emergency response 1, 3, 5, 8, 163, 166, 167, 170
empiricism 4, 61, 67, 68, 69
epistemology 6, 22, 49, 54, 68, 105, 143
ethics 8, 11, 19, 52, 57, 65, 164, 165, 166, 167, 170, 172, 190, 191, 192, 197, 198
ethnography 6, 9, 17, 106, 109, 112, 191
everyware 163

Facebook 67, 91, 137, 141, 158, 159, 169, 170, 173, 193, 196, 200, 204
finance 1, 19, 23, 56, 141, 158
firmware 1, 136

Flickr 125, 146
F/OSS 182, 183, 185, 186, 187, 193, 195, 197, 198
Foucualt, Michel 66, 120, 142, 181
Foursquare 1, 6, 7, 8, 18, 91–102, 106, 109–12, 139, 155, 156
Freebase 9, 203, 204, 207
Fuller, Matthew 4, 5, 10, 15, 61–70, 141

Galloway, Alex 51, 54, 56, 136, 141
game theory 5, 62
geodemographics 3, 10, 131, 215–33
geographic information system (GIS) 18, 19, 165, 168, 216
geopolitics 9, 200–13
GitHub 5, 75–86, 193, 233
Global Positioning System (GPS) 42, 43, 91, 110, 121, 122, 137, 139
Google 32, 55, 75, 86, 130, 193, 195, 196, 201–10, 212; Knowledge Graph 9, 211; Maps 42, 56, 200; Street View 8, 155, 156, 157, 158
governance 1, 8–10, 15, 16, 22, 23, 42, 56, 63, 105, 124, 133, 173, 178–87, 198, 203, 213; algorithmic 15, 16, 18, 131; anticipatory 15, 22; technocratic 23
government 1, 2, 4, 9, 19, 41, 49, 50, 55, 56, 65, 158, 163, 164, 166, 173, 178, 179, 181, 185, 187, 190, 191, 192, 194, 195, 197, 198, 204, 206, 207
governmentality 118
Greenfield, Adam 36, 41, 54, 105, 163, 180

Hackathon 3, 9, 50, 155, 186, 190–8
Hacking 4, 9, 37, 190–8
Hailo 7, 130, 134–37, 142, 143
hardware 1, 7, 10, 18, 20, 29, 51, 52, 64, 68, 69, 131, 132, 133, 134, 136, 137, 141, 142, 143, 180, 183, 186
Heidegger, Martin 6, 107, 108, 111, 113
hermeneutic 106, 110, 111
home 2, 16, 18, 27, 29, 32, 34, 36, 37, 38, 42, 45, 51, 94, 95, 97, 232

IBM 49, 54, 166
Ideology 11, 19, 56, 62, 64
imitation 74, 75, 76, 77, 80, 81, 84, 85, 86
indeterminancy 5, 72, 73, 74, 82

238 *Index*

infrastructure 1, 2, 3, 4, 5, 7, 8, 10, 11, 15, 16, 18, 19, 20, 22, 24, 27, 28, 30, 31, 32, 34, 37, 38, 40, 42, 43, 45, 50, 51, 56, 73, 80, 81, 86, 91, 131, 132, 134, 136, 137, 141, 142, 143, 158, 168, 178, 179, 180, 182, 183, 184, 185, 186, 187, 192, 200
innovation 2, 8, 15, 20, 30, 33, 64, 100, 119, 122, 127, 163, 165, 167, 171, 187, 190
Instagram 7, 8, 146, 147, 148, 151, 153, 155, 156, 158
instrumental rationality 4, 50
interface 1, 3, 4, 6, 7, 18, 19, 20, 21, 22, 34, 43, 50, 51, 52, 53–4, 55, 56, 57, 67, 92, 106, 111, 112, 116–27, 132–43, 146, 148, 157, 158, 159, 178, 179, 181
Internet of Things 3, 4, 22, 27–46, 73
interoperability 29, 30, 69, 163, 164, 166
iOS 32, 86, 139

Jerusalem 9, 201–11
Justice 8, 69, 164, 165

Kitchin, Rob 1, 2, 3, 15–24, 105, 106, 117, 118, 131, 132, 139, 141, 142, 163, 179, 200

labour 137, 141
language 9, 17, 20, 62, 73, 170, 178, 201, 210, 232
Latour, Bruno 67, 142, 171, 194, 206
Law 7, 9, 11, 17, 19, 23, 36, 37, 42, 82, 142, 178, 180, 197, 204
life-logging 7, 134, 137, 166
LinkedIn 192, 193
Living Plan-IT 51
location-based services 1, 42, 119, 126
location-based social networks (LSBN) 6, 91–103, 105–114
logic 4, 10, 34, 42, 61, 66–70, 118, 119, 121, 132, 133, 201, 204, 206, 211, 213

machine learning 27, 75
McLuhan, Marshall 118, 121
management 1, 2, 4, 10, 15, 16, 22, 27, 34, 37, 41, 46, 51, 56, 95, 180; automated 16
Manovich, Lev 7, 8, 15, 18, 117, 119, 141, 146–59
map 1, 2, 8, 39, 42, 49, 51, 52, 54, 56, 91, 102, 110, 111, 121, 138, 139, 140, 156,

157, 159, 167, 168, 170, 172, 186, 200, 221, 232
mass media 109
Master Touch 125
Materiality 131, 132, 134, 141, 143, 172, 197, 204
Mathematics 5, 10, 64, 65
measurement 10, 35, 50, 52, 116, 124, 149, 151, 173, 186, 194, 218, 219–20, 221, 225
metadata 132, 134, 136, 207
meters 1, 27, 35, 37, 137, 139
middleware 1
mobile phones 1, 8, 32, 33, 51, 55, 102, 148, 164, 165, 167, 168, 171
mobility (movement) 42, 43, 52, 53, 75, 76, 77, 78, 80, 86, 91, 93, 117, 118, 119, 131, 132, 134, 136, 138, 139, 141, 158, 164–66, 173, 195, 221
modality 8, 53, 139
model 2, 5, 7, 8, 10, 19, 30, 53, 61–70, 95, 126, 130, 131, 133, 136, 137, 142, 164, 184, 215–33
modernity 37, 69, 146, 180
Moves 7, 130, 134, 137–41, 142, 143

navigation 42, 43, 44, 50, 55, 66, 96, 102, 110, 111, 112, 119, 120, 122, 124, 125, 130, 153, 157–8, 181, 201
neoliberal 182, 187
networks 1, 2, 3, 4, 5, 6, 7, 8, 11, 19, 22, 27, 29, 30, 32, 33, 34, 36–40, 45, 46, 50, 51, 52, 55, 77, 106, 108, 109, 112, 113, 121, 122, 130, 131, 132, 134, 136, 142, 156, 171, 173, 183–86, 192; community 9, 179, 181, 182–86; distributed 36, 127, 181, 182, 184, 185; DIY 40; peer-to-peer 9, 178–87; radio 1, 136, 137, 182, 185; satellite 1, 29; wireless 3, 9, 27, 28, 32, 37, 52, 179, 180–87

object orientated programming 65, 68
objectivity 5, 11, 65, 132
On Broadway 8, 153–55, 159
ontology 11, 62, 105, 130, 141, 142, 143
openness 29, 40, 45, 191, 192, 193, 197, 198
OpenStreetMap 168, 172, 200
operating systems 1, 4, 10, 20, 31, 32, 44, 45, 50, 51, 52, 54, 56, 136
output areas 220–31
ownership 35, 36, 38, 186, 221, 232

Index 239

panoptic 120
participation 2, 4, 7, 8, 9, 41, 42, 45, 55, 116, 117, 118, 120, 122, 123, 124, 127, 170, 178, 180, 183–4, 190, 193, 194, 198, 212
peer production 181–87
performativity 7, 11, 94, 102, 116–126, 131
phenomenology 6, 106, 107, 110, 165, 167, 170, 172
photographs 52, 91, 92, 101, 124, 147, 148, 153, 155, 171
platform 1, 5, 7, 18, 20, 21, 37, 42, 44, 45, 56, 73, 74, 75, 76, 77, 78, 79, 80, 81, 82, 83, 84, 86, 91, 92, 93, 96, 99, 100, 101, 102, 109, 117, 121, 127, 134, 141, 200, 203, 209, 212
policy 10, 17, 19, 23, 57, 65, 133, 165, 171, 183, 194, 216
political economy 11, 19, 23, 131
politics 4, 8–10, 11, 18, 28, 38–41, 52, 55, 56, 57, 61, 64, 67, 69, 130, 131, 141–3, 158–9, 165, 178, 181, 182, 183, 186, 187, 191, 197, 198, 201
post-human 165, 167, 170, 172, 173
post-phenomenology 107
power 2, 5, 11, 15, 37, 41, 45, 56, 61, 66, 68, 72, 73, 75, 76, 81, 82, 118, 131, 142, 170, 178, 182, 203–4, 213
prediction 2, 65, 66, 74, 95, 166
privacy 22, 94, 95, 101, 124, 126, 166
protocols 4, 19, 29, 30, 33, 38–41, 45, 51, 52, 54, 56, 86, 122, 133, 134, 136, 141, 190
provenance 9, 201, 203, 204, 207–10
public space 82, 116, 117, 123, 124, 183

qualculation 8, 163, 164, 165, 167, 171, 172, 173

radical constructivism 67
real-time 112
recommendation systems 18, 93, 94, 95, 99, 100, 101
reductionism 4, 5, 10, 61, 63, 66, 68, 130, 233
reflexivity 117, 119, 120, 123, 126, 191
regulation 1, 2, 7, 15, 19, 22, 35, 37, 40, 66, 82, 101, 118, 131, 137, 142, 165
rematerialisation 6, 92, 102
representation 9, 10, 43, 46, 52, 54, 55, 64, 65, 123, 130, 132, 139, 142, 159,

181, 200, 201, 203, 204, 205, 206, 211, 212, 213, 215, 217, 231, 232
resistance 11, 22, 44, 100, 164
rhetoric 3, 23, 27, 28, 29, 36, 44, 69, 120, 121, 123, 180, 191, 195, 216

satellite 1, 29, 52
Saving Face 7, 116–20, 123, 124, 125, 127
scale 3, 8, 17, 22, 23, 24, 33–4, 38, 42–3, 53, 54, 55, 61, 63, 64, 68, 69, 77, 81, 132, 133, 137, 157, 165, 183, 218–19, 220
screens 1, 4, 6, 7, 49, 50, 52, 53, 54, 55, 111, 113, 116–127, 139, 158, 171, 179
search engines 3, 203, 204
security 1, 16, 22, 27, 38, 54, 136, 165, 166, 183, 190
segregation 5, 61–66
Selfiecity 7, 8, 148–53, 159
semantics 68, 70
Semantic Web 9, 200–13
sensors 1, 3, 19, 27, 28, 34, 35, 36, 51, 73, 105, 178, 179, 181
sentience 15, 49
Silicon Valley 56, 73
Simulation 2, 5, 61, 62, 63, 64, 65, 67, 68
Sloterdijk, Peter 6, 106, 107–109, 110, 111, 112, 113
smart cities 2, 3, 4, 8, 9, 18, 22, 23, 24, 27, 29, 36–8, 41, 42, 43, 44, 49, 50, 53, 54, 56, 107, 124, 126, 179, 180, 181, 183, 187, 191, 196, 198
smartphone 1, 5, 6, 34, 45, 51, 57, 105, 106, 130, 132, 134, 136, 137, 139, 143, 181
social: area analysis 215, 218; coding 5, 77, 81, 82, 86; gaming 95; interaction 1, 6, 91–103; responsibility 50, 193, 233; sorting 65, 131, 166
socio-spatial behaviour 1, 6, 11
software studies 15, 16, 17, 18, 20, 21, 24, 117, 141, 146, 156
Songdo City 41
space, production of 3, 15, 16, 187, 216
stack 4, 7, 20, 29, 45, 52–3, 54, 56, 130, 132, 134, 137, 139, 141, 143, 157
standardisation 32, 33, 132, 220, 221, 225
standards 4, 19, 31, 37, 132, 133, 136, 159, 168, 172, 201, 219

240   *Index*

statistical analysis 10, 27, 49, 67, 151, 157, 201, 207, 216, 217, 218, 220, 225
subjectivity 2, 19, 108, 109, 118, 125, 132, 217, 233
surveillance 1, 8, 16, 18, 38, 55, 116, 120, 124, 158, 159, 163, 164, 165, 166, 167, 171, 173, 180
Swarm 91, 93

TCP/IP 29
technological unconscious 2, 178
teleology 9, 11
temporality 4, 11, 30–2, 38, 43, 44, 45, 97, 113, 119, 120, 122, 125, 192
Tinder 1
Townsend, Anthony 2, 16, 58, 179, 181
transduction 106, 131
transgression 11
transport 1, 16, 35, 44, 52, 55, 91, 131, 132, 139
Tripadvisor 92, 100
Twitter 1, 7, 8, 91, 109, 155, 156, 157, 158, 159, 166, 168, 200

UNData 9, 201, 204, 207
Urbanism: abstract 4, 10, 61–70;
digital 8, 163–73; networked 2, 15, 18, 22; peer-to-peer 9, 179, 181, 182, 183; programmable 11, 22, 23, 24; splintering 131
USB 31, 32
utilities: energy 1, 16, 29, 32, 55, 191; lighting 1, 16, 30; water 1, 16, 30, 51

visualisation 7, 8, 18, 49, 50, 51, 52, 53, 54, 55, 56, 87, 119, 124, 125, 139, 146, 148, 149–55, 158, 159, 179
Volunteered Geographic Information 200

weather 1, 49, 55, 163, 167, 201
widgetisation 4, 49, 50, 196
Wikidata 9, 201, 203, 204, 206, 207, 210, 211, 212
Wikipedia 9, 182, 186, 200, 201, 203, 204, 205, 206, 210, 211, 212
wireless 27, 28, 32, 37, 52, 180, 183, 184, 187; community 3, 9, 179, 181, 182–83, 186
World Bank 170

Yelp 100, 200
YouTube 146, 159